The Common Gaze

The Common Gaze

Eric Stoddart

scm press

Published in 2021 by SCM Press
Editorial office
3rd Floor, Invicta House,
108–114 Golden Lane,
London EC1Y 0TG, UK
www.scmpress.co.uk

SCM Press is an imprint of Hymns Ancient & Modern Ltd
(a registered charity)

Hymns Ancient & Modern® is a registered trademark of
Hymns Ancient & Modern Ltd
13A Hellesdon Park Road, Norwich,
Norfolk NR6 5DR, UK

British Library Cataloguing in Publication data
A catalogue record for this book is available
from the British Library

ISBN 978 0 334 06004 8

Typeset by Regent Typesetting
Printed and bound by
CPI Group (UK) Ltd

Dedication

To John Kitchen and Calum Robertson, Director and
Assistant Director of Music, and to the choristers of
Old St Paul's Scottish Episcopal Church, Edinburgh
– whose commitment to beautiful music lightened the
darkness of writing about the Holocaust during the
2020 Covid-19 lockdown.

To Harry van der Weijde, Lana Woolford and Eleanor Smith
who, overnight, became a broadcast team to livestream
beauty in the darkness.

Contents

Acknowledgements

I wrote much of this book during the Covid-19 lockdown in the spring of 2020, but the research and conceptual development stretches back over a good few years. I am grateful to the University of St Andrews for a semester of research leave in the autumn of 2018, which provided me with the space not only to read but to think. To the colleagues who covered my various roles in the School of Divinity, not least T. J. Lang for being acting director of our distance-learning postgraduate programme, 'Bible and the Contemporary World', I offer my thanks.

I have appreciated immensely the support of those colleagues in St Andrews and much further afield who share my sense of urgency around issues of surveillance, religion and politics, particularly Mario Aguilar (St Andrews), Susanne Wigorts Yngvesson (Sweden) and David Lyon (Canada). They, as well as members of the Surveillance and Religion Network, which I jointly coordinate with Susanne, inspire me to keep on grappling with a rapidly expanding field.

A grant from the J. & A. Deas Fund (St Mary's College, University of St Andrews) helped significantly with my purchase of books directly related to this volume. I owe a debt of gratitude to friends without whom this book may well not yet have seen the light of day: Phil, Jubin, Kim, Patrick and Sheila.

Introduction

Test, track and trace

Test students to see if they have reached their cohort benchmark. Track students' individual and peers' progress over their years in school. Trace those not attaining learning goals or whose early-life indicators suggest they may be at risk of low achievement, and intervene with extra assistance.

Test workers' productivity. Track the effect on the company. Trace those who are a liability to efficiency.

Test a voter's susceptibility to a particular message. Track this campaign's spread. Trace voters who might be similarly persuaded.

Test a person's lifestyle stability for housing allocation. Track the system's effect on homelessness. Trace the clients who fall back into chaotic patterns.

Test a congregant's involvement in church life. Track the success of discipleship programmes. Trace members who need to be encouraged.

Self-test your running speed and stamina. Self-track your progress. Be traced by advertisers with equipment and programmes.

Test, track and trace has been a mantra of public health agencies responding to the Covid-19 pandemic but is a strategy for multiple forms of surveillance. Familiar too in the plots of crime movies, testing a suspect, tracking their suspicious movements and tracing their nefarious contacts is a well-trodden path accelerated, and complicated, by digital technologies.

Surveillance is, in David Lyon's definition, 'the operations and experiences of gathering and analysing personal data for influence, entitlement and management' (Lyon 2018a, p. 6). In advanced capitalist societies we encounter surveillance at numerous points in our everyday life but the intensity, fairness and consequences are not the same for all of us. Our ethnicity, income level and religion are among the factors that mean we can reap considerable benefits from surveillance systems or can be burdened with further weight of discrimination. In one area of life we might benefit while being disadvantaged in another. Some of our personal data we offer freely to digital platforms so that we can gain personalized information appropriate to our interests. We may not be so aware that our interests can also be influenced by what we then receive. As George Dyson so pithily observes, 'Facebook defines who we are, Amazon defines what we want, and Google defines what we think' (Dyson 2012, p. 308). We construct our identity by comparison with vastly greater audiences than did our pre-digital forebears. It may only be at the very back of our minds that the valuable data points we generate when we track our exercise regimes are our free work for informational capitalists monetizing the moves we make. At so many points we need to be identifiable, not just when we travel through international borders but in daily life when accessing particular buildings or proving our entitlement to welfare or health services.

If we ask what all this surveillance is *for* we receive answers that include some combination of national security, value for money, efficiency, convenience, profit, political advantage or the like. However, this can be taken to a deeper level when asked alongside the question, '*Who* are these systems for?' Surveillance for the common good is the answer this book explores. The United Nations Educational, Scientific and Cultural Organization (UNESCO) (UNESCO 2015, p. 77) uses the Christian moral theologian Lisa Cahill's expression to explain the common good as 'a solidaristic association of persons that is more than the good of individuals in the aggregate' (Cahill 2004, p. 8). Another prominent Christian ethicist, also within the Roman Catholic tradition, provides UNESCO with a further clarification: 'It is the good of being a community – "the good realized in the mutual relationships in and through which human beings achieve their well-being"' (UNESCO 2015, p. 77, quoting Hollenbach (2002, p. 81).

A common-good approach lifts us out of silos of individualist thinking that focus on how surveillance impacts upon human rights of, typically, privacy. Stepping back, as is the wont of much liberal democracy, from questions of what constitutes 'the good' in favour of leaving those as private rather than public questions, impoverishes a critical discussion of surveillance. Privacy features little in this book, precisely in order to keep our attention focused on what might lie beyond those trenches, used as they are for important forays against what are sometimes dubious government and corporate intrusions into our personal lives.

In a world in which being influenced, building our identity and being identified are interwoven and saturated with surveillance, this project proposes a new concept: the common gaze.

Surveillance under the sign of the cross, and more

In *Theological Perspectives on a Surveillance Society: Watching and Being Watched*, I draw on a feminist critical hermeneutic of care to probe behind contemporary surveillance. I am interested there in how surveillance is legitimated, particularly around conceptions of risk. Rather than draw on privacy as the central critique, I opt for the less-familiar social practice of (in)visibility – the skill of managing how we make ourselves, and are made, more and less visible in particular contexts. While others had, and have since, articulated a normative ethics of surveillance, my offer in 2011 is of a discursive ethic:

> It is an approach that understands the ethical moment to be one of continual interrogation of all that circulates around, impacts upon, and feeds back into interdependent human flourishing. This is not the application of a universal principle of caring in turn used as a criterion against which surveillance is judged *per se*. A critical ethic of care shows considerable family resemblance to a discursive ethic that attends to the particularity of people's situations; facing up to how we are being formed and forming one another, disclosing and refusing re-closure is the mode of being ethical. (Stoddart 2011, p. 51)

This is, in Michel Foucault's terms, ethics as 'the conscious [*réfléchie*] practice of freedom' (Foucault 2000, p. 284). In *Theological Perspectives* I draw on Jürgen Moltmann's injunction to consider God in terms of the history of the crucified God, Jesus Christ (Moltmann 1974, p. 321). This being how we are to name God propels me to argue that 'it is the crucified God who knows what it is to be under surveillance, and we are to understand his surveillance of us from the perspective of the Cross' (Stoddart 2011, p. 170).

David Hollenbach's injunction to do social ethics 'under the sign of the cross' (Hollenbach 1996, pp. 12–14) resonates with much of this new project. In his terms, 'the cross is the revelation of divine solidarity with every human whose experience is that of forsakenness and abandonment' (Hollenbach 1996, p. 13). Such an impetus pushes beyond the common good as just a means of imagining life together by giving priority to what is happening to those who are already poor, oppressed or unjustly marginalized. As Hollenbach extols the sign of the cross as opening 'the possibility of an ethics of compassionate solidarity' (Hollenbach 1996, p. 13), this book frames the challenge by adapting a core dimension of liberation theology to be *a preferential optic for those who are poor*. Such a move, to add the preferential option to common-good thinking, is advanced by Cahill when, in the context of bioethics, she articulates the common good on a global scale that means wealthier nations not trampling on the rights of other countries: 'the global common good also requires ... [a] preferential option for the poor as necessary for social transformation, going beyond rights and equality' (Cahill 2004, p. 19).

My argument in this book is in sympathy with Hollenbach, Cahill and other Christian thinkers who contribute a theological deepening of the common good. However, the belief in divine solidarity, upon which a social ethics is built, can prove highly problematic in the light of much human experience. Hollenbach contends that a theological common-good ethic 'surrenders the effort to construct all moral meaning as an extension of the temporary survival of the modern self into the hands of a compassionate Friend who saves us when we cannot do so for ourselves' (Hollenbach 1996, p. 14). But what happens when that Friend fails?

Surveillance under the sign of the cross must also be under the sign of Auschwitz. This one camp is symbolic of the attempt to oppress and later to exterminate Jews from the early 1930s until 1945. But as Johann-Baptist Metz argues, theological discussion is not undertaken in the light of a symbol or objectified category of 'the Jews' or 'Judaism'. Instead, those who were brutalized and killed 'have to be seen – the destroyed faces, the burned eyes, of whom we can only tell, which we can only remember, but which cannot be reconstructed in systematic concepts' (Metz 1984, p. 26). Where was this Friend whose gaze is crucial to Christian theological perspectives on surveillance? What does it mean to talk of a divine gaze that ostensibly failed? Considering the common gaze demands that we consider problematic assumptions made of God's gaze.

A note on method

The methodology of this book lies close to public theology, not in David Tracy's sense of arguments that are 'available in principle to any attentive, intelligent, rational and responsible human being' (Tracy 1983, p. 66) but as Elaine Graham contends, in not only doing theological reflection *about* issues of public concerns but 'do[ing] its theology *in* public, with a sense of transparency to those of other faiths and none' (E. Graham 2013, p. 232). It is practical theology in its following a cycle of reflection (common in the field represented, for example, by Thomas Groome in the USA (Groome 1991) or John Swinton and Harriet Mowat in the UK (Swinton and Mowat 2006)). Leaning more towards approaches that do not necessarily privilege orthodox theological perspectives, I use a cycle that begins with naming experience, appreciating how it is understood by non-theological disciplines, and only then progressing to consider biblical and theological perspectives in a move that articulates the ways in which, for example, sociology and theology affirm and challenge each other's interpretation of a particular practice. On such a basis, revised practice can be proposed. In my *Advancing Practical Theology*, I find a tendency for practical theology to lean more towards negotiation with, rather than a more radical confrontation of, injustice (Stoddart 2014b). In that book I draw on the liberative ethics proposed by Miguel De La Torre as 'a spiritual response to unexamined normative and legitimised social structures responsible for privileging a powerful minority at the expense of the disenfranchised majority' (De La Torre 2013, p. 3). In *The Common Gaze* I deploy a method that therefore submits practical theology to liberative ethics:

> Integral, then, to any cycle of reflection must be the voice, needs and contribution of those who are marginalised, disenfranchised or in other ways oppressed by Empire. This does not mean adding an extra step to the diagrams of the cycle of reflection, but radicalising each step. (Stoddart 2014b, p. 144)

It is this cycle of radical public practical theology that structures the three central chapters of this volume.

The path before us

This book has three parts: the first sets out the principal elements that I bring together as the common gaze, namely surveillance and the common good. Chapter 1 explores surveillance as a contemporary culture of the watched life and watching as a way of life. David Lyon's recent work on the culture of surveillance provides the main theoretical framework upon which we explore not only forms of surveillance but its supporting social institutions and structures. Turning then to biblical parables of watching, we focus particularly on the recovery of the lost sheep. This generates questions about failing shepherds misruling their metaphorical flock that have a twenty-first-century salience for the leaders of surveillance businesses as well as beginning to reposition the purpose of surveillance as primarily restorative rather than for security.

Chapter 2 uses the concept of social imaginaries to discuss, by way of the work of Michael Sandel, the value of the common good as a process of moral engagement. Roman Catholic Social Teaching provides us with a theological rendering of the common good within which God's preferential option for those who are poor can be expressed. By imagining the common good in the context of surveillance and digital poverty, we arrive at our definition of the common gaze: *surveillance for the common good, inflected with a preferential optic for those who are (digitally) poor.*

Part 2 comprises three substantial chapters addressing influence, identity and identification. Chapter 3 considers claims that democracy and, more particularly, citizens themselves, are being 'hacked' by micro-targeted political advertising. This use of surveillance enables the use of analytics against the datafied citizen by inferring characteristics and attempting to dull people's critical attention to information by riling them to anger. Cambridge Analytica serves as an example of what has been attempted in the weaponizing of information. We make an imaginative step into the biblical world of false prophets and the role of the crowd in the New Testament narratives to appreciate the fragility of human decision-making under influence. This leads us to posit artificial intelligence as an alluring opportunity offered in current, and possibly future, politics. With artificial intelligence playing an increasing part in data analytics we examine the argument that humans would be wise to devolve complex political decisions to machines more able to cope with the vast amount of information available that ought to shape policy. The theological perspectives of Brian Brock, Antje Jackelén and others enable us to resist claims that humans should stand aside. Artificial intelligence is not as intelligent as its proponents claim, being incapable of offering artificial alternatives to either salvation or love. What is left in artificial intelligence is therefore an inadequate basis for responsible decision-making. If politics means anything it cannot be undertaken on our behalf and so we lay claim to the motto 'nothing about us without us' as a theologically grounded resistance to pressure upon humans to abdicate in favour of machines.

In Chapter 4 we examine the self-quantification movement in which smartphone and wearable device applications let us count our steps, set workout goals and monitor our health indicators. Understanding these socio-technological developments as forms of identity construction, we come to see how a governed self is a monetized self. Shoshana Zuboff's model of surveillance capitalism shows how our behavioural surpluses are our work as prosumers in an information economy that reaches into so many aspects of life with the fervour of a colonizing power. The economic critique of ancient Rome expressed in the vivid imagery of the book of Revelation poses challenges to complicity by merchants in the trade of luxury supported by imperial pagan cults. We take the challenges facing Christians trading in Corinth to be indicative of that to which John the Seer is pointing to through his apocalypticism. Using as our inspiration the old question, 'What has Athens to do with Jerusalem?' we pose our own version, 'What does Silicon Valley have to do with Corinth?' Here we interrogate informational capitalism in the light of the Roman Catholic theology of work and dignity to challenge the selfishness into which self-quantifiers are being shaped. As a bulwark against market exchange and competition as the dominant paradigm for handling data, we explore the possibilities of a logic of gift and solidarity. Not without its own problems, we propose positioning self-quantification more within an economy of grace than exchange, particularly against neoliberal prioritizing of the market as a way of reasoning across hitherto non-monetized areas of life. Given that Christians are offered digital means of self-quantifying their spiritual progress, our practical theological sensibilities are exercised in the light of Jesus' injunction to avoid displays of piety. While devices may indeed nudge in positive directions, we suggest that they may encourage a datafied hypocrisy.

Chapter 5 tackles identification by posing the question of how algorithms might have liberative possibilities and not only the oppressive outcomes so clearly identified in the works of Safiya Umoja Noble and Virginia Eubanks. We share with them deep concerns about unjust discrimination arising from the degrees of legibility required particularly of those who are already disadvantaged economically and often also socially. While rejecting the rationalizing of people adversely impacted as collateral damage, we suggest that surveillance *of* surveillance offers scope for at least tracking where injustice needs to be addressed. At the heart of systems of algorithmic surveillance there lie processes of social categorization that are integral to the functioning of human societies through the ages – and no less so in the worlds of the Hebrew Bible and New Testament. By drawing on Mary Douglas's notion of uncleanness as something being out of its proper place, we turn to the ritual purity presented in Leviticus and in the ideational mapping of the Jerusalem Temple in Ezekiel. The work of the New Testament scholar Marcus Borg on Jesus' radical reframing of holiness as compassion rather than primarily purity offers us a theological reconsideration of surveillance categorization in current digital systems. Instead of the prevailing use of surveillance to impose order on a chaotic world of terrorists and fraudsters, we argue that information might be liberated, not for profit or control but for compassion. This brings us to the profound challenge of arguing for a common gaze that builds upon the compassion of God when the faces of the Jews and others murdered by the Nazis compel our respectful silence. We conclude that God's gaze in the camps failed – in terms of the transcendent and powerful God envisaged in much Jewish and Christian theodicies. The Jewish feminist theology of Melissa Raphael, articulated as the presence of Shekhinah in the resistance of people in the camps to being dehumanized, offers us an approach that is combined with the notion of relational transcendence proposed by the post-colonial Christian theologian Mayra Rivera. Miguel De La Torre's advocacy of hopelessness and Rowan Williams's call to wounded speech in the face of more recent atrocities leads us to articulate the common gaze as a wounded gaze and a way of watching *with* rather than *over* others. Conscious of the weight of tradition in the wide use of the term *surveillance* we nevertheless put a marker down for the neologism *comveillance* as a way of keeping the purpose of surveillance as solidarity more prominently in view.

Part 3 comprises two final chapters: Chapter 6, articulating the common gaze as a public practice, and in Chapter 7 as church practice. In the former we address concerns about the assumptions of the common good in liberal democracy working their way into the common gaze. More positively, we identify the potential contribution of the common gaze towards making democracy more resistant to hacking, and society more resilient in the face of unmanageable dangers. In the final chapter we turn the common gaze on Christian practice in challenging how the Church might welcome surveillance upon itself, at the same time as revising its use of surveillance in church growth and forms of political activism. We then return to the biblical passages that have featured throughout the book to propose how practices of reading need to be revised.

The common gaze matters because surveillance reinforces and introduces further injustices as well as delivering health, economic and caring benefits for which many are profoundly grateful. But surveillance is a system of values – not merely of technological devices. We need the common gaze to remind us how surveillance holds us. Zuboff captures what is at stake and how we envisage the common gaze as one way of responding:

When I speak to my children or an audience of young people, I try to alert them to the historically contingent nature of 'the thing that has us' by calling attention to ordinary values and expectations before surveillance capitalism began its campaign of psychic numbing. 'It is not OK to have to hide in your own life; it is not normal,' I tell them. 'It is not OK to spend your lunchtime conversations comparing software that will camouflage you and protect you from continuous unwanted invasion.' *Five trackers blocked. Four trackers blocked. Fifty-nine trackers blocked, facial features scrambled, voice disguised …*

I tell them that the word 'search' has meant daring existential journey, not a finger tap to already existing answers; that 'friend' is an embodied mystery that can be forged only face-to-face and heart-to-heart; and that 'recognition' is the glimmer of homecoming we experience in our beloved's face, not 'facial recognition'. (Zuboff 2019, p. 521)

Part 1

Surveillance as a Twenty-first-century Culture

The watched life

Surveillance may commence before our conception if our mother tracks her menstrual cycle using her smartphone. Her health and ours during pregnancy may benefit from medical monitoring. As we pass each educational milestone, our teachers record our progress. Our attendance, or lack of it, at college tutorials is visible to staff (and us) on virtual learning platforms. Our employer scrutinizes our efficiency and trustworthiness. If we become parents we likely enable tracking apps on our child's phone. During a global pandemic we watch national trends and possibly report our own symptoms and make ourselves traceable should we become a contagious contact. On entering retirement our receipt of state benefits enfolds us in another system of watching. Becoming frail in advanced age means we rely more and more on movement sensors to keep us that bit safer. Surveillance is available, often imposed, across our life cycle.

But proving our entitlement to services comes at a cost – not merely to us but to wider society. The United Nations' special rapporteur is sympathetic to the view that twenty-first-century Britain is creating a digitally Dickensian workhouse in which:

> British compassion has been replaced by a punitive, mean-spirited and often callous approach apparently designed to impose a rigid order on the lives of those least capable of coping, and elevate the goal of enforcing blind compliance over a genuine concern to improve the well-being of those at the lowest economic levels of British society. (Human Rights Council 2019, para. 13)

While smartphones can prove to be a lifeline to migrants on treacherous journeys (Alencar et al. 2018), those devices' digital emissions render travellers trackable and identifiable. Efforts to improve the safety of public spaces for women in, for example, the Punjab rely on mobile data communications in the form of a 'Public Safety app' by which women may audit local areas as 'safe' or 'unsafe' based, partly, on their experience of street harassment and violence. In privacy terms, users need to surrender personally identifiable information to civic authorities to register the app. Even if this application provides greater safety it can only be for 'a particular kind of woman – middle to upper class, able-bodied, English-speaking, tech-savvy and has access to the internet' (Khan 2018, p. 23).

This chapter deploys David Lyon's articulation of the culture of surveillance: 'How surveillance is imagined and experienced, and about how mundane activities ... are affected by and affect surveillance' (Lyon 2018a, p. 2). In an attempt to get at least a foot outside of a technological paradigm, we will draw on one of Jesus' parables of watching, commonly known as the lost sheep, and its implicit critique of those shepherds who are negligent in their care-full and careful tending of the flock. This will enable us to consider two cultures of watching: biblical and twenty-first-century. While the Bible might help us think critically about the culture, character (and proficiency) of model watchers (shepherds), Lyon's culture of surveillance will foster a critique of how we are being shaped (and shaping) our reliance on digital systems.

There is not a simplistic duality in which biblical cultures trust God to watch and twenty-first-century cultures trust surveillance. Neither is there a straightforward correspondence of terms from biblical parables to digital experiences. It is the case that shepherds are managing flocks and we are herded through physical spaces. We might also find a parallel in mixed flocks being sorted into ownership and we being sorted into categories by algorithms. Yet, any analogies break down once we appreciate that twenty-first-century sheep are not passively grazing but actively gazing.

Nevertheless, an imaginative reading of the lost sheep parable will lead us to affirm the best practices of watching over. Lyon's concept of 'the culture of surveillance' will begin to challenge how we read biblical themes of watching when the gaze is performative; producing particular types of watcher and the watched. It matters who is naming an experience of surveillance; whether one is near to the bottom of the economic scale or of low value in public perception.

Watching as a way of life

Culture of surveillance

David Lyon's contribution to the study of surveillance is singularly significant for our project for two principal reasons. Foremost this is because Lyon has been a consistent voice, arguably the most prominent advocate, of drawing the humanities to the discussion table. Although a social scientist, Lyon has recognized the importance of considering surveillance as ethical practices within diverse understandings of what it means for human beings to flourish. Here, alone, there is resonance with practical theology in its public mode, concerned with 'doing being human' (Pattison 2007, p. 20). The second reason that Lyon's analyses are compelling for this exploration is his attention to Christian perspectives on surveillance (Lyon 1995, 2014, 2018b). While making no claims to be an academic theologian, Lyon has highlighted the importance of appreciating that surveillance is practised by people of religious faith – not only in their communities of worship but in their vocations as computer scientists, politicians, business executives and educationalists (to name only a few).

For Lyon, surveillance can be concisely defined as 'the operations and experiences of gathering and analysing personal data for influence, entitlement and management' (Lyon 2018a, p. 6). The key component to this definition lies in its first part. Surveillance is not merely a set of, albeit very much more complex, technological operations. Most importantly, Lyon's definition attends to what it is like to be a subject of a surveilling gaze *and* what is someone's perception as one who deploys data-gathering and analysis towards others. Naturally, as his definition allows, a person can be both a subject and deployer of surveillance in multiple domains. Being a data analyst in a marketing organization likely means also being monitored by one's employer. A politician deliberating over new privacy regulations may well be a contributor to social media, subject to scrutiny by her political opponents. Lyon has extended his analytical toolbox by developing the notion of 'the culture of surveillance'. By this he means 'how surveillance is imagined and experienced, and about how mundane activities … are affected by and affect surveillance' (Lyon 2018a, p. 2). It will be helpful to unpack the main points of this theoretical framework.

'Watching has become a way of life', writes Lyon (Lyon 2018a, p. 4). This is a move on from both the surveillance state and the surveillance society. In its liquidity, surveillance takes different, and unfixed, forms (Bauman and Lyon 2013). Its endearing convenience to consumers renders it both soft and acceptable in contrast, perhaps, to the rigid, steely surveillance by the state. Data-gathering and analysis now leak between domains – where information garnered about grocery shopping can be engineered to be of value to political campaigns. As Lyon rightly observes: 'Without a fixed container, but jolted by security demands and tipped by technology companies' insistent marking, surveillance spills out all over, just because it is an organizing principle of these activities' (Lyon 2018a, p. 32). But not just those activities – liquid surveillance includes 'the kinds of social relationships that are possible within a surveillance culture' (Lyon 2018a, p. 33). Older analogies such as the panoptic penitentiary are displaced by 'performative surveillance' (Lyon 2018a, p. 34) as we engage in 'monitored performances', whether this takes place in a call centre, in our leisure activities recorded on a phone app or public protests we engage in as anti-surveillance activists (Lyon 2018a, p. 36).

Crucial, then, to the culture of surveillance are those ways in which we picture ourselves: our social imaginaries of 'social arrangements and relationships' (Lyon 2018a, p. 45). While social imaginaries include 'shared understandings about certain aspects of visibility in daily life, and in social relationships, expectations and normative commitments' (Lyon 2018a, p. 41), Lyon's definition, indebted to Charles Taylor (C. Taylor 2004), also includes practices: '*responsive* activities that relate to being surveilled and also *initiatory* modes of engagement *with* surveillance' (Lyon 2018a, p. 42, emphasis in original). Treating surveillance as culture enables Lyon to articulate a number of significant changes in how we imagine life organized by surveillance. It may be that what at first we find to be convenient surveillance (as in airport security) becomes in our minds an imposition with which our compliance is demanded. What was once a novelty (phones that could track our location) turns into a pressure upon us when it is normalized as an expectation of family or business relationships. We may elide, argues Lyon, from online to 'onlife' – 'network devices hav[ing] become embedded in the lived environment and taken up within the context of everyday interactions' (Lyon 2018a, p. 114). In this social imaginary of expectations and practices, what we once contested we might now meet with compliance (Lyon 2018a, p. 138).

Although not yet having given ourselves over to total transparency, Lyon sees glimmers of hope if we can retain (or perhaps in some cases acquire) a wider vision. This would mean noticing 'the wider contexts of small experiences of surveillance' that might 'undermine trust, generate disadvantage to some, or simply be an instance of treating others only in terms of disembodied, abstract data' (Lyon 2018a, pp. 177–8). Furthermore, in what is in effect a plea by Lyon that had been made by feminists in earlier contexts when they claimed that the personal is political, he encourages us to think how individual issues around surveillance might actually be public (Lyon 2018a, p. 178). In a third glimmer, Lyon argues that, despite the global forces in play, the local matters for 'the attitudes and actions of users make a difference' (Lyon 2018a, p. 178).

It is these three candles sputtering in the digital wind that speak directly to our project. We are concerned about the social fabric of trust and disadvantage, seeing in our case Christian theological and biblical imagination contributing to a critique of the personal as well the political. Our conclusions are aimed at fostering hope that we can make a difference to the culture of surveillance. This will require inflecting cultures of surveillance more towards issues of intersectionality, as previously advocated by Rachel Dubrofsky and Shoshana Amielle Magnet, who attend to 'the use of surveillance practices and technologies to normalize and maintain whiteness, able-bodiedness, capitalism, and heterosexuality, practices integral to the foundation of the modern state' (Dubrofsky and Magnet 2015, p. 7). Attending, as will our biblical reflections, to social imaginaries prior to the modern state will also give us scope to open conversation with surveillance in twenty-first-century societies with more critical distance from a technological paradigm.

Beyond the veil

What, then, is the culture of surveillance in more contextual terms? This will be the question we seek to unpack at numerous points in this book, but here we can put a stake in the ground by way of parliamentary and arms-length government bodies. These are, of course, nothing like the final word and, to some extent, represent the perspectives of elites. Nevertheless, their considered reflections, having taken evidence from a large cast of characters, warrant noting.

The UK's Surveillance Camera Commissioner, Tony Porter, draws our attention to the porous boundary between the police and the private sector, through which digital imaging data may now sometimes be permitted to flow:

> The overlap between police use of video surveillance platforms will become more entangled with that of private and commercial organisations. Clarity as to their use, intention and purpose is paramount if public trust is to be retained in the use of video surveillance camera systems by the police and others such as local authorities. (Surveillance Camera Commissioner 2019, p. 1)

Porter's concern is the veil that is drawn over quite what is happening at that porous membrane; lack of transparency is one thing but, as he goes on to observe, awareness on the part of the public of exactly which bodies – acting supposedly in their interest – are deploying these technologies is another:

> I have called for the need to recognise the burgeoning use of video surveillance platforms in many sectors, but particularly those in health, education and transport. The scale of organisations operating such systems in the public domain goes well beyond the limited range of 'relevant authorities' provided within the Protection of Freedoms Act 2012. That limitation is increasingly looking illogical and is rejected by the industry and operators themselves. (Surveillance Camera Commissioner 2019, p. 1)

Porter acknowledges that legal, regulatory frameworks struggle to update sufficiently quickly in response to technological developments. This situation is worrying because systems' 'inherent abilities to intrude upon a very broad spectrum of our fundamental rights and freedoms become far more detailed and sophisticated' (Surveillance Camera Commissioner 2019, p. 1). Such an approach would not be accepted with pharmaceuticals. Rushing a drug on to the market with minimal testing would (outside of a pandemic) be met with a public outcry; not so it seems when the principle is applied in the field of data analytics. Much the same would be said if car manufacturers were allowed to let market forces determine the safety of a new high-speed vehicle. It is said that the definition of a Scottish *gentleman* is that he is able to play the bagpipes but chooses not to. The UK's Surveillance Camera Commissioner makes the same point about private enterprise's complex data technology relationship with law enforcement: 'it is important that the mantra of "just because you can, doesn't mean you should" needs to be applied. Careful thought around how these challenges are to be managed going forward is required' (Surveillance Camera Commissioner 2019, p. 47). There is a culture of pitting data protection against security as if we can only have one *or* the other. This is perhaps like a teenager being reluctant to wear a reflective vest when cycling in the dark because 'it's not cool'. In reality, the yellow fluorescent vest could keep him safe enough to be cool. One wonders if a similar petulance from the security services was behind the FRA (the European Union Agency for Fundamental Rights) concluding in a report:

> Data protection rules and other rule of law principles should not be seen as potential hurdles to protecting the security of Europe's citizens, but instead as sources of mutual benefits for individuals and intelligence

services. Respecting these rights and principles paves the way for more accurate data collection and analysis, renewed trust among European citizens towards their intelligence services and, as a result, a more effective defence of national security. (FRA 2017, p. 135)

The Privacy Commissioner of Canada reached a similar conclusion but with respect to commerce:

We must reject the notion that rights-based laws impede economic growth or other important societal objectives. Fundamental rights are not an impediment to innovation or the delivery of government services in the digital age. In fact, a rights-based statute would serve to support responsible innovation by promoting trust in government and commercial activities. (Privacy Commissioner of Canada 2019, p. 3)

Where democratic transparency and accountability are presented as inimical to good government we can see corrupt authoritarianism added to a debased culture of surveillance. At its meeting in Johannesburg in March 2019, the International Conference of Information Commissioners concluded that even if there are regulatory regimens about personal information, these are not necessarily of substantial value to everyone in a country:

not all citizens are able to exercise the right of access to information equally. Women, refugees, internally displaced persons, people living with disabilities and other vulnerable and marginalised groups face particular challenges. Whether socioeconomic, political or historical in nature, these challenges impede both their right to access to information and access to information about them. (ICIC 2019)

The commissioners noted projects in this regard in Bangladesh, Brazil, Guatemala, Liberia and Nigeria. There is something both paternalistic and sinister about a culture of surveillance that, from those at the centres of power, can be framed in terms of illegitimate challenges to their accountability.

Before the veil

Surveillance culture is imagined and practised under the influence of social patterns and structures. It hardly needs saying that integral to much of our encounter with our own and others' personal information is the mediation of global corporations. There are regional differences where the state is more directly engaged with platforms, as in China. But there are deep footprints left by the major players such as Facebook, Google, Twitter, Instagram and Snapchat as they stride through our imagination. Only a decade ago we might have looked at someone askance whose most frequent contact with their friends was by pinning a photograph or a message on a noticeboard that they might pass by a few times during the day. The notion that we might keep returning to that noticeboard throughout the day to check if someone had added a tick or maybe a sticky star to our note would raise a few concerned looks. Using a noticeboard in such a way might be fine for a few office colleagues but is not how we would normally imagine our contact with our friends. To be fair, it was easy to lose touch with friends who moved away. Businesses would be cautious about making international phone calls and certainly among families this was kept for special occasions, if at all.

With friends to whom we lived closer, we made arrangements ahead of time to meet at a particular cafe at a set time – and accepted a convention of waiting ten, maybe fifteen, minutes should they be delayed. When riding the bus to meet a friend we listened in to others' conversations or sat in silence. We were out of contact until standing in front of our friend at the cafe as we had planned. Global technology platforms have given us means of contact that most of us never envisaged if we were growing up in the 1970s and even the very early 1980s. We can now connect (albeit often asynchronously) with people who might never before have remained within our category of friends.

National government is another social structure that is involved in our lives like never before. 'Signing on' for what was once called unemployment benefit really did mean signing a card in the dole office. However, the extent of the staff's access to other information about us was limited. We might be targeted for scrutiny if suspected of making a false claim – but this was staff-intensive and thus expensive to mount. The prospect of being caught up in an investigation sweep by the security services was something that only happened under communist regimes – state surveillance was something the baddies in movies did to their own citizens. Edward Snowden's exposure of democratic states gathering data on their own citizens was too close for comfort to the plot of *1984* the novel (Snowden 2019). Dystopic real-life has, to some extent, superseded dystopic science fiction.

Class social structures also shape our experience of the culture of surveillance. When we look later at algorithmic decision-making in welfare entitlement we will see how significant one's place on the socio-economic ladder can be in encountering data analysis of personal information relating to one's intimate relationships, finances (or lack thereof), criminal record (for minor infractions), as well as health – physical and mental. While poverty excludes one from so many privileges, pleasure and opportunities, the lack of money engulfs one in digital systems of monitoring that others, more well-off, usually can avoid. The same can be true if one's ethnicity is under suspicion – 'driving while black', 'flying while brown', and most recently 'coughing while Asian' are phrases that point to systemic discrimination, reinforced and reproduced by surveillance. The culture of surveillance is different depending on where the dimensions of one's identity interests lie.

Our national or local memories of surveillance also influence a culture of surveillance. Extreme sensitivities to abuses of surveillance by the Nazis and then communists in East Germany – juxtaposed with often more accepted surveillance by West Germany – prompt a particular imaginary around good and bad forms of state monitoring (Sperling 2011). Rigorous monitoring of the black majority's movements around South Africa by the apartheid regime, in collaboration with private security companies, embeds narratives that are particular to that country's twenty-first-century surveillance practices (Diphoorn 2016). Memory is a powerful dimension of a culture of surveillance; 9/11 in the USA, 7/7 in London, 12 October 2002 in Bali, and innumerable bombings in Iraq, Afghanistan and the wider region. Such events do not only provide political justification for close monitoring of the dangerous other but seep into a nation's collective consciousness. When 'icon' now so often means either a symbol on a computer screen or a celebrity-hero figure, it is worth reasserting its religious meaning. The photograph of a plane crashing into one of the World Trade Center towers or of a red London bus with its roof blown off becomes iconic in the sense that we look through and beyond the image. Icons connect us to an imaginary that in turns shapes our everyday perception. Our respective cultures of surveillance each have their own icons.

A culture of surveillance highlights the kinds of social relations that we imagine to be possible, mediated by global digital media corporations. Living an onlife implicates us in watching and being watched with regimes that frequently outrun the pace of regulatory bodies. A culture of watching is not new, and although its twenty-first-century innovations are important, turning attention to the biblical worlds can open somewhat forgotten perspectives.

Counting sheep who count

Watching parables

Lyon's culture of surveillance invites us to reflect on how we and others picture ourselves; our social imaginaries. We now turn to the Bible to begin asking that same question, but of the people in New Testament contexts. Here I want to think solely in terms of watching, not attempting a comprehensive account of the social imaginaries of the first-century AD eastern Mediterranean cultures. Taking a quick tour of various parables of watching before stopping to take time with the one about the lost sheep, we can begin to glimpse the shape of a different culture of watching.

We find some hint of apocalyptic and eschatological mindsets in the parable of ten watching virgins or bridesmaids. In Matthew 25 Jesus tells a parable:

> Then the kingdom of heaven will be like this. Ten bridesmaids took their lamps and went to meet the bridegroom. Five of them were foolish, and five were wise. When the foolish took their lamps, they took no oil with them; but the wise took flasks of oil with their lamps. As the bridegroom was delayed, all of them became drowsy and slept. (Matt. 25.1–5)

It is not snoozing that determines being wise or foolish, it is being prepared when woken that is crucial. Interestingly, neither is it willingness to share that differentiates wisdom and folly, for the parable goes on to tell of those with oil not decanting a portion of it on request to their neglectful sisters. We have here a culture of apocalyptic watching; a disposition of readiness for an in-breaking of God into history.

In the parable known to us as 'the rich man and Lazarus' we find a wealthy man looking up from Hades (in the triple-decker universe of the day) at the heavenly beatitude awarded a poor man whom he had neglected on his doorstep:

> There was a rich man who was dressed in purple and fine linen and who feasted sumptuously every day. And at his gate lay a poor man named Lazarus, covered with sores, who longed to satisfy his hunger with what fell from the rich man's table; even the dogs would come and lick his sores. The poor man died and was carried away by the angels to be with Abraham. The rich man also died and was buried. In Hades, where he was being tormented, he looked up and saw Abraham far away with Lazarus by his side. (Luke 16.19–23)

In an ethos of just desserts within a divine recompense and retribution paradigm, watching has consequences *now* and not only in the watchers' futures.

Religious scrupulosity hoves into view (although we will have much more to say about this when we talk in Chapter 4 about self-quantification) when watching is disabled by the infamous 'log in your own eye' (Matt. 7.4). Hypocrisy in watching was familiar to Jesus' audiences, who could image a scenario in which invitees to a royal wedding neglect to show up when summoned and compound this social slight by murdering the king's messengers. In the parable of the wedding banquet (Matt. 22.1–14) we alight on the propriety of social customs, particularly one's outfit at a wedding feast. Most oddly, a last-minute invitee, scooped off the streets to make up numbers, has a grisly fate because he is inappropriately dressed:

'But when the king came in to see the guests, he noticed a man there who was not wearing a wedding robe, and he said to him, "Friend, how did you get in here without a wedding robe?" And he was speechless. Then the king said to the attendants, "Bind him hand and foot, and throw him into the outer darkness, where there will be weeping and gnashing of teeth." For many are called, but few are chosen.' (Matt. 22.11–14)

Whatever theological interpretation is required of this parable, we learn that the contemporary culture of watching was recognizable for its monitoring of social mores. Non-conformity led to non-entitlement.

Watching to avoid ritual pollution, on what was to become famous as the road to Jericho, sat alongside alertness against being surprised by brigands. Looking 'with pity' (Luke 10.33) distinguished the Samaritan as the good man to his neighbour. Within the domestic sphere we can find people searching for objects and rejoicing greatly upon finding them. The everyday culture of watching is a communal affair:

'Or what woman having ten silver coins, if she loses one of them, does not light a lamp, sweep the house, and search carefully until she finds it? When she has found it, she calls together her friends and neighbours, saying, "Rejoice with me, for I have found the coin that I had lost."' (Luke 15.8–9)

But domestic watching can be familiar sibling rivalry; surely recognizable to those then, and through the ages, who have heard the parable of the prodigal son:

'Listen! For all these years I have been working like a slave for you, and I have never disobeyed your command; yet you have never given me even a young goat so that I might celebrate with my friends. But when this son of yours came back, who has devoured your property with prostitutes, you killed the fatted calf for him!' (Luke 15.29–30)

These parables of different types of watching give us a glimpse into the culture of the gaze that is predominantly an everyday experience; one reason for the long-lasting appeal of these parables as assumption-destabilizing rhetorical devices. However, I want to give more attention to cultures of political watching, as a means of talking about leadership responsibilities. In so doing we can engage the Bible in stimulating our imagination about broader, societal aspects of our contemporary surveillance culture.

Lost sheep; careless shepherd?

Now all the tax-collectors and sinners were coming near to listen to him. And the Pharisees and the scribes were grumbling and saying, 'This fellow welcomes sinners and eats with them.'

So he told them this parable: 'Which one of you, having a hundred sheep and losing one of them, does not leave the ninety-nine in the wilderness and go after the one that is lost until he finds it? When he has found it, he lays it on his shoulders and rejoices. And when he comes home, he calls together his friends and neighbours, saying to them, "Rejoice with me, for I have found my sheep that was lost." Just so, I tell you, there will be more joy in heaven over one sinner who repents than over ninety-nine righteous persons who need no repentance.' (Luke 15.1–7)

The focus of the parable is the shepherd, rather than the sheep; it is the shepherd who seeks and rejoices. The parable tells of behaviour that is, arguably, atypical for a shepherd in that he endangers the 99 for the sake of the one in anything but a sensible commercial decision. It could matter if first-century Palestinian shepherds *owned* their sheep. Some were hired hands (John 10.12–13) but they might have followed the Greek practice of a shepherd raising a few of the sheep among the flock as his own (Levi 1993, p. 115). We will, shortly, hold this parable in the light of Ezekiel's critique of the shepherds (that is, the leaders) of Israel (Ezek. 34.1). These fail to strengthen the weak, heal the sick, bind up the injured and neglect to bring back strays. Rather, as villains, they rule with harshness and force (Ezek. 34.4). In Ezekiel's vision, God is rescuing sheep *from* their shepherds (Ezek. 34.10); God acts as a good shepherd (Ezek. 34.11f.).

Luke 15 is about the gospel being for outcasts (Snodgrass 2008, p. 94) while Matthew's context for the parable is about loss from the Christian community (Matt. 18.12–14). Staying with Luke for the moment, the culture of watching here might point to a concern for the outcast, not further excluding one who is outcast. It is worth noticing that the Lucan context is actually one of surveillance. Jesus has been observed eating and drinking with 'sinners'. In a parallel passage in Mark 2.15, Jesus is clearly the host of (and not just eating with) 'sinners' (Bailey 1983, p. 143). The parable in Luke is Jesus' defence for what has been established through surveillance of him by his critics: 'The primary function of this parable for Jesus was a defence of his deliberate association with and eating with people known to be sinners' (Snodgrass 2008, p. 108). In John's Gospel the motif is developed into the shepherd surrendering his life for the sheep (John 10.11).

There is another difference between Matthew's and Luke's versions of the parable of the lost sheep: the sheep is 'going astray' in Matthew (18.12) but the shepherd 'has lost' his sheep in Luke (15.4, 6). In an intriguingly similar Midrashic tale, Moses follows a sheep who has bolted, for it wanted a drink (Shemot Rabbah 2.2). In such light we might want to ask why the sheep in Jesus' parable would have gone astray.

In another respect it is a parable of surveillance, for it prompts us to ask how the shepherd knew one was missing. Amy-Jill Levine calls this the parable of 'the Initially Oblivious Owner' (Levine 2014, p. 35). A regular habit of counting was required to ensure all were present; in human terms, a disciplinary process of accounting for the presence, and alerting to an absence, from the flock. Separation from the group is inherently problematic (whether understood as straying or being lost).

Shepherds of misrule

The New Testament parable has clear echoes from the prophet Ezekiel:

> You eat the fat, you clothe yourselves with the wool, you slaughter the fatlings; but you do not feed the sheep. You have not strengthened the weak, you have not healed the sick, you have not bound up the injured, you have not brought back the strayed, you have not sought the lost, but with force and harshness you have ruled them. So they were scattered, because there was no shepherd; and scattered, they became food for all the wild animals. My sheep were scattered, they wandered over all the

mountains and on every high hill; my sheep were scattered over all the face of the earth, with no one to search or seek for them. (Ezek. 34.3–6)

Such a relationship with the people is quite paternalistic and the context is of a theocracy with its problems of authoritarianism and repression of minorities (or even majorities) who deviate from religious law. Nevertheless, the imagery takes us to the heart of what a position of leadership is *for*. Ezekiel may be addressing his contemporaries or kings of Judah both past and present. Possibly Ezekiel refers not just to Zedekiah but the whole leadership stratum of Judah (Mein 2001, p. 97). Predatory misrule is perhaps a concept inspired by Zephaniah (3.3) and delinquent shepherds from Jeremiah (2.8):

> It was left for Ezekiel to combine the two themes – predatory rulers and delinquent shepherds – into the image of predatory shepherds feeding on their own flock, an extravagance typical of him; cf., e.g., 'children shall eat their parents' (5:10), or the nymphomaniacal adulteress of ch. 16. (Greenberg 1997, p. 709)

Sentinels or watchmen (such as those on the walls of Jerusalem, Isaiah 62.6–7) may become blind 'without knowledge' and 'silent dogs that cannot bark' at danger (Isa. 56.10). While these might be civic rulers, a prophet may contribute to this function: 'Mortal, I have made you a sentinel for the house of Israel; whenever you hear a word from my mouth, you shall give them warning from me' (Ezek. 3.17).

While shepherds watch

Confronting the corporate leader

A sheep and shepherd metaphor is immediately problematic in a twenty-first-century context because paternalism by leaders is bad enough. Rendering any link between subjects of surveillance and sheep is even more problematic. To start with, questions of human agency do not sit easily with ruminants bred for food and wool. As problematic as such analogies might be, we might usefully ponder what might be the relationship between digital shepherds and their data-flocks. If the CEO of a data-gathering company were to have the responsibilities of a shepherd, what might those be? What was expected of the better shepherds? Seeking the well-being of the flock comes first and foremost, involving protection and sustenance. Taken into the political realities facing people in Ezekiel's or Isaiah's times, leadership means attending to the interests of the community, rather than self-interest. In other words, a leadership that is not exploitative. Furthermore, given acute regional power struggles, the good ruler deals in realities rather than fantasies. We are so accustomed to surveillance being a commercial venture – even when practised by the state when it contracts private research and development companies to supply infrastructure. We will have much more to consider of surveillance capitalism in Chapter 4 but just for the moment we can pause and imagine a world different from the monetization of our personal data. We ought not to romanticize first-century AD farming – sheep were not kept for show but as an important element in the agri-economy that put food in the mouths of local communities in one way or another. However, there is a responsibility incumbent upon the leader as metaphorical shepherd to seek the good of the people as a whole. In the tradition of the Hebrew Bible, the good is inextricable from faithfulness to God's covenant.

If not God's covenant, what are the founding narratives of the technology industry that is led by today's CEO shepherds? Some have arisen from Cold War anxieties, some with roots further back in previous international conflicts. When surveillance technologies have their roots in military defence and aggression (such as in Israel/Palestine; see S. Graham 2010), it would not be surprising for a particular type of leader to be formed, or deemed suitable, for certain companies. The shepherds of Israel in the Hebrew Bible were most certainly charged with strategic military responsibilities, so at least those narratives find no essential problem in this regard.

A different, but sometimes related, foundational narrative lies in governance. Surveillance here manages large numbers of people in terms of public services, democratic participation and the like. Negatively, surveillance is to pacify by pre-empting discontent over perceptions of inequitable treatment. Positively, data gathering serves as a means of social justice in order that none are overlooked or treated unfairly. The qualities of a leader of surveillance corporations and institutions are rather different in relation to this foundational narrative. We are not referring to competence in terms of technical efficiency but people leading from deep wells of commitment to public service. A third foundational narrative is found in the origins of social network platforms. Giving first the benefit of the doubt, the roots of Facebook in peer-to-peer communication in college were relational. Putting people in touch, the platform then becomes the medium rather than the means. Interaction shifts from being facilitated in material space *by* virtual environments to taking place *in* virtual environments. There are, however, questions arising from the foundational narrative of social networks that lie in objectifying other college students (usually, but not invariably, objectifying women by men). Being 'in touch' as a euphemism for seeking out sexual relationships is perhaps a root that has grown into a feature of social networks more extensively. There is no need to deny the proclivity of people to sexualize a means and medium of communication whatever might have been the best-intentioned origins of social media.

What a culture of watching contributes is a focus on the shepherd as a leader. Looking via this particular biblical imaginary draws attention to the qualities of the surveillance leader, much more than to his or her proficiency as a technician (whether of digital or management systems).

Overwhelming the metaphorical shepherd

To consider a culture of watching in the light of a twenty-first-century culture of surveillance immediately throws up some profound challenges to any slippage of parabolic and metaphorical language into descriptions of God's gaze. The materiality of surveillance grates against the very different mode of expression of the first-century eastern Mediterranean culture. Christians in a world of the Internet of Things might couch their understanding of God not through overtly metaphorical language of a digital milieu but instead rely anachronistically on those of agricultural communities of the time of Jesus. Distance from that imaginary results in privileging first-century AD frames of reference and, rather too easily because these are placed in the mouth of Jesus, assigning them an illegitimate (and perhaps even accidental) descriptive force. It is as if the power of the metaphor of Jesus as the Good Shepherd overwhelms its rhetorical force.

The culture of watching in the Bible is given illocutionary force by appeal to an enchanted world of agents of God, and against God; a world of miracles, angels and evil spirits. A twenty-first-century culture of sur-veillance has its own reinforcement in terms of existential threat of the dangerous demonized Other. Steeped in centuries of Christian spiritual tradition, the Shepherd's watchfulness becomes an anthropomorphic rendering of the divine – a problem that we will review when we ask later, in Chapter 5, about the failure of this sort of divine gaze in the concentration camps of the Third Reich.

Finding lost sheep

If we bracket the problematic use of 'sheep' for twenty-first-century people with agency (albeit constrained), we can see in these biblical texts an imaginative pointer towards a possible primary purpose of surveillance lying in finding those outcast or lost in economic, social and cultural fields and clifftops. The force and harshness of which Ezekiel's shepherd rulers are found guilty offers an analogy with the unbending and fault-finding surveillance by the twenty-first-century state. While a good shepherd sought out the lost, digital automated shepherds are underregulated and guard the sheepfold to ensure the missing sheep can return only following scrutiny that demands to know where they have been; testing the criteria for readmission to the fold. The outcasts are discouraged from returning, the conditions of return being too intrusive (or expensive) under rigid shepherding. The digital shepherd is to seek the profitability, not the integrity, of the flock.

The good digital shepherds identify with the outcast, not compelling return but establishing needs that could enable return. More so, the flock itself is changed, for it is not readmission to what a sheep left but to a joyful welcome of a flock with a vision of being prepared for the future.

To make these imaginative connections is not to dismiss other purposes of surveillance, such as security. Rather, it is to recast the *primary* aim as restoration; security goals of identifying bad sheep are, at most, secondary. Good digital shepherds are commended as serving in an honourable vocation, but bad shepherds are to be tackled not promoted.

The Common Gaze as a Twenty-first-century Imaginary

Looking (out) for the common good

Jack and Jill – what happened next?

> Jack and Jill went up the hill
> To fetch a pail of water.
> Jack fell down and broke his crown,
> And Jill came tumbling after.

A possible future ...

Jack recovered to live a long life and a life that he always told his grandchildren had been a 'good life' despite his celebrity status. Seeing pictures of himself as a baby, in the arms of his grandfather, made him ponder when he'd become 'Jack', not the failed water carrier but at an existential level. When had he realized that he was Jack, an individual member of his family? He could not fix a date, not even pinpoint the year, when he gained sufficient interior distance from his mother to be aware of being a self. Not that identifying such a moment of realization was really that important to him. Jack knew he had grown into being Jack. He had developed his own sense of what a 'good life' meant for him and was thankful for a strong and supportive family who had nurtured his self-identity. That his family had known a good life meant that he had gone on to live well.

He and Jill had weathered the fuss around her laughing at his injury when she had come off unscathed by her tumble. Their families, like the others in their village, had always depended on one another. Jack remembered his teenage years fondly. 'The good life of my community', Jack would tell visitors, 'was integral to my good life.'

When he became a father himself, Jack was instrumental in raising funds for lighting on the path up to the well. It vexed him that the Hubbards had not contributed to the appeal and others had noticed too and accused them of free-riding on others' generosity. It was more important to Jack that the community had safe access to the water supply. Jack had worked hard to persuade the village that using the copse as a fuel source for flaming torches up the hill side was going to deny the next generation but one of not just the material for torches but the ecosystem upon which their whole way of life depended.

Looking back, Jack was glad that his village had wrestled together with the challenge of a lighting system that was sustainable. Although strained, their bonds as a community had deepened and it had felt wonderful to have worked it through together. A write-up in the regional newspaper had applauded Jack's village for realizing that working together on the project was good in itself. It was indeed the case that those in the village who needed to climb the hill for water benefited from the lighting, but everyone who had taken part in the debate and raised funds had benefited by participating. Together they had secured a good that was common in both its production and its benefits.

As Jack looked back on those heated debates he wondered if perhaps Jill had been right after all. By then a mother herself, she had disagreed about lighting the hill because it 'will change our way of life'. 'My family values the dark skies and don't want to be kept awake at night. It's our bedroom windows that look towards the hill top, not other people's', Jill had argued. The politics of the village had also had to handle the politics of nearby townships. Although it was solar power that ran the lights in Jack's village, the expertise for manufacturing the equipment lay elsewhere. Their region could support just one factory and Jack's election to the assembly gave his village a voice. However, the Muffets succeeded in building a coalition of delegates and secured the production plant for their town. It had taken Jack all his skills as a peacemaker to convince his village that the common good did not stop at the boundary of their own township.

Jack was well aware that he, Jill, the albeit reluctant Hubbards and the politically astute Muffets had not moved into the region as fully formed political actors who began a process of negotiation over their respective notions of the good life. They found themselves having to deal with an emerging situation. Furthermore, they had grown to be individuals from families that were themselves part of existing communities. Their sense of a common good had itself been shaped by prior practice of the common good. Their sense of self had been developed within a common-good-acting community; and that community life was shaped by their individual identities whether as Jack, Jill, old Mrs Hubbard or Miss Muffet. They inhabited a social imaginary of the common good.

Almost any surveillance practice throws up clashes of interest. Global corporations make substantial investment in developing new technologies and expect a handsome return. Governments work for political advantage in being able to take the credit for doing something when a public cry is 'something needs to be done' – either pushing surveillance strategies forward for national security or constraining them when privacy alarms are sufficiently loud. With our fetish for digital convenience and 'onlife' on the one hand, and our wariness around the safety of our personal information on the other, you and I have our interests. To talk about surveillance *for* one another opens a fresh perspective on the *telos* or end of the digital gaze. This chapter considers first how the notion of the common good offers a possibility for interrogating the various clashes of interest in twenty-first-century surveillance. In recognizing that 'we' is a category that can easily obscure deep disparities between people, we turn to Mary's Magnificat and Jesus' Nazareth Manifesto, which disclose God's preferential option – here an optic – for those who are poor. Bringing together a culture of the common good with a culture of surveillance leads to proposing the common gaze as an innovative analytical tool.

Social imaginary

When we stand at a busy street corner and watch passers-by, notice familiar trademarks on store-front signs, see a bus or two stopped at the traffic lights, spot the short queue at the ATM and hear a couple of protestors waving placards, we understand what is going on. We share a sufficiently similar imaginary with our society to be able to read the meaning in what we are watching, be that the behaviour of people, the authority of institutions, our identity as a city and perhaps as a nation, what it means to be human in this place at this time, and how political processes hold us, broadly, together. We do not stand at the corner and intentionally reflect upon these assumptions; they are, to use a musical analogy, a ground bass over which intricate melodies are harmonized.

Institutions need to be understood in terms of their function, but asking what these function *for* (the question about surveillance that lies behind this book) takes us into the realm of symbolic meanings (Castoriadis 1987, p. 136). The social imaginary sits in the confluence of culture, society and personality as what Jürgen Habermas calls 'lifeworld' (Habermas 1996, p. 80). Charles Taylor deploys the concept to give an account of the development of the modern, Western, way of seeing:

By social imaginary, I mean something much broader and deeper than the intellectual schemes people may entertain when they think about social reality in a disengaged mode. I am thinking, rather, of the ways people imagine their social existence, how they fit together with others, how things go on between them and their fellows, the expectations that are normally met, and the deeper normative notions and images that underlie these expectations. (C. Taylor 2004, p. 23)

For Taylor, there are four components to the modern social imaginary: economy, public sphere, popular sovereignty, and bills and charters of rights. A major shift in thought came when, instead of a feudal or manorial management of allocating what resources were needed by households or state, society imagined the economy as 'an interlocking set of activities of production, exchange, and consumption, which form a system *with its own laws and its own dynamic*' (C. Taylor 2004, p. 76, emphasis added). With the emergence of civic humanism the public sphere becomes an imagined space that 'knits together a plurality of such spaces into one larger space of nonassembly' from which something we call 'public opinion' is recognized without there having been meetings of all the public, and – we would add – prior to the creation of polling companies (C. Taylor 2004, p. 86). Popular sovereignty is built upon traditional rights of ancient constitutions (C. Taylor 2004, p. 112) but in a new form, legitimizing elected assemblies. Thus, 'the people' were invented as 'a new collective agency' (C. Taylor 2004, p. 143) replacing monarchical and other hierarchical structures. In the same development came the new idea of someone's direct access to the state by virtue of their citizenship (C. Taylor 2004, p. 159). Later, particularly after the Second World War, the social imaginary expands to include appeals to charters of universal human rights beyond those conferred by states (C. Taylor 2004, p. 172).

Taylor's key point for our discussion is that an expanded civic humanism no longer relies so heavily on networks of people who are physically close to another who thereby construct their identities on those relations. Rather, people think of more impersonal categories: how each relates to 'the state, the movement, the community of humankind' (C. Taylor 2004, p. 160). People build bridges beyond merely those fellow citizens of a state and extend the imagined space of mutual interest to a more global level (C. Taylor 2004, p. 178). This, it is important to note, can occur at the very same time in the opposite direction where there are movements seeking self-determination, such as Catalonia (vis-à-vis the Spanish state) or Scotland (in terms of the United Kingdom). Nationalism need not, however, be antithetical to global responsibilities.

The idea of the common good offers a way forward within this expanded social imaginary of many perspectives on not only its four components but also on the good life; what it means to flourish as individuals, societies and as a global community sharing the same planet as home.

The common good as moral engagement

Michael Sandel recognizes three broad categories of moral responsibility: natural duties, voluntary obligations and, his favoured position, obligations of solidarity (Sandel 2009). Natural duties are those we owe to another person because they are a person. This means treating others with respect, avoiding cruelty and not imposing our definitions of what is good for them; generally giving space for people to make their own decisions. We imagine one another as autonomous beings with whom we are together in a hypothetical social contract, hence our duties do not rely on consent, for, as Sandel puts it, 'No one would say that I have a duty not to kill you only if I promised you I wouldn't' (Sandel 2009, p. 224). It is within this way of looking around us and seeing how we fit together with those in our immediate vicinity, and more broadly in a democratic state, that notions of privacy are commonly framed; respect for one another's autonomy curtails surveillance or other forms of intrusion within the liberal, natural duties imagination.

The second category of moral responsibilities is of those entered into voluntarily and to which we have chosen to bind ourselves by obligation. So, you pay me to build an extension to your home and I accept that commitment to you – but I am not obligated to build homes for anyone else. It may be that in smaller tasks I am returning a favour, such as picking up flour at the one supermarket in town that has it during lockdown. No money need be exchanged for a particular obligation; the key is that I have consented.

Within the liberal framework that includes both natural duties and voluntary obligations, we respect one another's rights but it is none of our business to attempt to advance the other's good – unless we have jointly entered a relationship in which that is accepted. Stepping back to the level of citizenship, 'the average citizen has no special obligations to his or her fellow citizens, beyond the universal, natural duty not to commit injustice' (Sandel 2009, p. 224). For Sandel, this is too thin an account of the special responsibilities we have to fellow citizens (rather than those sharing the globe with us in other countries) and of how we are constituted as selves through unique interactions with those around us, over years and with our different cultural and individual histories.

Such a narrative construction of the self-in-relation means that the identities we develop ought not to be set aside, for 'they are part of who we are, and so rightly bear on our moral responsibilities' (Sandel 2009, p. 224). This is where the third category of moral responsibility enters the field: there are obligations of solidarity owed 'to those with whom we share a certain history' (Sandel 2009, p. 225). Because personhood is mutually constituted in relationship with particular others, these are not voluntary obligations that depend on acts of consent. For Sandel, such obligations arise within familial relations, but may also confront us in communal relations (in the sense of an actual perceived community, perhaps those in the part of town among whom we grew up, or more recently in networks of shared identities or interests).

To be neutral with respect to the good life is, in Sandel's view, a mistaken position because if I am constituted in relationship with other people then I cannot adequately think about what I consider to be the good without reflecting on 'the good of those communities with which my identity is bound' (Sandel 2009, p. 242). A refined liberal position, such as that of John Rawls (Rawls 1993) that accepts the importance of thick descriptions of loyalties and attachments in private, but not public, discourse does not satisfy Sandel's narrative construction of the self. So two ways of seeing remain. On the one hand, there is a perspective that recoils from the history of religious wars contesting the good, and thus emphasizes freedom to determine our own good. This view is that we fit together in public life by pulling back from others. On the other hand, there is an outlook that finds presumed neutrality with respect to the good to be disingenuous and, in effect, pulls people towards one another at the risk of smothering by a forced adoption of agreed goods.

An imaginary of the common good seeks to address both, sometimes polarized, expectations of one another in society:

> A just society can't be achieved simply by maximizing utility or by securing freedom of choice. To achieve a just society we have to reason together about the meaning of the good life, and to create a public culture hospitable to the disagreements that will inevitably arise. (Sandel 2009, p. 261)

For Sandel, this means broadening discussion of values beyond the usual topics, in the USA at least, of sex and abortion to include questions of poverty, health and war (Sandel 2009, pp. 262–3). The politics of the common good that Sandel advances pay particular attention to cultivating citizens who are concerned 'for the whole' and not 'purely privatized' notions of what it means to imagine life together (Sandel

2009, pp. 263–4). At the same time, Sandel concludes, it is important to limit 'market-oriented reasoning' that is being injected into everyday life, far beyond the customary economic aspects (Sandel 2009, p. 265). Addressing inequality is similarly important, and for Sandel in two ways. First, as affluent people secede from public services such as transport or health care, they are increasingly reluctant to support tax policies that fund services upon which poorer people rely. Second for Sandel is the resultant 'hollowing out of the public realm' (Sandel 2009, p. 267) by the loss of places such as parks and community centres where people from different walks of life encounter one another. Solidarity becomes more and more difficult to engender as physical distance, let alone the wealth gap, increases. The common good in this framework, argues Sandel, requires 'a politics of moral engagement' (Sandel 2009, p. 268) rather than what is more often one of avoidance of the difficult conversations around clashing views on the good.

The common good and God's preferential option

Catholic Social Teaching offers rich reflection on what theology might contribute to framing the common good. At its most basic, as Chrysostom observes: 'This is the rule of most perfect Christianity, its most exact definition, its highest point, namely, the seeking of the common good … For nothing can so make a person an imitator of Christ as caring for his neighbours' (Reich 2018, p. 40). For Thomas Aquinas, 'all things depend on God' (Aquinas 1945, p. 27; modified by Hollenbach for inclusive language in Hollenbach 2002, p. 4). As Hollenbach explains, the good that is to be sought is 'the very reality of God' (Hollenbach 2002, p. 4). In his *Summa* Aquinas is reaffirming the Aristotelian position that 'the good of the community is more "godlike" or "divine" than the good of an individual human being' (Hollenbach 2002, p. 4). While this requires political community, as Keys notes, 'Political community does not itself constitute that good, at least not according to Aristotle or Aquinas after him' (Keys 2006, p. 86).

The progress of persons

The Roman Catholic catechism (Roman Catholic Church 1999) defines the common good as 'the sum total of social conditions which allow people, either as groups or as individuals, to reach their fulfilment more fully and more easily' (§1906). It has three 'essential elements': respect for the person; the 'social well-being and development of the group itself' (§1908); and peace, 'the stability and security of a just order' (§1909). In what will be a recurring theme of this book, 'The common good is always oriented towards the progress of persons: "The order of things must be subordinate to the order of persons, and not the other way around" [*Gaudium et spes* 26, §3]' (§1912).

Such ordering seeks to maintain individual responsibility when forms of welfare support by the state might, on the one hand, abrogate people's agency, and on the other hand be a ready means by which people might abdicate their responsibilities. John XXIII, in *Pacem in terris*, articulated the Catholic view of the purpose of the state's authority: 'heads of States must make a positive contribution to the creation of an overall climate in which the individual can both safeguard his own rights and fulfil his duties, and can do so readily' (John XXIII 1963, §63). As states collaborate for the sake of the common good, 'the prosperity and progress of any State is in part consequence, and in part cause, of the prosperity and progress of all other States' (John XXIII 1963, §131). In the *Pastoral Constitution of the Church in the Modern World* (*Gaudium et spes*), the Second Vatican Council gives the definition of the common good, which we have seen is contained in the catechism. *Gaudium et spes* indeed alerts all people of good will to a two-pronged challenge to the pursuit of the common good:

> Growth is not to be left solely to a kind of mechanical course of the economic activity of individuals, nor to the authority of government. For this reason, doctrines which obstruct the necessary reforms under the guise of a false liberty, and those which subordinate the basic rights of individual persons and groups to the collective organization of production must be shown to be erroneous. (Second Vatican Council 1965, §75)

Neither the market nor socialist central planning are the answer for development that is in the common good. Each citizen's vote ought to be exercised with the common good in mind – and the freedom of that vote preserved: 'All citizens, therefore, should be mindful of the right and also the duty to use their free vote to further the common good' (Second Vatican Council 1965, §75).

Participation becomes a key dimension given particular prominence by John Paul II in his encyclical *Centesimus annus* (1991). This involves a movement by each person to offer the gift of his or her self, as an act of solidarity, to form authentic human community, which, in Catholic terms, is an authenticity found in community orientated to people's final destiny, which is God (John Paul II 1991, §41). Building upon his earlier philosophical writings as Karol Wojtyla, this pope argues that the corollary of self-giving is ensuring the opportunities for participation by others in the life and growth of the community (Wojtyla 1979, pp. 280–3). What safeguards us as persons acting with others is participation: 'the property by virtue of which we as persons exist and act together with others, while not ceasing to be ourselves or to fulfil ourselves in action, in our own acts' (Wojtyla 2008, p. 200). Community and the common good are, for John Paul, not the same. Community has a value that is discovered by 'observing the co-existence and co-operation of people as if from the perspective of the personal subjectivity of each of them. The common good, on the other hand, seems to be an objectification of the axiological meaning of each society, social group, etc.' (Wojtyla 2008, p. 240).

For Benedict XVI, Christian love includes, but is not limited to, political participation, for 'The mission of the lay faithful is therefore to configure social life correctly, respecting its legitimate autonomy and cooperating with other citizens according to their respective competences and fulfilling their own responsibility' (Benedict XVI 2005, §29). He returns to this in his *Caritas in veritate* (2009): 'The more we strive to secure a common good corresponding to the real needs of our neighbours, the more effectively we love them' (Benedict XVI 2009, §7).

Benedict is not shy of economic redistribution as an integral dimension of seeking the common good:

> Economic activity cannot solve all social problems through the simple application of *commercial logic*. This needs to be *directed towards the pursuit of the common good*, for which the political community in particular must also take responsibility. Therefore, it must be borne in mind that grave imbalances are produced when economic action, conceived merely as an engine for wealth creation, is detached from political action, conceived as a means for pursuing justice through redistribution. (Benedict XVI 2009, §36, emphasis in original)

'The whole person and all people' forms for Benedict a criterion of evaluating political, economic, cultural and religious activity (Benedict XVI 2009, §55). We might well conclude that it is possible to be both rich and poor; materially wealthy and spiritually impoverished. Those who are materially poor may have spiritual riches but theirs could also be a double poverty as a poverty of spirit and material condition. For Benedict, holistic development requires attending to spiritual and moral welfare *as well as* economic sufficiency: 'There cannot be holistic development and universal common good unless people's spiritual and moral welfare is taken into account, considered in their totality as body and soul' (Benedict XVI 2009, §76).

The third component, 'the stability and security of a just order', is a call towards conflict. It is not stability of an ordered society, indeed the justification often made by politicians for increased surveillance of populations. The common good is directed towards an order that is *just*. Those who benefit from an unjust order are rarely willing to surrender their advantage.

The preferential option

The Magnificat

Social imaginaries fall under judgement in the song of Mary, the mother of Jesus:

> My soul magnifies the Lord,
> and my spirit rejoices in God my Saviour,
> for he has looked with favour on the lowliness of his servant.
> Surely, from now on all generations will call me blessed;
> for the Mighty One has done great things for me,
>   and holy is his name.
> His mercy is for those who fear him
>   from generation to generation.
> He has shown strength with his arm;
>   he has scattered the proud in the thoughts of their hearts.
> He has brought down the powerful from their thrones,
>   and lifted up the lowly;
> he has filled the hungry with good things,
>   and sent the rich away empty.
> He has helped his servant Israel,
>   in remembrance of his mercy,
> according to the promise he made to our ancestors,
>   to Abraham and to his descendants for ever.
> (Luke 1.46–55)

God scatters proud people in the *thoughts* or, as liturgical versions often render, 'the imagination' of their hearts. Those who picture themselves as masters or mistresses of their success come under the divine gaze that disrupts and disempowers. Mary is given the voice of divine social reversal, and upending of thrones that upends perceptions of the divine favour. In his apostolic exhortation *Evangelii gaudium* (2013), Pope Francis, given his ministry in Argentina, sets himself against arguments that redistribution towards the poor must be curtailed for the sake of social peace: 'The dignity of the human person and the common good rank higher than the comfort of those who refuse to renounce their privileges' (Francis 2013, §218). This is socially and politically disruptive and meets with resistance from those already privileged. There might then be cause to maintain the status quo lest the consequent upheavals and possibly violent resistance are so destabilizing as to damage everyone, privileged and underclass alike. But to refrain from distributive justice because it is disruptive is to pursue a false peace. Maintaining conditions of injustice either through positive policies or neglect fails to address the grievances that drive violence. Without sanctioning violence on the part of those kept in an underclass, but recognizing it, Francis, in his 2015 encyclical *Laudato si'*, confronts with a call for a genuine social peace that is necessary for the common good: 'the stability and security provided by a certain order which cannot be achieved without particular concern for distributive justice; whenever this is violated, violence always ensues' (Francis 2015, §157).

Francis cuts to the chase on climate change:

> The failure of global summits on the environment make it plain that our politics are subject to technology and finance. There are too many special interests, and economic interests easily end up trumping the common good and manipulating information so that their own plans will not be affected. (Pope Francis 2015, §54)

The Nazareth manifesto

In strictly narrative terms, Jesus is surely his mother's son in the resonances between his Nazareth Manifesto and Mary's vision of an upending God.

> When he came to Nazareth, where he had been brought up, he went to the synagogue on the sabbath day, as was his custom. He stood up to read, and the scroll of the prophet Isaiah was given to him. He unrolled the scroll and found the place where it was written:

> > 'The Spirit of the Lord is upon me,
> >   because he has anointed me
> >   to bring good news to the poor.
> > He has sent me to proclaim release to the captives
> >   and recovery of sight to the blind,
> >   to let the oppressed go free,
> > to proclaim the year of the Lord's favour.'

And he rolled up the scroll, gave it back to the attendant, and sat down. The eyes of all in the synagogue were fixed on him. Then he began to say to them, 'Today this scripture has been fulfilled in your hearing.' (Luke 4.16–21)

In passing, we can note how the gaze features quite prominently. Those unable to see are to be granted the capability of gazing. The one making the claim that such a promise is now being fulfilled is the subject of the synagogue congregation's gaze when 'all eyes were fixed on him'. In the Nazareth Manifesto we hear a vision to address that from which deliverance is required. The common good is here in its disruptive mode; people in need are being oppressed and the coming reign of God confronts this situation, in favour of those who are poor, captive, blind and oppressed. On the other hand, the year of the Lord's favour is indeed for all, but not at the expense of those who are in particularly straightened circumstances.

Anna Rowlands sums up the value of the Catholic Church's teleological account that places political and civil participation in relation to the fellowship of salvation, which, in the light of the Magnificat and Nazareth Manifesto, means that:

This faith-based vision is also characterized by its orientation towards the biblical preferential option for the poor ... The common good is therefore measured less according to the greater good for the greatest number and more against the wellbeing and participation of the least. (Rowlands 2015, p. 10)

The preferential option in liberation theology

In the 1960s and 1970s the 'preferential option for the poor' is developed, in sympathy with the Second Vatican Council of the Roman Catholic Church's concern for the Church to be of, and attentive to, people who are poor. However, 'the preferential option' pushes this much further, given the political and economic situation of dictatorship and exploitation in Latin America. The Latin American Episcopal Conferences of 1968 and 1979, giving institutional support for what was developing in the activism of clergy and religious, and in the academic writings of those such as Gustavo Gutiérrez and Enrique Dussel, presents the option as not excluding anyone, yet giving a priority in approaching the needs of those in poverty and thus a preference to addressing their needs (a verb as well as a noun), 'una preferencia y un acercamiento al pobre' (CELAM 1979, §733).

For Gutiérrez, poverty is material, subjugation to nature, exploitation by others, and a lack of prosperity that others experience (Gutiérrez 2001 [1974], pp. 254–5). This extension includes the denial of access to 'certain cultural, social, and political values' (Gutiérrez 2001 [1974], p. 255); it is not confined to the economic domain. Not only is there the indignity of having to beg and to rely on the charity of others (Gutiérrez 2001 [1974], p. 257), fraud and violence are directed against the poor. 'In the final analysis,' writes Gutiérrez, 'an option for the poor is an option for the God of the kingdom Jesus proclaims to us' (Gutiérrez 2001 [1974], p. 18). Enrique Dussel makes a significant distinction between the practice of society and of community. Society describes, for Dussel, 'the condition of the individual (labour, toil, and so on) in the prevailing order of domination and sin', whereas community is the practice of 'face-to-face relationships of persons standing in a relationship of justice' (Dussel 1988, p. 28). Poor and rich are, here, dialectical terms (Dussel 1988, p. 23); there are no poor people without some people being rich. Poverty is therefore not a necessary functional component of economic systems but the oppressive actions of the rich. For Dussel, this dialectical theory of poverty is integral to the accounts, and importantly critiques, of poverty in the Bible:

> The constitutive act of the 'poor' in the Bible is not lacking goods, but *being dominated*, and this *by the sinner*. The poor are the correlative of sin. As the fruit of sin, their formality as 'poor' constitutes the poor and oppressed, and as such, the just and holy. (Dussel 1988, p. 22, emphasis in original)

The dialectical model of poverty is at the centre of liberation theology – and of its defence of the preferential option. As José Míguez Bonino argues, 'poverty is not a disconnected fact. It is the inevitable and quite normal result of a total situation determined by the laws, goals and structures of the economic system which we have developed' (Míguez Bonino 1977, p. 8).

An imaginary of the common gaze

Imagining the common good

As the insights of recent popes have demonstrated, the common good is pitted against powerful counter-forces in politics, economic reasoning and the social expectations of the privileged. To talk, as we propose here, of a 'culture of the common good' (Camdessus 2012) is a bold vision that chimes with Anna Rowlands' plea also for 'the imagination of the Common Good' (Rowlands 2015, p. 14). But, as Patrick Riordan argues, 'The common good of the polis is heuristic, naming that which is sought, but which is not yet attained' (Riordan 2008, p. 27). It may well be true that the common good is noticeable precisely because we so rarely observe it in practice; the positive instances stand out because we do not expect to see them. Nevertheless, and perhaps because of a paucity of the common good in political discourse (beyond issues around climate change and before the global pandemic of 2020), Riordan is correct to contend that 'we need terms which allow us to speak about realities we do not yet know, but are in the process of exploring and discovering' (Riordan 2011, p. 212). Esther Reed argues that 'the common good is more verb than noun' (Reed 2015, p. 59).

It is important, as Rowlands contends, that considerations of the common good do not neglect the phenomenological; 'how it feels to *inhabit*' this notion (Rowlands 2015, p. 5, emphasis in original). A culture of the common good is a counter to the functionalism and managerialism that Rowan Williams believes are interwoven with secularism, and instead is 'a willingness to see things or other persons as the objects of another sensibility than my own, perhaps also another sensibility than our own, wherever "we" are, even if "we" is humanity itself' (Williams 2012, p. 13). Shaping in an imaginary of the common good takes place amid forces of which many may be quite unaware and so there is 'a genuine question about how what people say they want, or who people say they are, is manipulated and largely determined by different kinds of economic and political power' (Williams 2012, p. 25). As we will see in subsequent chapters, influence through the hacking of the citizen is a significant threat to the common good.

An imaginary of the common good, as we are developing it here, means that it 'contains rather than brings to an end discussion' (Sagovsky and McGrail 2015, p. xxvi). Incorporating a religious dimension means, in Williams' terms, 'contributing to the imagination to resource and renew motivation within our common life' (Williams 2012, p. 21). This is not solely interior but expressed in 'a habit of commitment to the good of the other, which creates and sustains mutual trust' (Williams 2012, p. 117). Such an approach is more radical than it might at first appear. When viewed from the perspective of God's preferential option for those who are poor, there arise awkward questions about who needs to be part of such discussions and what deliberate bias is required for particular categories of people to be so involved. The current Archbishop of Canterbury, Justin Welby, writes about the common good as 'a foundation of stability in society and a source of hope' (Welby 2018, p. 39). The latter may well be the case, but hope for whom? People with much to lose in terms of social status and economic privilege have hopes for a stable society. When one has little, in terms of both status and economic privilege, one may have quite different hopes: yearnings for greater equity and removal of systemic barriers. Stability is, as we have seen, rather absent from both the Magnificat and the Nazareth Manifesto. Being cast down from one's throne could scarcely be described as stability.

The imagination within the culture of the common good clashes with other political imaginations, particularly those that are unable to envisage effective community (O'Donovan 2017). Such conflict, inevitable as it is in the formation of community, can be particularly uncomfortable for Christians who spend so much time within generally homogenous faith communities – not simply in terms of shared faith but shared race and class (McClintock Fulkerson 2012, p. 425). A common-good imagination is shaped by the market because, as Lisa Isherwood argues, our desires have been so enslaved (Isherwood 2015, p. 287). In her counterclaim of flesh becoming word (as the obscured other side of the familiar Word becoming flesh), Isherwood contends that 'this rooting of the divine within and between us is a foundational act of resistance to markets which take advantage of our uprooted desires' (Isherwood 2015, p. 287). When the culture of the common good leans towards preserving privilege for some people, Isherwood's insight points in the direction of destabilizing the status quo. Such resistance may be costly when it is called forth from encounter (possibly by way of digital mediation) with actual people who are disadvantaged by political, economic, cultural and religious systems. The agonies in the bodies of those who are poor – and the divine between us – is highly suggestive of a culture of the common good that requires a paradigm shift rather like the one we envisage for surveillance from the cross.

Embodiment, or what we might otherwise call concrete practices, is one element, but this goes hand in glove with reflexivity, a discipline that citizens as a whole, according to Elaine Graham, need to develop, in terms of religious literacy, in the pursuit of the common good in diverse contexts that may well be suspicious (often rightly so) of religious perspectives (E. Graham 2017). However, concrete efforts might be acclaimed as expressions of the common good but, in effect, reduce reflexivity. Helen Cameron concludes thus in discussing emergency food parcels, donated as part of organized systems of food banks in the UK: 'The food parcel can divert our attention from the commercial organisations that stake a claim on the incomes of the poor. It can mask the poor performance of government agencies tasked with providing a safety net for every citizen' (Cameron 2014, p. 201). Cameron is drawing our attention to philanthropy as in some ways an expression of the common good, but in other ways, neutralizing the more radical impact of incorporating a preferential option for those who are poor. A culture of the common good might well be counter-intuitive to certain Christian sensibilities. Cameron hits the nail on the head when, in drawing on the parable of the prodigal son, she observes that 'the one figure in the parable we know we are not meant to criticise is the father. His generosity is the paradigm for both sons and for us' (Cameron 2014, p. 200). To avoid masking accountability of those on their thrones, a culture of the common good requires to fight on unexpected fronts.

Digital poverty

In a study of major north-eastern US cities in 2012–13, Seeta Gangadharan identified those whose broadband connectivity makes them 'privacy-poor, surveillance-rich'. Digital poverty is, here, partly a lack of knowledge in the sense that marginal users are concerned about privacy, and may have an awareness of their paucity of practical ignorance about the consequences – and at the very same time this dimension is absent from instruction programmes offered to them (Gangadharan 2017, p. 603). There is, for these users, a poverty of privacy, which is viewed as a luxury rather than a right. Their vulnerabilities are 'most acute when applying to and maintaining eligibility in welfare programs, often at the last minute' (Gangadharan 2017, p. 604). This is a poverty of control over the information flows concerning their lives lived dependent upon institutional systems (Gangadharan 2017, p. 604).

Contrary to naive expectations, using public terminals does not mean one is immune to tracking (Gangadharan 2017, p. 606). Exploitation by unscrupulous service providers is also significant. For example, a user in the study encountered a purportedly free résumé service: 'on the last page, the service demanded money from the user in order to receive the complete résumé. Lacking funds, the user abandoned the effort, left without a résumé at the price of this personal information now in possession by the service' (Gangadharan 2017, p. 606).

Digital poverty can mean divulging personal details in desperation when job-searching (Gangadharan 2017, p. 609). Gangadharan concluded that marginal users adopted information and communications technology with hope and resignation, 'a hope that learning how to use email and surf the web, for example, will lead to better jobs, and resignation that [they] will encounter some of the same predatory targeting [they have] experienced before' (Gangadharan 2017, p. 610).

Jan van Dijk has conceptualized digital inequalities in four dimensions: immaterial – life chances, freedom; material – capital (economic, social, cultural) and resources; social – positions, power and participation; and educational – capabilities, skills (van Dijk 2013, p. 107). He draws on Charles Tilly's notion of 'opportunity hoarding' (Tilly 1998), which goes hand in hand with exploitation. Using a network approach to offer a more relational view, with information as a positional good, van Dijk concludes that 'unequal competencies and skills are reinforced by unequal positions in social, economic, cultural and political networks and they lead in turn to an unequal division of material resources' (van Dijk 2013, p. 120).

Digital poverty therefore comprises, at least, the following dimensions: (a) lack of (and fear of) access; (b) access on terms of less privacy (lack of education in controlling personal information); (c) lack of IT skills leading to reliance on help from others (e.g. librarians for uploading CVs and personal information); (d) lack of interest paid to one's personal information because companies or the state do not bother about you; and (e) lack of access to employment recruitment sites and to government services.

In John Paul II's encyclical of 1991, in which he returned to the preferential option for the poor, it is interesting to see his critique of the perpetuating cycle of exclusion: 'for the poor, to the lack of material goods has been added a lack of knowledge and training which prevents them from escaping their state of humiliating subjection' (John Paul II 1991, §33).

A preferential optic for those who are poor

The common gaze is surveillance *for* others. This shift in preposition from *of* to *for* encompasses a fundamental reframing of the intention of surveillance strategies. It is a social imaginary that attempts to gain critical traction on the priorities of surveillance and the privileges a surveillant gaze reproduces. It is not surveillance *of* the common good. In its dependence on a culture of the common good, the common gaze assumes that watching out for one another is an intrinsic not an instrumental good. There are occasions of watching that are for particular purposes of, for example, identification and entitlement. However, at its core there is an irreducibly social good (C. Taylor 1995) of watching out for others that cannot be achieved by individuals by themselves. The preposition is here also crucial. It is watching *out for*, not watching per se that is commended in the common gaze. Yet although we can thus go with Jean-Paul Sartre, who remarked that 'My apprehension of the Other as an object essentially refers me to a fundamental apprehension of the Other in which he will not be revealed to me as an object but as a "presence in person"' (Sartre 1956, p. 340), the gaze remains integral to power (Sturken and Cartwright, 2018). The proposal of the common gaze, therefore, includes deliberate reflection upon what such power means in specific contexts.

To watch over, or to practise surveillance *for* one another, is an expression of our fundamental interconnectedness. This means that watching over others is not disengaged or disinterested in others' material circumstances. As Marita Sturken and Lisa Cartwright explain, 'a gaze is, in one sense, a kind of look. You may turn your gaze upon objects, places or others. Whereas a glance is quick, a gaze is sustained' (Sturken and Cartwright, 2018, p. 103). But it is looking out for others with the awareness that this is necessary in a contingent and often unjust world. For so many of us, our capabilities are constrained and we are denied even the basics for flourishing as human beings. Here we can go with John Finnis, who argues that 'in voluntarily acting for human goods and avoiding what is opposed to them, one ought to choose and otherwise will those and only those possibilities whose willing is compatible with a will toward integral human fulfilment' (Finnis 1999, p. 44).

It is a theological claim that looking out for one another is not only an intrinsic or basic good of family, friendship or religious community (cf. Finnis 2001, p. 5) but also of political communities. It is in making watching over one another instrumental that surveillance is so readily practised as surveillance *of* others. Our personhood is constituted in our relationships with others – and this is often most immediately in the closer circles of kin and community. But our civic and political communities are composed of other *people* who are only derivatively *citizens* (or non-citizens, as the case may be). We can put this another way: in the eyes (or gaze) of God we cannot dismiss an other because she does not share our citizenship. In terms of the parable of the sheep and the goats (Matt. 25), we are watching over Christ ('you did it to me'). In this sense, the common gaze penetrates political identity and thereby sets a different categorization: rich or poor. The needs of those who are poor are thereby primary, although not paramount. Rich people come *after* and not before poor people. In the words of Gustavo Gutiérrez: 'The canticle of Mary combines a trusting self-surrender to God with a will to commitment and close association with God's favourites: the lowly, the hungry' (Gutiérrez 2005 [1984], p. 127).

The common gaze is also a gaze of those who are poor, not only the rich watching out for them. Practising the common gaze discloses internalized marginalization in a process described by Paulo Freire's conscientiation (Freire and Ramos 1972), W. E. B. Du Bois's black double-consciousness

(Du Bois 1926), and Michel Foucault's internalized disciplinary mechanisms (Foucault 1979). Yes, there is indeed an 'inspecting gaze' and thus:

> There is no need for arms, physical violence, material constraints. Just a gaze. An inspecting gaze, a gaze which each individual under its weight will end by interiorising to the point that he is his own overseer, each individual thus exercising this surveillance over, and against, himself. (Foucault 1980, p. 155)

However, I think we can venture a more positive angle on the gaze than does Foucault. To be subject to a gaze that enfolds one when one needs the beneficial option for those who are poor is to be inspected by love. It is, and here Foucault is correct, to internalize that surveillance, but it is surveillance *for* you, not primarily *of* you. There is no need to abrogate this to the realm of mystical experience. As Sigurdson reminds us, the gaze is 'anything but abstract; instead it is culturally, historically, and not least physically situated. The gaze is a way of establishing relationships of different sorts; it *is* in fact a relationship' (Sigurdson 2016, p. 292). Because it is a social imaginary of imagination *and* practice, the common gaze is a preferential optic for those who are poor. Certainly this could degrade to paternalism but not necessarily so. It is a gaze of those shaped by the Magnificat and the Nazareth Manifesto.

The common gaze is returned by those upon whom it falls. In this mode it is what bell hooks would call an oppositional gaze, resisting oppression even when that is not what might be intended:

> Spaces of agency exist for black people, wherein we can both interrogate the gaze of the Other but also look back, and at one another, naming what we see. The 'gaze' has been and is a site of resistance for colonized black people globally. (hooks 2015, p. 116)

A preferential optic for those who are poor (more widely, those who are oppressed) is grounded in subjectivity precisely because of the theological claims of Mary's song and her son's manifesto. Without such a foundation, the common gaze is but another version of an objectifying 'imperialist gazing' (Kaplan 1997, p. 14). What Ann Kaplan asks in terms of race and ethnicity can be asked also of categories of 'rich' and 'poor': 'What happens when white people look at non-whites? What happens when the look is returned – when black peoples own the look and startle whites into knowledge of their whiteness? What mirroring processes (going both ways) take place in inter-racial looking?' (Kaplan 1997, p. 4).

The common gaze is radical for wherever one finds oneself on the socio-economic spectrum. And yet surveillance *for* others hovers rather too close to paternalism and even neo-colonialism. There is scope for adding the preposition *with* in order to break the domination that even well-meaning looking-out-for can embody.

A problematic optic?

The preferential optic is revolutionary?

A prominent criticism of liberation theology was made in 1984 by the Congregation for the Doctrine of the Faith, at that time under the Prefecture of the then Joseph Cardinal Ratzinger. One accusation was that despite its deep concern for the poor, liberation theology was constructed from an ideology of violent revolution:

> So the aspiration for justice often finds itself the captive of ideologies which hide or pervert its meaning, and which propose to people struggling for their liberation goals which are contrary to the true purpose of human life. They propose ways of action which imply the systematic recourse to violence, contrary to any ethic which is respectful of persons. (Congregation for the Doctrine of the Faith 1984, II.3)

The Catholic Church is not pacifist; its just-war tradition (Roman Catholic Church 1999, §2309) gives conditions for legitimate defence but assumes waging war by governments not by groups without such recognized authority. Violence is thus the preserve of the state and not revolutionary or protest groups. The issue becomes more problematic when two or more groups within a state are contesting the power to be the state, and thereby obtain the monopoly on violence reserved to public authorities. Movements for national autonomy for regions of a unitary state such as the Basques vis-à-vis Spain are a case in point. The 2020 riots in the USA in response to the alleged murder (at the time of writing) of George Floyd by a white police officer illuminate the theological challenge: can illegal state violence be opposed by illegal mob violence?

There is a temptation for those on the sidelines, even allies of a cause, to call for pacifism from those actively engaged in confronting and seeking to overturn a violent public authority. In the much more limited terms of our discussion of surveillance, the preferential optic is indeed derived from the preferential option which has antecedents and some theoretical underpinnings from revolutionary Marxism (mediated through liberation theology). Pacifism is an honourable position but we should be wary of

requiring it of those under oppression, whose brutalizing and dehumanizing we ourselves do not share. The Holocaust (of which more later)
causes us to ponder whether or not we would condemn violent insurrec-
tion movements within Germany or Poland had these arisen to resist the
surveillance system of the Nazis against the Jews.

The preferential optic has a limited view of sin?

The Congregation took liberation theologians to task also over supposed
implications that suffering is to be understood only as poverty (Congregation for the Doctrine of the Faith 1984, IV.5). The problem here was
that if sin is limited to 'social sin', in the sense of it being oppression by
imposing or maintaining adverse social conditions, then salvation and
regeneration depend on changed economic and political systems:

> Nor can one localize evil principally or uniquely in bad social, political,
> or economic 'structures' as though all other evils came from them so
> that the creation of the 'new man' would depend on the establishment
> of different economic and socio-political structures. (Congregation for
> the Doctrine of the Faith 1984, IV.15)

The Congregation admit that freedom in Christ 'should necessarily have
effects on the social level' (Congregation for the Doctrine of the Faith
1984, IV.13) but this flows *from* liberation in the human heart.

The question for the preferential optic of the common gaze is, then,
what it makes of the relationship between social and personal sin. The
common gaze has little interest in setting liberation from social and personal sin in sequential terms. The key here is that in the parable of the
sheep and the goats in Matthew 25, Jesus pointedly portrays the righteous
as not knowing they are righteous; they went about being compassionate. If we must frame the common gaze in terms of sin, then sin occurs
in dehumanizing others by a surveillance gaze. Systemic dimensions are
present but, while these shape operatives, designers, marketers and purchasers of surveillance technologies, it is *people* who are taking decisions.
A decision might be to automate a system of filtering for entitlement to,
for example, welfare payments, but this is still a human decision.

Preference is reverse discrimination?

Adjudging that liberation theology is so heavily reliant on Marxist ideology, the Congregation consider it necessary to confront any importation
of class struggle into the Church:

It is not the 'fact' of social stratification with all its inequity and injustice, but the 'theory' of class struggle as the fundamental law of history which has been accepted by these 'theologies of liberation' as a principle. The conclusion is drawn that the class struggle thus understood divides the Church herself, and that in light of this struggle even ecclesial realities must be judged. (Congregation for the Doctrine of the Faith 1984, IX.2)

The rich become, it is claimed, a class enemy to be fought, avoiding the injunction to love one's neighbour, one's fellow Christian, and indeed one's enemy. This has implications for the common gaze because oppressed and oppressor could be too easily framed as dichotomous when intersectionality alerts us to the possibilities of being denied in some aspects of one's identity while having advantageous affirmation in other dimensions. Furthermore, to give preference to some, even oppressed, people over others may merely reverse discrimination. Much here depends on properly understanding the concept of 'preferential'.

Stephen Pope makes a helpful distinction between cognitive and moral notions of 'preferential'. We are always viewing a situation, and speaking, from *a* perspective. To take sides therefore is a conscious step of appreciating that not taking a side is actually to take a side (Pope 1993, p. 247). In this cognitive sense, a preferential optic is to acknowledge that we are always looking in a particular way, not least by way of our social imaginary. It is also to recognize the need for active engagement (Pope 1993, p. 247) with or on behalf of a particular group. In the moral sense, this might be understood as reverse discrimination unless attention is given to the fact that people have not only different levels of need but various capabilities to address those needs from within their oppressed status; capabilities that may include degrees of intelligence and/or constrained access to resources (Pope 1993, p. 252). The common gaze is preferential in both cognitive and moral senses.

Summary definition of the common gaze

The common gaze is surveillance for the common good, inflected with a preferential optic for those who are (digitally) poor. The common gaze is not a substitute for the common good, but an expression, in cultures of surveillance, of the common good.

Part 2

3

Influence: Hacking Citizens

A nudge and a wink

The last secret ballot

A howling gale at 6.30 in the morning made attaching the notice-boards to the railings more than a little challenging for election officers Margaret McPherson and Tom Finlay. They got the slightly battered 'Polling Station' secured first before tackling the trickier task of hanging the new three-metre-long banner over the entrance. Until 10 that night, voters would pass under the bold, blue lettering, 'If you've nothing to hide, you've nothing to fear.'

'My first election was the last secret ballot,' Margaret remarked.

Tightening the last rope, Tom looked over: 'Better to face reality?'

'I suppose so.'

'They got so good at inferring voting intentions that it didn't make sense to pretend it was secret any more.'

Relieved to get in out of the wind, Margaret unpacked her voters' roll ready for opening in a few minutes: 'I wasn't ashamed at voting Green but wanted to choose who I told.'

'But it's easier for advertisers to show their clients how effective they've been. We're more accountable too as voters when people know who chose who.' Tom was poised with his hand on the door and could see the queue of two sheltering as best they could against the rain that had now started.

Three hundred miles south, the Prime Minister of England and Wales highlighted the fourth item on his Cabinet agenda: replacing elections – a status report from the Secretary of State for Digital, Culture, Media and Enterprise.

Surveillance of the democratic process and surveillance as part of democratic processes is not about what happens in the polling booth. Rather, it is about the surveillance that takes place continually and long before a citizen arrives to cast a vote in a particular election. We are talking here about the hacking of democracy, and in particular hacking citizens to influence, arguably to manipulate, their decisions at the ballot box. This is hacking in the sense of exploiting a vulnerability in a system to gain unwarranted access.

Brittany Kaiser, former Director of Program Development, Cambridge Analytica, the company that was often the focal point of accusations of data mishandling and investigations into political influencing, sums up her involvement:

> I had made choices in all this. But unlike the very people who were the targets of Cambridge Analytica's devious and brilliant messaging, I, too, had been a perhaps unwitting victim of an influence campaign. As with so many others, something had made an impression on me, I clicked on it, and that had sent me through a wormhole of disinformation, and I made choices I never would have thought I was capable of making. (Kaiser 2019, p. 350)

The British investigative journalist Carole Cadwalladr recognizes the marathon in which regulatory systems find it nigh on impossible to keep up with the technological advances in data collection and processing in politics and commerce: 'what the Cambridge Analytica story exposed, by accident, from Facebook's reaction in the months that followed, is the absolute power of the tech giants' (Cadwalladr 2018). With staff of *The New York Times*, Cadwalladr was a finalist in the 2019 Pulitzer Prize in National Reporting, the citation for which read: 'For reporting on how Facebook and other tech firms allowed the spread of misinformation and failed to protect consumer privacy, leading to Cambridge Analytica's theft of 50 million people's private information, data that was used to boost Donald Trump's campaign' (Pulitzer Prizes 2019). Cadwalladr was also named as one of a team who won the investigative reporters' award of Gerald Loeb Awards 2019 for 'Facebook, Disinformation and Privacy', which also included Nicholas Confessore, Matthew Rosenberg, Sheera Frenkel, Cecilia Kang, Paul Mozur, Jack Nicas, Gabriel J. X. Dance, Michael LaForgia and Brian X. Chen of *The New York Times*. (UCLA 2019).

Concern among politicians is only intensified by observations about the liquid-like flow of surveillance from one domain to another from the UK Information Commissioner, Elizabeth Denham, who in her oral evidence to the Digital, Culture, Media and Sport (DCM&S) Committee investigation into 'Disinformation and "fake news"' in November 2018 remarks: 'We do not want to use the same model that sells us holidays and shoes and cars to engage with people and voters. People expect more than that' (DCM&S Committee 2018b, Q4011). In her message that opens her November 2018 report to the UK Parliament, Denham drives home the fundamental issue: 'Citizens can only make truly informed choices about who to vote for if they are sure that those decisions have not been unduly influenced' (ICO 2018c, p. 4).[1]

The fictional vignette featuring the election officers Margaret McPherson and Tom Finlay with which we begin this chapter is dystopic but it chimes well with anxieties over real-world events. Data-politics today unfold with complex twists and turns involving multiple characters with diverse objectives. A true-life gaze upon democracy continues to unfold. The aim of this chapter is to illuminate the ways in which citizens as voters are enfolded in streams of data that are selected, captured, analysed and inferences enacted by artificial intelligence (AI). We first consider how voters are in the cross-hairs of this particular gaze, offering a definition of datafication. This will lead into examining the claims of how democracy is being hacked. Drawing upon the main conclusions of principal parliamentary investigations in the UK, we will come then to the particular story of Cambridge Analytica and what has been termed 'weaponized information'.

This will bring us then to biblical texts on false prophets and how 'the crowd' feature often in the New Testament narrative. False prophets are here associated with those implicated not just in disinformation but in manipulation of others. 'The crowd' will let us see how shaping of the masses is not a prerogative of digital worlds. We will then move on to attempt a theological critique of propaganda, being a combination of weaponizing information and hacking democracy. Roman Catholic contributions on the ethics of advertising and communication will inform our inquiry, but with most attention being paid to Jacques Ellul's argument for the necessity of propaganda. AI is portrayed by many as a decision-making system superior to that of humans. Drawing on existing theologies of AI and technology, particularly those of Brian Brock and

---

1 Denham concluded the ICO investigations in a letter to the chair of the Digital, Culture, Media and Sport Select Committee on 2 October 2020. The further work her office had undertaken since April 2019 confirms, she writes, 'my earlier conclusion that there are systemic vulnerabilities in our democratic systems' (ICO 2020, Letter, §2). In Annex 2, Denham reports back on activity undertaken by SCL Elections and Cambridge Analytica. She surmises that there appears to be an exaggerated claim by SCL about the number of data points it held per individual on 230 million Americans (ICO 2020, Annexe 2, §10). One particular conclusion is both concerning and of significance for future developments by companies processing data for political purposes: 'We also identified evidence that in its latter stages SCL/CA was drawing up plans to relocate its data offshore to avoid regulatory scrutiny by ICO' (ICO 2020, Letter §11).

Antje Jackelén, will engage us with the main issues and the importance of ethical decision-making that remains embodied.

In conclusion, we will challenge the toxic combination of oligarchy and its interests in manipulating the public's negative emotions.

Gazing on democracy

The citizen

Datafied citizenship

Datafication, more generally rather than specifically of citizens, can be defined as 'the technical ability to turn increasing amounts of social activity and human behaviour into data points that can be tracked, collected and analysed [and] has led to significant changes across government, business and civil society' (Hintz et al. 2019, p. 42). It may coincide with dataism, a belief in the objectivity of quantification and uncritical trust in the institutions that collect and analyse data (van Dijck 2014, p. 198). Popularly, dataism manifests as the view that, 'It's data so it must be true', an outlook closely aligned to the populist mantra, 'We don't need experts' because 'The data speaks for itself'. In such reasoning we are all experts because we all have the data (or should be given access to the data).

Datafication is not so simple as digital communications allowing people to collectively organize (Hintz et al. 2019, p. 144). The latter is better described as digital citizenship, but these possibilities of citizens organizing and government delivering services electronically are but one dimension of the broader concept of datafied citizenship: 'the categorizations, assessments, profiles and scores that data processes enable complement forms of citizenship that are assigned by the state, rather than generated by citizens themselves' (Hintz et al. 2019, p. 153). This is a departure from more limited understandings of citizenship in digital environments, where the emphasis is on self-creation and self-assertion of our citizenship (Hintz et al. 2019, p. 21). As Arne Hintz and his colleagues correctly observe, there is the potential for both empowerment and democratization in citizens' uses of digital platforms to challenge a state's authority (Hintz et al. 2019, p. 32). We might here think of the campaigns of the transnational Extinction Rebellion movement or more localized protests such as Hong Kong's 'umbrella revolution'.

Datafied citizenship, however, alerts us to the digital footprint or data emissions left behind when people organize and protest using technologies that facilitate their communication while under surveillance. This is not to say that active citizens are necessarily fully transparent to the state. Some campaigners will make judicious use of encrypted communications and low-tech face masks in order to partly circumvent government restrictions. Nevertheless, Hintz identifies a chilling effect (although not a freezing into silence) among some citizens: 'in our interviews with political activists, it becomes clear that many of them feel a sense of disempowerment in the face of what they perceive as being ever-greater visibility of their activities' (Hintz et al. 2019, p. 117). In what is a recurring observation in this book, we find that the distribution of surveillance among citizens is not equitable; here, more legitimate citizenship action may well result in more attention from the state's gaze.

But knowing who is and isn't a citizen is a challenge for the state and, when the challenge is national security, a different form of datafied citizen can be constructed. John Cheney-Lippold contrasts the US National Security Agency's attempt to create a data-based assessment of 'foreignness', authorizing 'legal' surveillance if a targeted data subject was deemed to be at least '51 percent foreigner' (Cheney-Lippold 2017, p. 157). The 51 per cent was an interpretation of law, not a reference to a solid statutory basis (Gellman and Poitras 2013; Greenwald 2014, pp. 108–16). Cheney-Lippold calls this *jus algorithmi*: 'a formal citizenship that, unlike soli and sanguinis counterparts, is not theorized as ordained and stable. It's a temporal, informationalized citizenship that is constantly reevaluated according to users' datafied behaviour' (Cheney-Lippold 2017, p. 157).

For Cheney-Lippold this is not '*the* datafied subject' but 'datafied subject relations': it is a more general frame and one that recognizes that our lived experiences may not always align closely with our algorithmic identities (Cheney-Lippold 2017, p. 158, emphasis in original). Algorithmic 'citizenship' in such circumstances assumes someone is a foreigner (in other words, a threat) until proved a 'citizen' (Cheney-Lippold 2017, p. 159).

Continuity and discontinuity

Datafied and algorithmic citizenship points towards both continuity and discontinuity with existing models of citizenship. Establishing citizenship has advantages for individuals who are thus able to claim particular rights (of protection, fair trial, voting and, in some states, welfare provision). On the state's side, registration of births, marriages and deaths enables the governance of a population that has different levels of entitlement; knowing who is *not* a citizen can be as important as knowing who is.

Citizenship is very easily taken for granted by those who rarely find themselves undermined, but profoundly precious to those for whom it serves as a bulwark against the worst excesses of oppression. The modern notion of universal suffrage can be contrasted with citizenship as a privileged status of a ruling group in the ancient Athenian city-state of Aristotle (Aristotle 2017, Book 3). The threat of a return to something akin to this more limited model is a shadow cast, as we shall later see, by data analysis and micro-targeting of voters, funded by oligarchs. Visions of self-government rather than papal or imperial control that energized citizenship assertions by Marsilius of Padua in his *Defensor paces* of 1324 (Marsilius of Padua 2018) and Nicolo Machiavelli (in the late fifteenth and early sixteenth centuries) in his *The Prince* and *The Discourses* (Machiavelli 1989) might need to be reservoirs of hope from which we draw in a twenty-first-century climate of global corporations governing the flows of our datafied citizenship, as Shoshana Zuboff argues, not wholly unlike colonizing powers (Zuboff 2019). We return to Zuboff when we consider surveillance capitalism in Chapter 4.

When claims of 'national security' are deployed to justify intrusive, and sometimes arguably illegal, monitoring of citizens, the spectre of Thomas Hobbes' protective liberalism of the seventeenth century looms large (Hobbes 1968, pp. 227–8). The need for a strong state with authority conferred to it by the people who voluntarily surrender in order to be kept safe is a contemporary clarion call to which algorithmic citizenship might be deemed a suitable response. Objecting to the Hobbesian argument, John Locke, publishing his *Two Treatises* in 1690 (Locke 1988), set the ground of developmental liberalism (Held 1996, p. 82), contending for political activity that secures the framework for freedom within civil society so individuals may achieve their private goals. John Stuart Mill's nineteenth-century defence of representative government articulated its importance for people's free development of their individuality, including their investment in democracy (Mill 1989 [1859]; see Held 1996, p. 100). In a culture of surveillance we can wonder about quite how 'private' are citizens' private goals when we are being shaped as consumers (of politics as well as of food and furniture) by data analytics telling us what we might also like to purchase.

Twentieth-century expansions of suffrage against patriarchy, racism and totalitarianism often came at a high price of people's self-sacrifice. But painting surveillance as a hindrance or as a malignant intrusion would be a mistake. It has contributed and continues to contribute positively. The traditional notion of citizenship was based around *jus sanguinis* or *jus soli* (either one's parents were citizens or one was born within the borders of a particular nation state). Thus, we find the importance of being registered and thereby recognized as part of a community. There arises the problem of being unregistered or registered in a place to which one no longer has or wishes access, as well as the problem of being registered as not-of-a-place. This is to be registered as stateless because one's homeland has been denied recognition or one's own status is indeterminable (for political as well as perhaps administrative reasons). Hannah Arendt recognized a shift after the atrocities of the Second World War in much public discourse towards 'the right to have rights':

> We became aware of the existence of a right to have rights (and that means to live in a framework where one is judged by one's actions and opinions) and a right to belong to some kind of organised community, only when millions of people emerged who had lost and could not regain these rights because of the new global political situation. (Arendt 1958, pp. 296–7)

We ought not to underestimate the importance of digital infrastructures in facilitating registration and thus assertion of rights by those in perilous situations. The United Nations' 1954 Convention relating to the Status of Stateless Persons and the 1961 Convention on the Reduction of Statelessness clearly predate most digital bureaucracy, but even if complete digitization is not yet possible (due to the exigencies of war and internal national conflict) the datafication of citizenship has a significant positive contribution towards the right to have rights. Beyond areas of conflict, people can be stateless where women may not transfer their own nationality to their children. Should a father be unknown, missing or deceased, children can find themselves stateless under the jurisdiction of, currently, 25 states around the world (UNHCR 2020).

Where there has been acknowledgement of multicultural forms of citizenship since the late twentieth century there have been instances of powers of self-government devolved to minorities within states, legal protections and public financing of minority cultures, and some guaranteed representation for ethnic minorities within existing political institutions (Kymlicka 1995). For this to be possible, data gathering and analysis that is targeted at minority groups renders them more visible for special treatment. The other side of this coin is that such hyper-visibility makes individuals and communities targets for prejudice that could be verbal and/or physical abuse. People being harangued for speaking a language other than English on public transport in the UK points to the resistance towards minority representation when racism is normalized by politicians and parts of the media. At the very same time, CCTV systems on public transport may assist in identifying a racist abuser and bring the person to trial. Similarly, surveillance by other passengers who record the encounter on their phones could contribute to justice for the abused – and simultaneously endanger a fair trial if the abuser is publicly shamed via social media.

Our citizenship is complex, whoever we are, because we practise it and others practise theirs at multiple sites of contested identity, such as class, gender, sexuality, age, ethnicity and physical or mental capacity. As Chantal Mouffe rightly concludes, citizenship has to recognize the politicization of the social and of the personal; being a citizen is not confined to a narrow segment of life in a constitutional settlement (Mouffe 1993, pp. 83–5).

The gaze

Hacking democracy

The datafied citizen is vulnerable to manipulation; democracy is susceptible to being hacked. There are two dimensions to hacking: one being actions to identify weaknesses in a computer system, the second being exploiting a weakness in order to gain an advantage. Both these are implied in the notion of democracy being hacked. It is necessary, even vital, to know where there are, in this case digital, vulnerabilities in order that these might be removed as far as possible by programming revisions, hardware adaptions and regulatory regimes. Of equal importance is knowing where assailants have already found points of susceptibility to abuse in democratic processes and deployed surveillance strategies to obtain an advantage.

We first consider the main findings of the principal parliamentary investigations. The UK parliamentary Digital, Culture, Media and Sport (DCM&S) Committee undertook one such inquiry in 2018 and 2019, 'Disinformation and "Fake News"'. In its final report it concludes:

> Electoral law is not fit for purpose and needs to be changed to reflect changes in campaigning techniques, and the move from physical leaflets and billboards to online, microtargeted political campaigning. There needs to be: absolute transparency of online political campaigning, including clear, persistent banners on all paid-for political adverts and videos, indicating the source and the advertiser; a category introduced for digital spending on campaigns; and explicit rules surrounding designated campaigners' role and responsibilities. (DCM&S Committee 2019, p. §211)

Polling Day itself was not the focus of this investigation, not least because in the UK there is little use yet of electronic voting systems; paper-based voting remains the norm. So it is not a question of the integrity of the voting system per se but of what happens further upstream. Although it may be that, in effect, election campaigning never really ceases, there are still more intensive periods in which efforts are made to influence voters to cast their ballot for one, rather than any other, party or position. In this sense we can talk about citizens being hacked as a strategy within a broader effort to secure advantage in democratic decision-making. The DCM&S Committee found inadequacies in electoral law that were intended to create or maintain something of a level playing field between political opponents. Regulations around spending, accounting for such spending, and identifying the provenance of political pamphlets, hoardings and broadcasts served reasonably well in analogue elections; where, even with regional or city-focused advertising, the public were addressed en masse. The committee concluded that recent innovations of digital advertising undermined many of these existing core principles, of which current legislation had failed to keep abreast.

Inferring

One of the key findings of the DCM&S Committee investigation turned around the use of inferred data; personal information drawn from a number of sources and mined by statistical methods to generate correlations that purport to say more about categories of voters than simple tabulation might reveal:

> In the UK, the protection of user data is covered by the General Data Protection Regulation (GDPR). However, 'inferred' data is not protected; this includes characteristics that may be inferred about a user not based on specific information they have shared, but through analysis of their data profile. This, for example, allows political parties to identify supporters on sites like Facebook, through the data profile matching and the 'lookalike audience' advertising targeting tool. (DCM&S Committee 2019, §42)

This process takes the aphorism 'a person is known by the company they keep', and expands 'company' to include not only friends but ideas, preferences and characteristics. Each of these may be a data point, and each, on its own, is covered to a greater or less extent by regulations in the EU and UK for data protection. The problem that the DCM&S Committee identifies is that statistical correlations produce new data; such inferred data is not so well protected under existing legislation. It is as if I carefully tend the secluded ground to the rear of my house. I have ownership rights over the bulbs and seedlings I plant, the soil into which I plant them, the fertilizer I spread to encourage growth, and flowers and shrubs that burst into life each spring, but I do not have ownership over 'the garden' as the cumulative experience of each of these components. In such a scenario, an unscrupulous photographer could fly a drone over my garden, take pictures and sell these for his own, but not my, profit. Legal realities aside, the point is that value from the whole is separated from value of the individual parts. There is effort by a third party (in this analogy the photographer) but without my consent as gardener. The analogy rapidly breaks down if probed too closely to posit my foolishness in signing a 100-page document in which one (unread) sentence transferred the creative rights to my garden.

The UK Information Commissioner's Office had taken a different line from the DCM&S Committee on inferred data in its 2018 report, 'Democracy Disrupted':

> Our investigation found that political parties did not regard inferred data as personal information as it was not factual information. However, the ICO's view is 'that as this information is based on assumptions about individuals' interests and preferences and can be attributed to specific individuals, then it is personal information and the requirements of data protection law apply to it'. (ICO 2018a §3.8.2)

Ours is not the task of deciding on this issue but we do note that the Information Commissioner, Elizabeth Denham, in giving evidence to the DCM&S Committee on 6 November 2018, makes an important, albeit intuitive, distinction between the contexts in which the public are comfortable about organizations using inferred data. She states that there has been:

> A disturbing amount of disrespect for personal data of voters and prospective voters. What has happened here is that the model that is familiar to people in the commercial sector of behavioural targeting has been transferred – I think transformed – into the political arena. That is why I called for an ethical pause so that we can get this right. We do not want to use the same model that sells us holidays and shoes and cars to engage with people and voters. People expect more than that. This is a time for a pause to look at codes, to look at the practices of social media companies, to take action where they have broken the law. For us, the main purpose of this is to pull back the curtain and show

the public what is happening with their personal data. (oral evidence, Q4011, cited in (DCM&S Committee 2019, §45))

Denham is suggesting a qualitative (and arguably an ethical, if not yet legal) difference between people's practices as citizens and as consumers. When we consider surveillance capitalism in some detail in the next chapter, it will become obvious quite how much against the tide Denham is trying to swim. In some ways we have been here before; an institution inappropriately commercializing its role. It took the Protestant Reformations in the sixteenth century to confront the Church selling indulgences. On the one hand we have the injecting of commercial interest into democratic processes. On the other hand (or perhaps more accurately, unknowingly in the other hand), this interjecting is occluded: 'citizens can only make truly informed choices about who to vote for if they are sure that those decisions have not been unduly influenced' (ICO 2018c, p. 4). This, as we noted at the beginning of this chapter, is a particularly crucial point of Denham's. John Stuart Mill's hopes for developmental democracy may well be dashed on some very jagged digital rocks. It is indeed hard to practise diligent citizenship if you are unaware when, and how, your opinions are being nudged in particular directions. This is not citizens becoming mere puppets of data-analysis corporations. We might laud the team leader who can get her team performing a task *her* way, although the team keep thinking it has been *their* idea all along. However, should this skill of people-management be writ large with democratic decision-making at stake, this nudging is cast in a more sinister light.

The Information Commissioner's Office report in 2018 concluded that political parties are being disingenuous in their approach of voters:

> Data protection law does not stop data controllers from getting and using information from publicly available sources. However, they need to ensure that the way they do it complies with all the requirements of the law. Even where a party got the personal information from publicly available sources, they must still provide a privacy notice to individuals. The ICO is concerned about political parties using this functionality without adequate information being provided to the people affected. (ICO 2018a, §3.8.5)

In a domestic setting we would be justly furious at an electrician who installed 80 per cent of our light switches so they are safe to use, but leaves the remainder wired incorrectly and giving us a shock on touch. Political parties having a cavalier approach to democracy are dangerous. The ecosystem of political campaigning directed at voters is not designed to fail safe. It is not like four-engined aircraft that can, *in extremis*, continue flying to land safely on just one. The ICO makes the significant point that transparency and thereby accountability for the use of personal information is not to be construed as a hindrance to democracy – but rather a vital component of it.

Lest we think hacking is a problem solely for the UK or the USA, the DCM&S Committee delivered a litany of countries in which they believed that one company, SCL Elections, and associated companies had been involved:

> Australia; Brazil; Czech Republic; France; Gambia; Germany; Ghana (2013); Guyana; India; Indonesia; Italy; Kenya (Kenyatta campaigns of 2013 and 2017); Kosovo; Malaysia; Mexico; Mongolia; Niger; Nigeria; Pakistan; Peru; Philippines; Slovakia; St Kitts and Nevis; St Lucia; St Vincent and the Grenadines; Thailand; Trinidad and Tobago. (DCM&S Committee 2019, §275)

This brings us to the particular story of Cambridge Analytica; for the account of which we rely here on parliamentary reports, with some supplementary annotation from recently published insider narratives, and from *Guardian* and *Washington Post* investigations.

Cambridge Analytica

Cambridge Analytica (CA) had its origins in SCL consultancy, a company that had used 'specialist communications techniques previously developed by the military to combat terror organisations, and to disrupt enemy intelligence and to give on the ground support in war zones' in political campaigns in different parts of the world (DCM&S Committee 2018a, §95). From this background, CA was 'to focus on data targeting and communications campaigns for carefully selected Republican Party candidates in the United States of America' (DCM&S Committee 2018a, §95). We can pick up the story from the point where, on 25 October 2018, the ICO 'imposed the maximum penalty possible at the time – £500,000 – on Facebook ... for lack of transparency and security issues relating to the harvesting of data' (DCM&S Committee 2019, §57). This related to processing of data between 2007 and 2014 (ICO 2018b). The ICO explained its position on Facebook's appeal, in a statement to the DCM&S Committee:

> We fined Facebook because it allowed applications and application developers to harvest the personal information of its customers who

had not given their informed consent – think of friends, and friends of friends – and then Facebook failed to keep the information safe ... It is not a case of no harm, no foul. (quoting evidence given as Q4284, DCM&S Committee 2019, §57)

So there are separate issues of the harvesting and sharing of Facebook data. What is of interest to us here is how CA used (or claimed to be able to use) this and/or other data. There are two strands worth focusing on at this point. We have information being disseminated that is palpably false. At the same time, there is what the DCM&S Committee calls 'the relentless targeting of hyper-partisan views, which play to the fears and the prejudices of people, in order to alter their voting plans' (DCM&S Committee 2018a, §92). It is this practice that the DCM&S Committee believes to be 'arguably more invasive' (DCM&S Committee 2018a, §92). Cambridge University researchers had been constructing psychological profiles about the US electorate, a fact revealed by Harry Davies at the end of 2015 (Davies 2015).

Alexander Nix, the former CEO of Cambridge Analytica, described their micro-targeting business in his evidence to the DCM&S Committee on 27 February 2018:

We are trying to make sure that voters receive messages on the issues and policies that they care most about, and we are trying to make sure that they are not bombarded with irrelevant materials. That can only be good. That can only be good for politics, it can only be good for democracy and it can be good in the wider realms of communication and advertising. (quoted in DCM&S Committee 2018a, §97)

What was key in this process was the capability to present, said Nix in his oral evidence to the committee, 'a fact that is underpinned by an emotion' (Nix, oral evidence Q662, quoted in DCM&S Committee 2018a, §98). The DCM&S Committee heard an explanation by Nix of how voters' shopping choices, preferred media outlets and cars they drove, and multiple other data points, could be matched with first-party research held in large data-sets. Nix's point was encapsulated: 'We can go out and ask audiences about their preferences ... indeed we can also start to probe questions about personality and other drivers that might be relevant to understanding their behaviour and purchasing decisions' (DCM&S Committee 2018a, §98).

Categories of voters were created, such as 'Openness', 'Conscientiousness', 'Extraversion', 'Agreeableness' and 'Neuroticism' (DCM&S Committee 2018a, §98). These data-gathering and analysis techniques exist alongside others, whether used by CA or by other companies. The DCM&S Committee investigation drew attention to the 'Facebook Pixel', which is a piece of code that can be embedded in websites:

> The Pixel can be used to register when Facebook users visit the site. Facebook can use the information gathered by the Pixel to allow advertisers to target Facebook users who had visited that given site. AIQ definitely utilized Pixels and other tools to help in data collection and targeting efforts. (DCM&S Committee 2019, §181)

The committee investigated Aggregate IQ, a Canadian digital advertising web and software development company, and concluded that a data-scraper tool existed that had the capacity to extract data from LinkedIn:

> There is a folder called 'LinkedIn-person-fondler-master', which is an application that scrapes LinkedIn user data. Within the repository is a file containing information on 92,000 individuals on LinkedIn. These names could then have been used to gather the user's location, position and place of work via the LinkedIn scraper tool. Using Facebook's ad targeting, AIQ would then have been able to reach these users via targeting of locations, place of work and job positions. (DCM&S Committee 2019, §187)

Knowing for sure quite how effective SCL/CA's involvement in political campaigns has been has proved difficult, but SCL have, in documents seen by the DCM&S Committee, claimed with regard to mid-term elections in the USA in November 2014 'a 39% increase in awareness of the issues featured in the campaign's advertising amongst those who had received targeted messages' (DCM&S Committee 2018a, §110). The need to know the effects of involvement in specific political campaigns is crucial – although perhaps not possible. In any event, what came to be known as the Cambridge Analytica and Facebook scandal unfolded in a way that suggests that much is at stake, and this is not easily dismissed. *The Guardian/Observer* and *The Washington Post* has run an extended investigation and the timeline in 2018 (Cadwalladr 2018) makes for salutary reading:

> March 2018: the *Observer* revealed that CA had harvested profile information of more than 50 million Facebook users.
> April 2018: the CEO of Facebook, Mark Zuckerberg, testifies to Congress, telling US representatives 'it was my mistake, and I'm sorry.'

May 2018: CA declare bankruptcy and Facebook suspects 200 apps as part of the company's investigation into the misuse of data.

June 2018: CA's ex-CEO Alexander Nix speaks to the UK parliamentary committee.

July 2018: the UK's ICO issues an interim report criticizing a number of political organizations for misusing personal data in campaigning.

October 2018: Facebook is fined £500,000.

November 2018: an international 'grand committee' of MPs from nine countries attempt to call Zuckerberg to testify but are sent only Facebook's European Policy chief.

Affect heuristic

In October 2019, two former CA employees published their accounts: Christopher Wylie, *Mindf*ck* (Wylie 2019) and Brittany Kaiser, *Targeted* (Kaiser 2019). Both go into considerable detail as to the unfolding saga, indeed intrigue, of the company and its relationship with US billionaire funders. It is hard to disentangle their personal self-justification, confession and mea culpa from reporting of events as other, less-embedded and self-interested, parties might perceive them.

The major point we can draw from those accounts is the use of the *affect heuristic*, which Wylie presents as a core component of recent micro-targeting approaches, 'where people use mental shortcuts that are significantly influenced by emotions' (Wylie 2019, p. 76). The intention is to shift people into a mode of 'identity-motivated reasoning' (Wylie 2019, p. 77) in which the targeter takes advantage of a perceived (or real) 'social identity threat' (Wylie 2019, p. 78).

In theoretical terms, the affect heuristic is a widely recognized phenomenon within risk perception, drawing to a considerable extent on James Russell's influential approach to studying affect. Core affect is 'a neurophysiological state that is consciously accessible as a simple, nonreflective feeling', whereas emotion is multi-layered (Russell 2003, p. 147). Of most relevance to our discussion of micro-targeting is the observation that 'fear is mainly associated with uncertainty in judgment and anger is mainly associated with evaluation and control' (Wu et al. 2018, p. 1333). However, it is actually subtle emotions that guide in most situations. But on occasions we are aware the stakes are higher, so 'When risk judgment or decision making is complex and psychological resources are limited, it is simpler and more effective to use the affect heuristic rather than probability theory to make judgments' (Wu et al. 2018, p. 1333).

Affect heuristic helps us understand what has unfolded on our screens, particularly, but not limited to, Facebook during the Brexit referendum and the 2016 US presidential election campaign. A campaign team want to motivate a community to vote for their candidate. The team needs to get people angry, because when people are angry they are less likely to weigh up information or rationalize on a broader perspective. TV stations employ hyperbolic, rage-filled commentators not merely as entertainment but as a political strategy. How better to enrage viewers than to keep telling them that they are part of 'ordinary Americans' or 'ordinary British people' (or whoever) who share the frustrations of unemployment, or of problems at work, or crime in their neighbourhood? 'You're not alone, "we" think this too.' If a targeter can get someone angered at a grievance that is touching on his or her identity – and, importantly, their sense of group identity – then the target will lap up information without thinking twice about it. That information deepens their rage and dulls their critical thinking. The targeter does not need to worry too much about the target being influenced by alternative explanations. If someone tries to 'debate' unemployment, cultural intrusion, dangers from immigrants, then the target perceives this 'debate' as an attack on his or her identity together as 'ordinary voters'. The target reacts to debate by becoming more entrenched because those with different information (especially information that contradicts what the targeter told them to get them enraged) are perceived to be attacking the target's freedoms.

So, in political micro-targeting, it is not only a matter of misinformation but misinformation wrapped in emotional manipulation. Information is thereby weaponized.

Weaponizing information

Information warfare

The hacking of citizens and of democracy can be set within the broader theoretical framework of information warfare and, specifically, the weaponizing of information. Kevin Desouza and his colleagues offer a taxonomic view of the actors (Desouza et al. 2020) in terms of roles and reach, motivation, unit and plausible deniability. Actors may instigate an act of information warfare that may include providing support by, for example, funding it or providing human resources. Some group or other will actually conduct the attack – and this may or may not include the instigators and supporters. Further options for actors are involving themselves in concealing the attack by means of, for example, shell companies. It is, however, possible that other actors such as news media unknowingly amplify the effects of the attack by how they respond. The focus of information warfare might be within the actors' own country but it may attempt to reach outside to other countries (some of which will have coverage of international treaties and international organizations, while others may fall outside those larger jurisdictions). Motivation can be political, military, economic or ideological, or some combination thereof. The Desouza et al. taxonomy identifies individuals, groups and organizations, giving particular attention to hitherto largely ignored private military contractors that 'have the advantage of ensuring that they meet stringent security requirements of a state actor, whilst still being able to conduct operations that are state-supported and are hard to trace back to the original sponsor' (Desouza et al. 2020, p. 5). Some states may sponsor information-warfare actors as part of their intelligence and security services. Others may offer arms-length support to groups. Some actors are non-state and more likely to be motivated by ideological concerns. (ISIS weaponizing social media as a recruitment and radicalization tool is an example of the non-state actor.) It is in order to maintain a stance of plausible deniability that state support, and also sponsorship, will be maintained with as much possible secrecy as is considered politically advantageous.

In the Desouza et al. taxonomy, information warfare makes use of one or more of four levels. Level 1 is taking information systems offline, possibly by a ransomware attack, which, in effect, takes a target's data hostage. Level 2 involves casting doubt on the veracity of the output of a target's information systems. Here we have efforts at manipulating algorithms such as biometric identification processes or encouraging collective human behaviour that nudges machine-learning systems to a desired, or simply any other, output. Level 3 is again manipulation, but this time of the interpretations and context of information. This can be putting valid information in an artificially generated false context such as a digitally manipulated specious location. The Level 3 lever also includes inserting invalid information (fake news) within a true context. Now that video and audio manipulation is so sophisticated it is possible to fool people into believing that a politician said something quite damaging to their prospects: 'evidence' of 'actual' footage is deployed to prove the point but in reality those words were never spoken. Level 4 is fully weaponizing information systems, causing major interruption to regional or national services, not merely of a targeted company or individual (as in Level 1).

The hacking of democracy we are examining maps well to Levels 2 and 3. The realm of fake news and disinformation most certainly targets the ways in which voters interpret all information that comes their way or that they actively seek out. Even those not taken in may unwittingly contribute to nudging the algorithms that deliver 'news' to others' as well as their own social media feeds. What we have here is political advertising as psychological operations (PSYOPS).

PSYOPS

In war there is truthful information from open and acknowledged sources, fabrications from unknown sources, and a grey area in which PSYOPS take place. In the grey area there is information generated and received; some of it truthful, some of it false (Smyczek 2005, p. 215). In the law of war there is a custom of chivalry which PSYOPS have to navigate. Under chivalry there is prohibition of perfidy which is 'an unlawful battlefield deception' (Smyczek 2005, p. 235), as well as feigning or misuse (Smyczek 2005, p. 233f.). In what reads like a description of how democracy is being hacked by political micro-targeting within the USA and UK (and elsewhere), Joshua Kastenberg provides the example of current US military strategy that might be 'feeding allied deception into an adversary's deception operation where it is known that the adversary is testing a U.S. force's response. The posting of fictitious news releases is one example' (Kastenberg 2007, p. 64).

There are, however, as we would expect, lawful deceptions or ruses permitted under Geneva Protocol 1. Our interest is in perfidy:

> Article 37 of Protocol I to the Geneva Conventions (Protocol I) prohibits the killing, wounding, or capturing of belligerents by perfidy. One example would be the misuse of agreed symbols that invoke a protection provided by the law of armed conflict. Similarly, the use of protected persons for offensive military operations may rise to the level of perfidy. (Kastenberg 2007, p. 67)

As weapons from the battlefield are deployed at home by actors with ostensible allegiance to their own country, it is sobering to notice how some of the military conventions are not likewise imported. As Vian Bakir et al. observe:

> there is minimal conceptual development with regard to manipulative modes of OPC [organized persuasive communication] involving deception, incentivization and coercion. As a consequence, manipulative OPC within liberal democracies is a blind spot, rarely recognized let alone researched, and with the result that our understanding and grasp of these activities is profoundly curtailed. (Bakir et al. 2018, p. 312)

It seems to me that there are parallels here about weaponized information directed against political opponents and wavering electors. There is a misuse of symbols, in this case the symbols of democratic discourse. Fake news undermines a cornerstone of democracy; an educated and informed electorate. The symbol of 'news' is so badly misused that doubt is cast over the entire ecosystem of political information. The circumlocution from the battlefield, 'persuasive communication' (Bergier and Faucher 2016), has its value to the unscrupulous users of weaponized information on the home front. This may seem overly dramatic, but Ron Schleifer argues that 'in the beginning there was propaganda, then it became psychological warfare, and today it is political marketing. There is really no substantive difference among the three terms: Their aim is to achieve political goals by way of psychological persuasion' (Schleifer 2014, p. 152).

The techniques that Schleifer identifies as shared by PSYOPS and political marketing are: emotions, personal attacks, guilt feelings, encouraging desertion, creating divisiveness and demonization. Organization techniques include front organization, coalitions, events and boycotts. Messages aiming to persuade contain buzzwords, legal jargon, atrocity propaganda, weakness message framing the receiver as an oppressed underdog. Whether waged by nationals or external actors, 'PSYOP is extremely effective against Western democratic regimes, since it poses as an acceptable political campaign' (Schleifer 2014, p. 157).

Sarah Maltby and Helen Thornham analyse leaflets issued in Afghanistan in which photographs of people are used to suggest what an ideal citizen looks like. Part of this tactic includes undermining the enemy's will to fight by 'influencing the enemy's perceptions of their own actions (e.g. by undermining the legitimacy of their leadership or eroding their moral power base) and influencing the perceptions of civilians in the battle space' (Maltby and Thornham 2012, p. 35). There is a short step to attempting to dissuade lightly committed voters to stay at home rather than support a particular candidate. Fake news about what a candidate has said or intends to do may indeed influence a voter's perceptions of their own actions.

Political micro-targeting

In PSYOPS as political micro-targeting there is a behaviourist assumption (of which we will have more to say in our theological analysis of artificial intelligence later in this chapter). There is also a political philosophy that substitutes marketing and manipulation for discourse. This goes hand in glove with privatizing political campaigning (a 'fragmentation of the marketplace of ideas' (Zuiderveen Borgesius et al. 2018, p. 89)), so one's neighbour sees different messages from the ones you see and does not necessarily know what you are being shown. In the current version of populism, the procedure and approach is not about the polis as a debate among citizens. Instead it comprises targeted messages from one party to individuals: 'A political party could also misleadingly present itself as a one-issue party to each individual. A party may highlight a *different* issue for each voter, so each voter sees a different one-issue party' (Zuiderveen Borgesius et al. 2018, p. 87). A knock-on effect is the fragility of any claim of a political mandate 'if citizens are voting on the basis of different policy promises' that could well be incompatible (Hillygus and Shields 2008, p. 14).

It seems to me that this form of political persuasion is amoral in that it weaponizes information without regard to veracity. It is only the effectiveness of a message, not its veracity, that matters. Furthermore, it weaponizes people; fellow citizens are framed as enemies rather than opponents. It relies on the ignorance of people who are datafied and manipulated. These processes devalue solidarity by making political decision-making too much like a list of musical preferences on Spotify; the social consequences of decisions are almost immaterial. Using 'dark posts' to disillusion a candidate's followers aims to suppress voting participation and can ignore certain voter groups (Zuiderveen Borgesius et al. 2018, p. 87).

The marketing of political micro-targeting can sound more like the hawking of magic than the science it purports to be: with the correct incantation (data analysis software) you can alter events. Experts are divided on the efficacy of micro-targeting, some thinking developers' claims are myths (Hoffmann et al. 2019, p. 17). In a 2018 analysis, Michele Settanni, Danny Azucar and Davide Marengo conclude that 'the relationship between digital traces of online behavior and psychological characteristics is quite strong, apparently stronger than the association found by scholars studying the link between personality and offline' (Settanni et al. 2018, p. 226). A study of German voters reached a different conclusion, but, crucially in my view, these participants had agreed to have their internet use monitored over four months, making them a rather different group from those who are not otherwise self-policing their browsing. The German sample may be more mainstream than other voters who might be easier to influence. Also, this is a study of predicting voting behaviour rather than influencing such voting behaviour. Ruben Bach and his colleagues found that, 'generally speaking, our findings do not indicate that political behaviours such as those studied in our article can be inferred from records of users' online activity in an almost deterministic way' (Bach et al. 2019, pp. 14–15). However, the team were careful to note, 'our results are limited to the German case, and results may differ for countries with different political systems (e.g. the two-party systems of the U.S.) or more (or less) polarized and partisan media' (Bach et al. 2019, p. 16).

Political parties can find that they have to cede power to intermediaries who control the technology (Zuiderveen Borgesius et al. 2018, p. 88). It is possible that at the next election a party could be outbid by the opposition and the crucial contract now made with their opponents. Alternatively, to outbid the current contract holder may require inordinate expense because, for example, 'Total digital advertising in the presidential race was expected to reach $1B by November, 2016, most of which was spent at Alphabet (Google, $400M) and Facebook ($350M)' (Thorson et al. 2019, p. 73). The fundraising arms race, with concomitant political indebtedness to large donors, seems likely only to be accelerated.

The crucial point is that micro-targeting does not need to work all the time, only just enough in specific swing seats where a tiny difference can have huge consequences. First-past-the-post and electoral-college systems do seem particularly vulnerable, 'where minor shifts in the popular vote can produce exaggerated swings in seats won' (Bennett 2013). Proportional representation is more difficult to game. On the other hand, micro-targeting can mobilize citizens, be more efficient and cost-effective for political parties and, in terms of public opinion, both 'expose voters to information that is most relevant for their voting decision' and 'voters can use their limited attention to process political information more efficiently, and therefore can make better-informed decisions' (Zuiderveen Borgesius et al. 2018, p. 86). And it is worth remembering that 'people do not live in digital bubbles' (Zuiderveen Borgesius et al. 2018, p. 91) but still learn political information from sources other than being micro-targeted. Nevertheless, I think it remains an open question as to the extent to which citizens, as electors, are in the sights of 'digital gangsters' (DCM&S Committee 2019, §139). As Clara Alves Rodrigues remarks, 'Facebook and Google's technology is challenging democracy. The capitalisation of human experience leads to significant disruptions that have to be carefully addressed' (Rodrigues 2019, p. 40).

In summary, there are many important issues. Data-gathering platforms, especially global players, have undue influence in democratic processes, part of which is their encouraging a shopping or consumerist model for politics. Processing political opinions is handling sensitive personal information (ICO 2018a, pp. 38–9). Especially where these are part of generating inferred data it is deeply concerning when surveys finds that many citizens are unaware of micro-targeting practices (in general and not just in political campaigning) and do not have easily deployed tools for controlling what is piped down the data stream to them (Ipsos MORI 2020, p. 29).

Hacking biblical decision-makers

The Bible has narratives about people being influenced by others with fear-mongering and political disinformation. On some occasions it is a few leaders who are advised by other religious and political actors. Our attention here will be on those categorized as false prophets. At other times the masses, or at least a section of them, are subject to influence. In the New Testament they are 'the crowd', and our attention will turn to them in the later part of this section.

False prophets

> In the prophets of Samaria
>   I saw a disgusting thing:
> they prophesied by Baal
>   and led my people Israel astray.
> But in the prophets of Jerusalem
>   I have seen a more shocking thing:
> they commit adultery and walk in lies;
>   they strengthen the hands of evildoers,
>   so that no one turns from wickedness;
> all of them have become like Sodom to me,
>   and its inhabitants like Gomorrah.
> (Jer. 23.13–14)

In order to draw on biblical imagination we do not have to find parallel political systems in the Bible – otherwise there could be little, if any, stimulation to critical thinking beyond the limited range of models in those texts. Tribal confederacy, theocracy and empire certainly have resonance for many readers of the Bible today, but would not address the political contexts of many others living in one or other form of democratic polity. Although people might not be directly electing their leaders in most periods of the biblical narratives, those leaders required at least the acquiescence of the people or, perhaps more significantly, the support of military leaders or the 'elders', to rule: 'Prophets are kingmakers, dynasty guarantors, and political and religious advisors to the kings' (Barstad 2009, p. 28). This is without incorporating the dynamic of prophetic critique coming from court prophets and freelance prophets.

Without overplaying any parallels, there is propaganda voiced by monarchs, their spokesmen (usually men) with prophets and prophetic schools vying for (or simply assuming) legitimation of divine authority. The time of Jeremiah offers a series of narratives that can generate an imaginative appreciation and critique of prophetic utterances into, in this case, a non-democratic polity. The fate of the nation lies, so the prophetic framing goes, in the hands of God, who is responding to the loyalty or disloyalty to the covenant commitments on the part of the nation (embodied in the monarch, or tied to the monarch in a form of collective responsibility). People may be unfaithful to God, so might the king, but so might be some prophets or priests. In instances of syncretism or outright apostasy, the people have not spoken in a referendum nor have they chosen leaders to take them in this direction. But in a patriarchal, tribal structure the decision has, in effect, been made on their behalf by their elders.

Within the prophetic framework of Jeremiah, there are those giving good advice and those giving bad advice. The advisors (prophets being a significant, although not the sole, category) may be wise or foolish; foolish or disingenuous; misled or deluded. Political decisions are, in this framework, also religious decisions; the covenant is always in play as the (intended at least) defining principle of these two kingdoms (northern and southern Israel). Information and counsel are given that may be 'false' or 'true' – in terms that speak of their source – from Yahweh or the dreams of men. It is not difficult to hear echoes of 'fake news' in the denunciation of 'false prophets'. It may be the king and his closest advisors, rather than the people as a whole, who are the targets of 'news' here. At the very least we are broaching questions of the authenticity of information or advice that is intended to influence the behaviour of those who are in a position to make political decisions.

Looking at verse 13 as a critique of prophets of the northern kingdom (Samaria), William McKane takes 'senseless' via 'tasteless' (lacking salt) through 'intellectual discrimination' rather than 'good aesthetic taste' (McKane 1986, p. 573). In McKane's reading, 'the prophets of the northern kingdom camouflaged ("whitewashed") falsehood by laying claim to prophetic authority' (McKane 1986, p. 574). In McKane's view these men are rebuked because of their failure to 'condemn breaches of morality' (McKane 1986, p. 575). There are then two possible interpretations for McKane. The prophets are evildoers themselves or they are deceiving themselves by supposing they speak with divine authority: 'they are not guilty of a calculated deceit, but they are deluded, for they equate the vividness and strength of their own insights and visions with the word of Yahweh' (McKane 1986, pp. 578–9).

Taking a different perspective, Robert Carroll does not think that the context set up in verses 1–2 is analysing a historical situation (Carroll 1986, p. 444). However, verses 5–6 are about legitimating Zedekiah, promising peace and security during his reign (Carroll 1986, p. 446). But Carroll asserts:

> it can hardly be referred (*sic*) to Zedekiah *simpliciter*. The word-play on that king's name preserves the memory of Zedekiah and incorporates him into the future hope, but the historical Zedekiah is only an echo in that hope, an echo contributed by the Jeremiah tradition. (Carroll 1986, p. 447)

Carroll is proposing that we have here a redaction of the Jeremiah tradition after the destruction of Jerusalem in order to address later conflicts: 'Just as in a later period accusations of witchcraft characterized the political ideologies of Christian Europe so in the exilic period accusations of being a false prophet were an effective means of countering opponents' claims' (Carroll 1981, p. 195). As Carroll points out, it was acutely difficult *at the time*, when prophets clash, to have criteria of truth and falsity: 'It is therefore rather hard on the prophets criticized in 23.9–32 that they should be accused of failing to turn the people when the genuine prophets fail to achieve that turning too. Both sets of prophets, true and false, achieved the same result' (Carroll 1981, p. 171). A prophet could have been wrong without necessarily lying: 'To accuse him of lying is to be committed to an ideological notion of truth' (Carroll 1981, p. 178). To further compound the difficulties, Ezekiel 14.6–9 presents God as the one deceiving a prophet who is sought out by an idolater. Both prophet and seeker are destroyed.

The problem of false prophets appears also in the New Testament, in the context of apocalyptic anxieties:

> When he was sitting on the Mount of Olives, the disciples came to him privately, saying, 'Tell us, when will this be, and what will be the sign of your coming and of the end of the age?' Jesus answered them, 'Beware that no one leads you astray. For many will come in my name, saying, "I am the Messiah!" and they will lead many astray. And you will hear of wars and rumours of wars; see that you are not alarmed; for this must take place, but the end is not yet.' (Matt. 24.3–6)

The key component here is the possibility of being led astray by those claiming an authority that is not theirs. These voices are against the backdrop of the prevalence of rumours about wars. In the Epistles we find warnings about 'false teachers ... who will secretly bring in destructive opinions' (2 Peter 2.1). The nascent Christian communities are instructed to be on their guard against 'many false prophets [who] have gone out into the world' (1 John 4.1). In the letter to the church at Thyatira (Rev. 2.18–29), a woman prophet/teacher is singled out for condemnation as one leading the Christian community astray; a Jezebel (Rev. 2.20). The apostle John is the 'itinerant outsider' while the woman is 'the resident insider' (Thimmes 2003, p. 132) who is 'beguiling' those who ought to be proving loyal to John (Rev. 2.20). Whether or not this woman (named only by this label) is guilty of that which John charges her is not our concern here. The evident conflict and perceived danger of maleficent influence over believers points to the complex dynamics of groups – all so familiar over the subsequent centuries of church life.

The crowd

We can broaden out the sphere of influence upon groups or masses by considering the role of 'the crowd'. The people murmur against Moses (Num. 16.41; 20.24; 26.9 etc.), and clamour for the golden calf (Exod. 32; 33.3–5). In Matthew's Gospel we find that the crowd follow Jesus (Matt. 4.25), are astounded at him (Matt. 7.28) and are filled with awe at Jesus' healing of a paralysed man (Matt. 9.8). The people are amazed at deliverance from a demon (Matt. 9.33) but are also characterized as 'harassed and helpless' (Matt. 9.36). They ponder whether Jesus is the Son of David (Matt. 12.23) and believe that John the Baptist is a prophet – to the extent that King Herod fears this crowd (Matt. 14.5). In Mark's Gospel we do not learn much about the crowd – except for their 'running together' (Mark 9.25) when Jesus rebukes the demon that keeps a boy from hearing and speaking. In Luke, we find the crowds where some are trying to touch Jesus, 'for power came out from him and healed all of them' (Luke 6.19). Jesus asks his disciples, 'Who do the crowds say that I am?' (Luke 9.18).

In John's Gospel there are divided views within one crowd: 'And there was considerable complaining about him among the crowds. While some were saying, "He is a good man", others were saying, "No, he is deceiving the crowd"' (John 7.12). At one point the Pharisees hear the crowd muttering in favour of Jesus: 'many in the crowd believed in him and were saying, "When the Messiah comes, will he do more signs than this man has done?"' (John 7.31). The Pharisees' response is to send temple guards in what turned out to be an aborted arrest attempt (John 7.45) in the face of a crowd divided over Jesus' credentials (John 7.43).

The crowd turns out to be fickle, particularly those assembled outside Pilate's residence, and, in response to his invitation, choose Barabbas for clemency (Matt. 27.15–26; Mark 15.11–15; Luke 23.18; John 18.39–40).

In Acts 14.19, 'Jews came there from Antioch and Iconium and won over the crowds. Then they stoned Paul and dragged him out of the city, supposing that he was dead.' Paul had no little trouble in Ephesus with crowds (Acts 19).

Crowds are not in any sense campaigners for democracy, nor are they exercising any democratic rights of assembly, speech and so on. These are groups – seemingly not identified as a particular sector of society such as Pharisees, scribes or others. More amorphous, forming and dispersing perhaps on a geographical basis, in the sense of being based on local towns, crowds are described as showing awe, being divided, not always consistent in their view. Of course, the various crowds are not composed of the same people on each occasion. Rather, the crowd is indicative of a collection of ordinary people who are interested, stirred, confused by what they hear and see.

Decision-making

The prophets may be closest to political advisers or spokesmen at centres of power. I also wonder if the prophets are not akin to some of our political commentators. It seems to me that there are a variety of intentions that could be attributed to prophets within the royal or 'public' court. There is competing political commentary circulating – whether within the royal court regarding the respective value of various foreign allegiances or among the people in terms of Jesus in the context of messianic claimants and rumours of war that might herald a great apocalyptic event. There appear to be at least two, interrelated motivations: strategic advantage over opponents/enemies, and ideological analysis of unfolding or unfolded events. This might be to bolster the authority of a particular political party, or to bolster the legitimacy of a particular theological reading of contemporary or past events. We might go as far as to say that in the biblical texts there are competing analyses of analysis. It is indeed important to appreciate that the Bible tells of symbolic, and therefore political, worlds that are distant in so many respects from post-Enlightenment reasoning. However, those twenty-first-century faith communities that continue to see the world as enchanted and use divination may well find themselves closer to the world of these biblical texts.

Alongside wisdom sought from political advisors/prophets, biblical figures make decisions by casting lots, for example: 'Then Saul said, "O LORD God of Israel, why have you not answered your servant today? If this guilt is in me or in my son Jonathan, O LORD God of Israel, give Urim; but if this guilt is in your people Israel, give Thummim." And Jonathan and Saul were indicated by the lot, but the people were cleared' (1 Sam. 14.41). Lots are also cast in the selection of Matthias as a replacement apostle for the disgraced Judas Iscariot (Acts 1.26). Political and military acumen feature frequently in the stories of the Judges and Kings. There is the Wisdom tradition extolled in the book of Proverbs as guidance for rulers, among others: 'By me kings reign, and rulers decree what is just; by me rulers rule, and nobles, all who govern rightly' (Prov. 8.15–16).

Dreams and their interpretation are another method of decision-making, for example Jacob's dream of a ladder reaching to heaven (Gen. 28.12). All of these are practised under the canopy of covenantal obligations, whether as the foundation of Israel's or of the Church's identity in God. The question of which guide (person or system) to trust never goes away. The consequences of being guided wrongly cast a shadow over the narrative. The crowd, as a recurring character in the New Testament drama, have to make decisions. This might be about how they respond directly to Jesus' or his disciples' message about the kingdom of God, brought into sharp focus by parables that leave one having to reconsider one's prior assumptions. The decision might lie in whether or not to attempt to approach Jesus for healing. At a more political level, given Jesus' emerging role and status in the complicated relationships between Jewish teachers, leaders and Roman authorities, members of the crowd have to weigh up relative dangers of aligning with one side or the other. The crowd are dealing with sometimes patchy information, spread by word of mouth from particular perspectives. Uneducated fishermen are among Jesus' main spokespeople and the crowd might not be blamed for treated such testimony as inherently suspect. They hear contrasting interpretations in denunciations from religious leaders and testimony from people who have been healed at Jesus' hands.

The writers of the film *Monty Python's Life of Brian* captured the challenge for the crowd that I attempt to problematize when they mishear 'Blessed are the peacemakers' as, the now widely recognizable, 'Blessed are the cheesemakers' (Jones 1979).

The crowd, those in the biblical narrative rather than in Terry Jones's film, bears remarkable similarity to what we see and participate in as members in twenty-first-century conflicts of influence. We are trying to interpret events around us, particularly when those call for a decision. We are subjected to diverse attempts to shape, manipulate, inform and educate. Our task now is bringing together the weaponizing of information with the insight generated from imaginative reading of the biblical texts. In order to achieve this we first consider a theological perspective on propaganda, before turning to query claims that algorithmic decision-making is superior as a system to human reasoning; a theology thus of artificial intelligence.

The great allure

Propaganda

We are considering how democracy, and more particularly the citizen, is being hacked by data analytics in a new approach to persuasive speech. First, we unpack a theology of propaganda, before turning to question whether or not there is a decision-making process that is better than the claimed fragility of human intelligence.

Distortion and dignity

The Roman Catholic Church's Pontifical Council offers theological reflection on advertising in 1997. It recognizes that political advertising has a legitimate role in supporting and assisting democratic processes. Obstruction, however, occurs when political competition is limited 'to wealthy candidates or groups, or require[s] that office-seekers compromise their integrity and independence by over-dependence on special interests for funds' (Pontifical Council for Social Communications 1997, §11). There are two facets here: squeezing out marginal voices, and politicians being in hock to vested interests. So data analytics is continuous in the sense that it is an extension of previous means of influence. The Council also observes that obstruction also arises with distortion and disinformation:

> instead of being a vehicle for honest expositions of candidates' views and records, political advertising seeks to distort the views and records of opponents and unjustly attacks their reputations. It happens when advertising appeals more to people's emotions and base instincts – to selfishness, bias and hostility toward others, to racial and ethnic prejudice and the like – rather than to a reasoned sense of justice and the good of all. (Pontifical Council 1997, §11)

The Council recognizes what might, using a contemporary metaphor from data encryption, be called a backdoor to human decision-making: concupiscence, 'an inclination to evil' (Roman Catholic Church 1999, §405) within which we are called to 'the most fundamental passion [which] is love, aroused by the attraction of the good' (Roman Catholic Church 1999, §1765). The Council is warning that although passion in politics is important, passions, unless lured by love, are seduced by evil. Political advertising is not expected to be impartial but profoundly aware of its power *not* to use concupiscent attraction to evil, and instead to deploy its power to attract to the good, not here meaning the policies it advertises but the methods the industry uses. It is in the light of its theological anthropology that the Council can claim: 'it is morally wrong to use manipulative, exploitative, corrupt and corrupting methods of persuasion and motivation' (Pontifical Council 1997, §14). The Council sets the bar high for ethical advertising, for it 'may not deliberately seek to deceive, whether it does that by what it says, by what it implies, or by what it fails to say' (Pontifical Council 1997, §15). Insinuations or silence, the currency of much political advertising and now micro-targeting, are to be scrutinized as much as are statements.

George Brenkert argues that the Pontifical Council (PC) might be injecting paternalism towards those to whom adverts are addressed: 'All responsibilities assigned by the PC with regard to advertising fall on advertisers; all rights accrue to consumers ... moral principles might override what consumers want' (Brenkert 1998, p. 326). Debra Ringold argues against overstating the industry's 'power to create needs' (Ringold 1998, p. 334). Furthermore, she contends that there are self-correcting mechanisms of competition within the advertising industry, which means that marketing meets consumers' preferences (Ringold 1998, p. 334). However, Brenkert makes a stronger case when he postulates how the Council might respond to charges of paternalism by pointing out that advertising does not take place on a neutral, level playing field. His words from over 20 years ago, prior to the explosion of data analytics and micro-targeting, have even more salience today: 'the market is ... a morally charged and skewed field on which consumers might get harmed' (Brenkert 1998, p. 327). Voters, to take the focus of our concern, are not in a position always, if ever, to know the extent to which they are being shaped by political advertising. Of course, questions of freedom of speech arise, and Gene Laczniak takes the view in his contemporaneous reflection that political advertising ought not to have featured in the Pontifical Council's paper, as 'by questioning the ethics of political speech, the church raises a frightening spectre' of what else the Church might want to censor (Laczniak 1998, p. 322). Laczniak raises an important concern, but it is not paternalistic or in any way to denigrate people's self-determination to insist on a regulatory safety regime for the use of, for example, radioactive materials. Granted, these are dangerous to all people in ways that can be accurately quantified. With political advertising, however, definitions of what is harmful or beneficial are more contestable. Furthermore, as Brenkert observes, 'In some cases, the same information might be destructive for one person, help another grow, and be indifferent to a third' (Brenkert 1998, p. 328). Laczniak's position would render political discourse amoral, with the consequence that the wealthiest is, in effect, the winner who takes all. With data-analytical techniques concealed within proprietary 'black boxes' (Pasquale 2015) for commercial secrecy, it is hard to see why political advertising should be awarded an ethical pass.

Quite where we position advertising hyperbole, especially within political discourse, is unclear in the Pontifical Council's paper. (As Patrick Murphy notes, there can be excess of truth as well as a deficiency; boastfulness as well as deception (Murphy 1998, p. 318).) For Brenkert, manipulation has not occurred if a consumer correctly understands the hyperbole of an advertising claim, but in such cases 'cynicism and skepticism, rather than directness and candour, are rewarded' (Brenkert 1998, p. 328).

Micro-targeting is only one element of political advertising but we can usefully turn our attention to another world leader, the pontiff of social media, Mark Zuckerberg, and his 17 October 2019 Georgetown University speech (Zuckerberg 2019). He presents his two main ideas: voice and inclusion. In his defence of free political expression he argues that movements like #BlackLivesMatter and #MeToo went viral on his platform, 'and this just wouldn't have been possible in the same way before'. Zuckerberg states that, contrary to perceptions of centralized power, platforms such as Facebook 'have decentralized power by putting it directly into people's hands'. He discloses Facebook's strategy of giving priority to the credentials, that is, the 'authenticity', of the speaker rather than focusing on the content of their messages. Zuckerberg makes the valid point that most of us would not want to live in a world 'where you can only post things that tech companies judge to be 100% true'. Indeed, but he has considerable optimism in the capabilities of you and me to sift truth from fiction from our vantage point on the playing field that is so tilted in favour of the wealthy and powerful:

> We don't fact-check political ads. We don't do this to help politicians, but because we think people should be able to see for themselves what politicians are saying. And if content is newsworthy, we also won't take it down even if it would otherwise conflict with many of our standards. (Zuckerberg 2019)

Zuckerberg positions his platform's permitting of political advertising as a public service for the underdog: 'But political ads are an important part of voice – especially for local candidates, up-and-coming challengers, and advocacy groups that may not get much media attention otherwise. Banning political ads favours incumbents and whoever the media covers' (Zuckerberg 2019).

He makes a distinction between voter suppression (in the USA restricted by the 15th Amendment), which Facebook will not permit, and freedom of speech (covered by the 1st Amendment). He claims to be 'inspired by' both amendments but fails to address any connection between the two that might play out on his platform. It seems that we have to keep coming back to the lack of level playing field between citizens and data-analytic companies (and their rich backers). Aaron Sorkin, the writer of *The West Wing* TV series, puts the issue colourfully in an open letter in response to Zuckerberg when he challenges having 'crazy lies pumped into the water supply that corrupt the most important decisions we make together' (Sorkin 2019).

In June 2020, in the wake of the killing of George Floyd and subsequent widespread public protests, a number of Facebook staff staged a virtual walkout, supported (anonymously, as befits their contract conditions) by some moderators, in protest at Zuckerberg's refusal to remove posts by Donald Trump they believed to be breaking company policies against incitement to violence (Hern 2020).[2]

If Brenkert is correct, as I believe he is, that political hyperbole demands judicious evaluation, then we have to differentiate between cynicism and scepticism in current usage. A good scholar must be a sceptic by thinking critically and testing different ideas. A cynic will jump to the conclusion that no one can be trusted to bring truth to the table so, as a result, she falls back on her gut reaction. Alert citizens need to be sceptics, as subjects of surveillance that scrapes their data for political micro-targeting. Brenkert thinks that the Pontifical Council is offering an ethics of virtue rather than an ethics of principles (Brenkert 1998, p. 330). I would agree and contend that cultivating virtue requires a discursive or disclosive ethic lest we fall into privileging Christian theological insights. In the common gaze, the disclosive is more appropriate for our multi-cultural and multi-perspectival engagement. There is an urgency here, given appeals to baser instincts of hate and anger, the problem of unknown influence in the democratic process, and the problem of oligarchs funding the data analytics that are the weapons of information wars in campaigning.

Political advertising now takes place within the broader ecosystem of social media. Pope Francis acknowledges the importance, and potentially positive, contributions of this form of communication:

---

2 On 7 October 2020, Facebook announced that it would 'temporarily stop running all social issue, electoral or political ads in the US after the polls close on November 3, to reduce opportunities for confusion or abuse' (Facebook 2020). This is, at the time of press, for an unspecified period of time and is in addition to other measures implemented in September and early October 2020, such as banning additional content that seeks to intimidate voters.

> The digital world is a public square, a meeting-place where we can either encourage or demean one another, engage in a meaningful discussion or unfair attacks ... The internet can help us to be better citizens. Access to digital networks entails a responsibility for our neighbour whom we do not see but who is nonetheless real and has a dignity which must be respected. (Francis 2016)

Our participation in political persuasion, whether by surrendering our data, sharing news (fake or genuine) or engaging in online discussions, is deeply ambivalent. It is hard to focus on the dignity of anonymous persons, especially when constructed as enemies within our own country. Francis alights on a crucial theological reading of online communication: 'Truth, therefore, is not really grasped when it is imposed from without as something impersonal, but only when it flows from free relationships between persons, from listening to one another' (Francis 2018). Dignity is thus not an abstract notion but a practice of solidarity and communication of self, what, in his 2019 letter on World Communications Day, he pithily rendered as the move from giving a 'like' to an 'amen' (Francis 2019).

Loneliness and complexity

Ours is not a world in which the 'bare facts' will or ought to suffice. We not only need narratives by which to construct our reality but there is a proper and necessary role for persuasion, even what customarily might come under the banner of propaganda. Jacques Ellul, Protestant theologian and sociologist, offers an insightful extended treatment (Ellul 1973 [1965]). We focus here on his chapter, 'The Necessity for Propaganda'.

For Ellul there is not an active propagandist and a passive crowd: 'The propagandee is by no means just an innocent victim. He provokes the psychological action of propaganda, and not merely lends himself to it, but even deserves satisfaction from it' (Ellul 1973 [1965], p. 121). Government needs to plead its case to its citizens and 'because information alone is ineffective, its dissemination leads necessarily to propaganda' (Ellul 1973 [1965], p. 127). People are invested not only rationally or financially but emotionally in what government does:

> in a democracy, the citizens must be tied to the decisions of the government. This is the great role propaganda must perform. It must give the people the feeling – which they crave and which satisfies them – 'to have wanted what the government is doing, to be responsible for its actions, to be involved in defending them and making them succeed, to be "with

it"' [quoting Léo Hamon, 'Le Pouvoir et l'opinion,' *Le Monde*, April 1959]. (Ellul 1973 [1965], p. 127).

This is an important feeling that, according to Ellul, has two components: an objective and a subjective. Objectively, we are confronted with complex situations that do not lend themselves to simple observation but require copious data, knowledge of possible strategies and mature consideration. However, we are very well aware, if we are honest with ourselves and others, that we are not merely insufficiently well informed but are incapable of working this out for ourselves. We want to participate in political decision-making but matters are not reducible to the few variables that we are able to handle. This is the point at which we draw on an affect heuristic (see above) to attempt to handle the complexity. Not only are we offered propaganda but it is wrapped in an emotional package that dulls our critical capacities under a threat (perceived or real) to our group identity. What makes matters worse still is how off-kilter the perception of facts about our communities can be.

Even a cursory glance at the 'Perils of Perception' reports being produced annually by IPSOS Mori alerts us to just how inaccurately the public guess proportions of, for example, Muslims in their country. The French have the greatest level of misperception when asked about the percentage of people in their country who are Muslim, the average guess being 31 per cent when the reality is 7.5 per cent. People in Great Britain, asked the question about their own country, guess 15 per cent when the reality is 4.8 per cent (Duffy 2018, p. 113). Ellul's view is that citizens need propaganda so that we can participate but propaganda 'hides their incapacity beneath explanations, judgments, and news enabling them to satisfy their desire without eliminating their incompetence' (Ellul 1973 [1965], p. 140).

The subjective situation is expressed in terms of 'loneliness inside the crowd'. Ellul merits quoting at length:

That loneliness inside the crowd is perhaps the most terrible ordeal of modern man; that loneliness in which he can share nothing, talk to nobody and expect nothing from anybody, leads to severe personality disturbances. For it, propaganda, encompassing Human Relations, is an incomparable remedy. It corresponds to the need to share, to be a member of a community, to lose oneself in a group, to embrace a collective ideology that will end loneliness. *Propaganda is the true remedy for loneliness.* It also corresponds to deep and constant needs, more developed today, perhaps, than ever before: the need to believe and obey, to create and hear fables, to communicate in the language of myths. It also responds to man's intellectual sloth and desire for security – intrinsic characteristics of the real man as distinguished from the theoretical man of the Existentialists. All this turns man against information, which cannot satisfy any of these needs, and leads him to crave propaganda, which can satisfy them. (Ellul 1973 [1965], p. 148, emphasis in original)

Ellul is, from his Protestant theology as well as his sociological analysis, more pessimistic about human nature than Roman Catholics, or technocrats such as Zuckerberg. Being cut off from God includes being cut off from one's fellow human beings. The 'intrinsic characteristics of the real man' are, I surmise, Ellul's theological anthropology in play. His citizen is cast adrift, reaching to clutch at the comfort of myths, as did Americans about the Communist peril at the time of his writing in the mid-1960s (Ellul 1973 [1965], p. 154). Whether or not one goes all the way with Ellul in attributing the human desire to urbanize and technologize as rebellion against God (Ellul 2003 [1970]), there is something potentially sinister about the justification that propaganda can provide for the human decision-maker who is overwhelmed by the complexity of situations, his or her need to find a cover story for inadequacy, and the isolation of modern (technologized) life:

Propaganda attaches itself to man and forces him to play its game because of his overpowering need to be right and just. In every situation propaganda hands him the proof that he, personally, is in the right, that the action demanded of him is just, even if he has the dark, strong feeling that it is not. Propaganda appeases his tensions and resolves his conflicts. It offers facile, ready-made justifications, which are transmitted by society and easily believed. At the same time, propaganda has the freshness and novelty which correspond to new situations and give man the impression of having invented new ideals. (Ellul 1973 [1965], p. 158)

If humans are so ill suited as decision-makers for the world we have created, are there better candidates to whom we might, or even ought, defer? Thus we turn to a theological consideration of just such a possibility: artificial intelligence.

Artificial intelligence

Generally speaking, AI is being developed as either narrow/weak or broad. (For a helpful history and overview, see Dormehl 2016.) Narrow or weak AI is focused on a specific set of tasks within a defined context. For example, a traffic-management system can be programmed to draw on multiple sources of data and, to warrant the designation 'intelligence', learn from this data. 'Learn' in this sense means refine its algorithms to make more nuanced decisions about traffic flows. Confined to this task it is narrow AI; there is no aim on the part of the programmers to enable this system to function beyond traffic management. Broad AI is the sort of AI that gets most attention in science fiction and philosophical discussion. This type of AI is developed with a view to it being able to function across multiple domains, rather than limited to a particular task; think of the film *I-Robot* or the character Data in the *Star Trek: New Generation* television series. Our attention is on broad AI, in particular the claims that it offers a way of transcending the perceived limitations of human decision-making.

Life is algorithm?

Yuval Noah Harari offers a view on the possible future for humanity in relation to AI: 'The most important question in twenty-first-century economics may well be what to do with all the superfluous people. What will conscious humans do once we have highly intelligent non-conscious algorithms that can do almost everything better?' (Harari 2017, p. 370). The 'almost' will be a key in our critique, and we will want to stretch the gap considerably. But, for the moment, let us understand what Harari expects to be the argument in favour of delegating as much as possible to AI.

Primarily, his claim is about mammalian decision-making processes. These require emotions in order to survive and reproduce in complex environments. These emotions are 'biochemical algorithms' (Harari 2017, p. 97), which in turn means that 'humans are algorithms' (Harari 2017, p. 98). Just to focus on humans, what we perceive as freedom to make choices is an illusion because there is no gap between determinism on the one hand and randomness on the other: 'Free will exists only in the imaginary stories we humans have invented' (Harari 2017, p. 329). Our responses are determined in the sense of being biological, algorithmic responses to stimuli. There is no self at the core of the human being that chooses its desires. Rather, 'there is only a stream of consciousness, and desires arise and pass away within this stream' (Harari 2017, p. 332).

Integral to Harari's position is the substrate independence of mental processes:

> Organisms are algorithms ... algorithmic calculations are not affected by the materials from which the calculator is built ... Hence there is no reason to think that organic algorithms can do things that non-organic algorithms will never be able to replicate or surpass. As long as the calculations remain valid, what does it matter whether the algorithms are manifested in carbon or silicon? (Harari 2017, p. 372)

An analogy here would be saying that calculating '2+2=4' on a piece of paper is the same as placing two pairs of stones in a line and counting them up. Using a binary system of computer coding also reaches the same answer. It does not matter what medium you use, counting is independent. In Harari's position, every thought we have is part of a chain of algorithmic decision gates that, in our case, happen to be in carbon-based life but could be in silicon-based computer components (of sufficient complexity of course). The ambition is not merely to replicate human intelligence but to design something that will exceed human imitations.

Our interest here is on a specific aspect of artificial intelligence ambitions: delegating political decision-making to machine-learning systems even if, in some respects, these are more efficient and accurate than humans. There are challenges on biological claims but most of our attention will be in developing a broader theological response.

Life is more than algorithm

Antonio Damasio engages directly with the claim that living organisms are algorithms, accepting that although algorithms are involved in the construction of living organisms and their genetic operations, 'they are *not* algorithms themselves' (Damasio 2018, p. 201, emphasis in original). Algorithms, in Damasio's view, are but 'steps in the construction of a particular result' (Damasio 2018, p. 201), not the result itself:

> Living organisms are consequences of the engagement of algorithms and exhibit properties that might or might not have been specified in the algorithms that directed their construction. Most important, living organisms are collections of tissues, organs, and systems within which every component cell is a vulnerable living entity made of proteins, lipids, and sugars. They are *not* lines of code; they are palpable stuff. (Damasio 2018, p. 201, emphasis in original)

What Damasio is arguing is analogous to the difference between a piece of sheet music and a performance. It is important, contra the immortal response of the comedian Eric Morecambe attempting Grieg's Piano Concerto, to the conductor André Previn ('I am playing all the right notes, but not necessarily in the right order') to recognize that a performance is more than even rendering the correct notes and dynamic levels. A performance is an experience – for players and audience – that exceeds musical phrases. We could put this another way to capture what Damasio is arguing about the palpability of living organisms: lines of code are not poetic. A poem touches us not only because meaning in the phrases is flexible. A poem is heard by people who respond emotionally. Yes, chemical components are involved in our operating as living organisms but 'feelings reflect the *quality* of those operations and their future *viability*' (Damasio 2018, pp. 201–2, emphasis in original). The emotions evoked by poetry are experienced by people whose body's frailty confronts them with a contingent horizon of mortality. To be fair, some people may experience similar feelings when seeing a piece of elegant computer coding. But the point is the same; there is no need to adopt a reductionist view. Hubert Dreyfus in his seminal paper 40 years ago made this very point:

> Indeterminate needs and goals and the experience of gratification which guides their determination cannot be simulated on a digital machine whose only mode of existence is a series of determinate states. Yet, it is just because these needs are never completely determined for the individual and for mankind as a whole that they are capable of being made more determinate, and human nature can be retroactively changed by individual and cultural revolutions. (Dreyfus 1979, p. 282)

Damasio argues that 'substrates count', as do contexts (Damasio 2018, p. 201). Life, and human intelligence, occur within particular substrates of carbon-based biochemistry: 'The substrate of our life is a particular kind of organised chemistry, a servant to thermodynamics and the imperative of homeostasis. To the best of our knowledge, that substrate is essential to explain who we are' (Damasio 2018, p. 201). We are able to offer a mental account of those substrates, and so phenomenology matters to Damasio because 'there is no evidence that such artificial organisms, designed for the sole purpose of being intelligent, can generate feelings just because they are behaving intelligently' (Damasio 2018, p. 202). To put this another way, if we are algorithms who are conscious of being algorithms then we are not algorithms.

Damasio is making a helpful distinction between 'emotive processes' and 'feelings'. The latter are 'mental experiences of organism states, including the states that result from emotions' (Damasio 2018, p. 203). How we feel feelings is not to explain feelings. Damasio also invites us to consider what we conceive of as the best levels of human thoughtful action. 'Predictability and inflexibility' may be integral to algorithms but this is not the sort of thinking we extol in human behaviour. The bureaucrat who responds, 'Computer says "no"' is valued in certain, perhaps quite limited, spheres. But creativity, surprise and intuition are prized in what we appreciate as intelligence (Damasio 2018, p. 204). Damasio takes Harari to task for dissolving human distinctiveness: 'the scope of human suffering and joys is uniquely human, thanks to the resonance of feelings in memories of the past and in the memory they have constructed of the anticipated future' (Damasio 2018, p. 205). Here Damasio is, as I understand him, pointing to hope as, if not a unique human capacity, at least in combination with the complex culture and self-awareness we can practise, what distinguishes us from other life forms. Hope, in this framework, is not an emotive process (of chemical reactions in our brain) but a feeling, of which emotive processes are a part, but only a part. Intelligence requires feeling; feeling relies on emotive (algorithmic) processes; without fragile, self-aware embodied selves there may be emotive processes but not feelings, so whatever decision-making capacities are constructed this is not intelligence. Such capacities may be significant, but as something other than intelligence.

So from Damasio we have, in effect, artificial decision-making (as sophisticated as it might be in revising its operating algorithms in response to situations encountered) *standing in* for human intelligence. There is a further standing in, that of a technological device 'stand[ing] in for a person as a communicator', a step that 'potentially erases and devalues the human that once stood in its spot' (Guzman and Lewis 2019, p. 10). As Joshua Reeves remarks with a disturbing metaphor of extraction, perhaps with connotations of illegality: 'The automation of our communicative culture thus threatens to siphon the biopolitical surplus from human communication: our political potential as speaking subjects is diminished as our social production is increasingly carried out with, by, and between machines' (Reeves 2016, p. 156). This is more than our reimagining how we relate to a technological system: it is how we imagine our fellow human beings and who we ourselves are (Guzman and Lewis 2019, p. 9). Humans, were we to step into the future postulated by Harari and transhumanists, would not only be spectators of decisions and their outworking but barriers to the making of intelligent choices. Our forebears showed the way by stepping back from much manual labour upon the development of machinery. We rightly consider it a boon of industrialization that we can travel faster than a horse and benefit from pharmaceutical advances. This has involved humans stepping back and making space for technology to stand in for our relatively puny and unsophisticated capabilities. The extent to which we should replace ourselves in political and social decision-making is another matter altogether.

But is it replacement or augmentation? Hardt and Negri argue that it is a mistake to impose 'an ontological division and even opposition between human life and machines' (Hardt and Negri 2019, p. 109). It is not simply, they argue, that we contrast techniques external to ourselves, that is, machines, but we construct internal 'intellectual tools' that increase the capacity for complex thought (Hardt and Negri 2019, p. 109). We can put this bluntly: someone in the seventeenth century does not think as we in the twenty-first do. The analytical constructs in which we have been trained would be alien technologies to the mind to our predecessors. It is not simply that we know more or our metaphysical assumptions (such as religion) are different. We have intellectual tools that mean we are, apart from digital technologies, 'machinic humanity' (Hardt and Negri 2019, p. 114). (Here we adopt Hardt and Negri's term from their discussion of the socializing of production, away from the factory.) We take their point and thus need to consider where augmentation, in effect, is replacement.

On being helped to clear out his garden shed Joe might claim that he has used this same broom for 40 years, but 'it's had seven new heads and five new handles in that time'. In one sense Joe is correct – it is, from his perspective of memories associated with sweeping his garden over the lifetime longer than that of his children, the same broom. But a dispassionate observer finds no such continuity. The components of the broom have been replaced time after time; it is not the same broom over 40 years. Similarly, at what point does machinic humanity cease being humanity?

Stand aside?

Artificial responsibility

Should we stand aside in favour of AI as a superior decision-making system? This would be to resign from a responsibility that it is not ours to cede because, contends Benedict XVI, to define the goals of humanity from within any ideological framework is wrong. The key for Benedict is that humans 'are a gift, not something self-generated' (Benedict XVI 2009, §68). Although we are to be 'actively involved in [our] own development' we individuate 'on the basis of a "self" which is given to us' in relation to other people – figures who are outside of our control (Benedict XVI 2009, §68). But, argues Benedict, we are outside of our *own* control in the sense that we must deal with what God, in the moral law, has written on our hearts. In other words, we are not entitled to delegate the definition of who we are to any human ideology (be it technology, communism, fascism, capitalism or something else). There is a powerful impetus towards bettering life through technology, and where this contributes to authentic development Benedict commends it (Benedict XVI 2009, §69), but it is not enough in his view to leave the defining of 'betterment' to technology. Benedict aims to keep technology subservient to authenticity; otherwise expressed as truth. While deploying technologies for improving human life, in what might often be very harsh environments, development includes the indispensable component of critical reflection upon not only actions but the underlying assumptions and criteria of decision-making embedded in a device or system:

> The 'technical' worldview that follows from this vision is now so dominant that truth has come to be seen as coinciding with the possible. But when the sole criterion of truth is efficiency and utility, development is automatically denied. True development does not consist primarily in 'doing'. The key to development is a mind capable of thinking in technological terms and grasping the fully human meaning of human activities, within the context of the holistic meaning of the individual's being. (Benedict XVI 2009, §70)

In Benedict's terms it is impermissible to adopt a technological practice simply because it achieves the purpose set it by the technician, even if the output at first appears to promote freedom from hardship or limitation. We ought not to decouple ourselves, or abdicate, from thinking critically about, in our case, AI and its capacity to process more information to identify deeper correlations: for 'human freedom is authentic only when it responds to the fascination of technology with decisions that are the fruit of moral responsibility' (Benedict XVI 2009, §70). It might be argued that in the realm of automated decision-making such moral reflection happens much further upstream at design and coding, so downstream responsibilities are pre-empted. But as we will see in Chapter 5, removing human intervention can reproduce or even exacerbate social injustice. In terms of our immediate consideration of political decision-making, Benedict's discussion of using technology for development puts a brake on abdicating in favour of AI. What Benedict says about international development of countries and communities applies to any suggestion that AI might be better at politics than us:

Development will never be fully guaranteed through automatic or impersonal forces, whether they derive from the market or from international politics. *Development is impossible without upright men and women, without financiers and politicians whose consciences are finely attuned to the requirements of the common good.* (Benedict XVI 2009, §71, emphasis in original)

Humans, moulded in response to the moral law written in their hearts, are integral to decision-making about technology. This is not reserved to experts – as important as they are in Benedict's model of development. When we extend our horizon to democratic processes and social life as a whole, John Paul II presents us with the importance of participation, not for him primarily on the grounds of political theory but on his Christian anthropology:

A man is alienated if he refuses to transcend himself and to live the experience of self-giving and of the formation of an authentic human community oriented towards his final destiny, which is God. A society is alienated if its forms of social organization, production and consumption make it more difficult to offer this gift of self and to establish this solidarity between people. (John Paul II 1991, §41)

It is more than making political decisions through any number of ballots; it is a matter of giving oneself to others at multiple levels of social encounter. To abdicate to AI would be a step of self-alienation, a retreat away from politics and into oneself. Of course, we are not yet confronted with the option fully to abdicate in favour of AI, and such a day may be much further away than enthusiasts for transhumanism hope. Nevertheless, it is valuable to consider that horizon and then step back to the present. To let ourselves 'be abdicated' even in any single election cycle by advocates of algorithmic political influencing is to put our society in reverse gear. Theologically, alienation from others is alienation from oneself and from God. It is our responsibility to give the gift of ourselves to others in the participation that includes political decision-making. Abdicating in awe (or perhaps fear) of the possibilities and conveniences of AI is to surrender to artificial responsibility; in both senses, of ersatz and technological.

Artificial salvation

Alienation is also a theme for the Protestant Brian Brock in his critique of technology, and it is helpful to consider the intentions to deliver freedom that appear, from a theological point of view, to be a fabricated deliverance.

Brock warns of technology becoming 'the cage for [humans'] own self-isolation' when pride induces awe and technological achievements that purport to offer power over the conditions of life, displacing God (Brock 2010, p. 231). In Brock's view, technology is attributed the power of salvation but by a route that is mechanistic and distancing from God and others, rather than requiring one to risk one's self in relationship: 'it asks us to find salvation by controlling space to find intimacy, controlling time to make meaning, and seeking power over others to establishing our subjectivity'; an inversion of the gospel (Brock 2010, p. 231). Technologies generate 'estrangements' and encourage a 'deadening narrowness' to our perceptions, evaluation and enjoyment of life in digital cultures (Brock 2010, p. 6).

The constrictions that shrivel life in its fullness occur, in Brock's view, at three 'nodal points in human relations': governance and law-making; business and industrial decision-making; and individual consuming and production (Brock 2010, p. 10). Christians are unable to affirm the ways in which the technological paradigm defines reality and morality, as well as its underlying assumptions such as the nature of society and of creation, particularly in terms of how Christians treat their own and others' bodies, as well as the earth (Brock 2010, pp. 20, 324). While technology offers many opportunities, Brock is concerned about the way freedom is conceptualized, in many ways a concern akin to that of Catholic Social Teaching on authentic human development: 'Theologically defined, freedom is not to have "potential," or to have "options," or to get to "do what feels right," but to be given a form that allows genuine human action, makes human activity *productive*, gives it *traction*' (Brock 2010, p. 170).

Brock is not against technology per se, for he appreciates its possibilities for facilitating our encounters with other people through devices that are not merely exerting our power over people but 'finding ourselves in the love of the other' (Brock 2010, p. 213). Nevertheless, he draws an analogy between idols that offered possibilities of control over dangerous and unpredictable environments and the proffered power of advanced technologies (Brock 2010, p. 230). For Brock, human predilection to self-congratulation and reliance on our achievements strikes at the heart of the false salvation that is on offer: 'Pride draws humans magnetically to awe at the work of their hands, *incurvatus in se*. This is the true anti-doxology that enslaves, when human awe and praise are again claimed by the secondary, by the subservient, by the merely human' (Brock 2010, p. 231).

Such turning inwards rather than outwards to God finds ample opportunity – and reframed as a positive trait – within technological thinking and the practice of technological life. Instead of rescue from the human condition being in God's hands, as an act of God's grace, we throw ourselves back upon our own resources. Contrary to the practice and vision of sabbath, technological work becomes a means of deliverance, not least through productivity in which we place our own and others' bodies under tight control. Where we retreat into the distance from others that technology offers us as an alternative to face-to-face encounter, we deny ourselves and others the possibilities of the full life to which Christ calls through his own breaching of the walls of separation:

> The false promise of the technological way of being, and the root of its destructiveness, is its replacement of this faith for reliance on a mechanism promising salvation without the risking of self in relationship. It asks us to find salvation by controlling space to find intimacy, controlling time to make meaning, and seeking power over others to establish our subjectivity. (Brock 2010, p. 231)

For Brock, digital technology reinforces turning inwards rather than turning Godwards, but judicious critical reflection that (for him) is grounded in the worshipping community of Christian faith stabilizes what would otherwise be volatile interaction with particular devices. To surrender our responsibilities for political decision-making to AI would, in Brock's terms, be idolatry. Furthermore, even being under the influence of AI is dangerous as a way of political thinking. Fomenting rage through manipulation of the affect heuristic is the antithesis of risking oneself for another. More than pulling back, micro-targeting by weaponizing information goes on the offensive to damage the other. Viewed in the light of Christian salvation, such practices are not only of no benefit to the perpetrators who are hindered from turning outwards to God but cause harm to others.

Antje Jackelén, however, is not closed to the possibility of *techno sapiens* as another form of life. She argues against placing natural evolution and technical evolution in opposition, favouring instead an appreciation of the way in which these processes interact (Jackelén 2002, p. 295), acknowledging that, from one perspective, 'our body appears to be a very ineffective and hazardous tool for storing ... precious information' (Jackelén 2002, p. 295). Jackelén's concerns here anticipate a situation well beyond the technological enhancement of humanity; a humanity 3.0 (or 99.0 for that matter). Even at the moment, AI in medicine can contribute to overcoming disease and, in speech devices, enable some people with disabilities to communicate effectively. Such aspects are, for Jackelén, similar to the marks of the messianic age as it was envisaged in Matthew's Gospel, where Jesus' response to John the Baptist's disciples was to point them to evidence of the blind seeing, the lame walking, the deaf hearing, the dead being raised and the poor having the good news brought to them (Matt. 11.2–6). There is, therefore, a dimension of salvation possible within AI technologies, and Jackelén leaves the door open to consider that 'the development toward *techno sapiens* might very well be regarded as a step toward the kingdom of God' (Jackelén 2002, p. 293). But, asks Jackelén, who benefits and who pays the price for these technological developments (Jackelén 2002, p. 294)? The poor as in the gospel announcement received good news, but, she reminds us, it would be naive to assume that technological developments necessarily combine with social justice; they may widen the gap between rich and poor. AI benefits may end up being only for some, and not all; for the already privileged rather than the systemically disadvantaged people in society.

Recognizing the physical and mental limitations of humans makes enhancements attractive and, in Jackelén's view, not to be dismissed as mere temptations. This will likely require extending the definition of life in a way that is not dissimilar to our referencing the 'life' of books and musical works (Jackelén 2002, p. 295). Indeed, she argues, an impetus for post-biological beings could be defended, given that 'a living being is not to be equated with its biological origin' (Jackelén 2002, p. 295). Jackelén is particularly helpful for our discussion of the relative capacities of humans and AI to process information adequate for political decision-making when she draws attention to the different ways humanity is problematized:

> Science and theology agree that humans are imperfect, defective. But the concepts they build on this common ground differ considerably. Science concludes that human beings are in need of improvement. Theology concludes that human beings are in need of forgiveness and transformation. Science wants to achieve an optimization of information processing; theology aims at holiness, salvation, or *theosis* (a kind of divinisation). Science thinks in terms of good and better (in quantifiable terms, not morally); theology thinks in terms of old and new (old creation, new creation). (Jackelén 2002, p. 296)

She is at her most optimistic when, rightly declining to place notions of improvement necessarily in opposition to those of forgiveness, Jackelén contends that AI decisions, because they could take everything into account, would 'eliminate much of the injustice caused by human decisions' (Jackelén 2002, p. 296). Speculation as to the preservation of personality and its history in a technologized form prompts Jackelén to acknowledge that there would be considerable implications for Christian doctrines such as the resurrection. Indeed, Ian Barbour, in an article a couple of years prior to Jackelén's, considers the transporter technology of *Star Trek* and argues against this being an adequate conceptualization of what it means to be human, particularly in the light of what God knows of us and what, by analogy, resurrection of the body of a person could involve. To put words into Barbour's mouth, but ones that encapsulate his contention, resurrection is not a version of 'beam me up, Jesus':

> the proposal appears reductionistic in its assumption that higher levels of selfhood are explainable by (and can be reconstituted from) information at the molecular level. I suggest that God knows us at all levels, including the highest level of our selfhood and subjectivity, and not just at the molecular level. God's relation to us is more personal than an inventory of molecules. (Barbour 1999, p. 381)

Brock is troubled by an ersatz salvation; Jackelén is exercised by the prospect of salvation of the artificial. She turns to the tradition of non-corporeal imaging of God to suggest that 'biological reality does not necessarily have to be a feature of Godlikeness' (Jackelén 2002, p. 298). Instead, relationality might be, argues Jackelén, a better avenue to follow but with a twist: 'in my view, relational capacity and a creativity that goes together with – and often results from – imperfection are crucial marks of the image of God' (Jackelén 2002, p. 299). In other words, to be relational requires incompleteness, even, as Jackelén states, imperfection. Out of brokenness we reach to another's brokenness – which suggests that the capacity and capability of AI precludes relationality.

Furthermore, as Jackelén articulates, relationality points away from a purely biological (indeed algorithmic) understanding of humanity. She appreciates the ritualizing or mystificating capacity of humans, along with our ability to make objects and devices, and to play. These, together with relationality and rationality, constitute us. The human is *homo liturgicus*, *homo faber*, *homo ludens* and *homo sapiens*. Being these, imperfectly in each aspect, would not be possible if we abdicate decision-making to AI. More immediately, to imbibe and internalize our relative inadequacy as decision-makers is to sacrifice too much for the sake of artificial salvation.

Artificial love

AI proponents evaluate us and find us wanting on an attenuated understanding of intelligence. Anne Foerst poses the important question of who gets to define 'intelligence', and in her feminist critique confronts the male mathematicians who were at the forefront of AI development and adopted their own skills as definitive:

> they ignored the fact that other people might select totally different skills for defining intelligence. Especially women, because of their daily experience, might choose different abilities: They often value social skills more highly than abstract, disembodied tasks. According to the feminist critique, the skills chosen by mathematicians are not only disembodied but estranged from any human's daily experiences in his or her bodily surroundings. (Foerst 1998, p. 101)

Eric Trozzo points to a further attenuation of the meaning of the self within data-algorithmic paradigms. He uses Bernard Stiegler's differentiation between 'consisting' and 'existing' that problematizes advanced capitalist reduction of what is valuable to what is calculable (Trozzo 2019, p. 131). 'Consisting' here means exceeding calculation; trust and time being two examples. Datafication therefore involves creating a faux predictability because only what can be measured is admitted: 'pure calculation holds no space for hope in the future, for unforeseeable possibility to rupture the current trajectory of probability' (Trozzo 2019, p. 131). Where Stiegler's use of the symbol of 'God' is to speak of 'novelty and vibrancy', Trozzo injects theological dimensions, principally by way of Jürgen Moltmann's distinction between *futurum* (based on linear projection of what will be, from what is of this world) and *adventus* (that which is coming from the future, from the future of the crucified God, breaking into this world) (Moltmann 1985, pp. 132–5). So Trozzo identifies a threat to humanity as creatures in which hope in God might take root and grow. Datafication may have value, but it is only *futurum*. Giving data and calculability priority easily eclipses the possibilities that are generated by the kingdom of God; possibilities not limited to human history. This means, as I explore elsewhere in the context of social categorization of persons as risky on the basis of algorithmic sorting, asking how anyone might be shaped by their future, not only their past: 'categorisation has the potential, if not vigorously critiqued, to posit a future for individuals and groups that obscures the shadow of the cross cast back from the resurrection future' (Stoddart 2014a). A person is, in the terms deployed by Trozzo, confined to existence and denied admission to consistence.

Trozzo develops his critique using Eberhard Jüngel's Lutheran theology that distinguishes between a person's actions and their true humanity (Trozzo 2019, p. 133). In such a model, actions flow from identity and it is thus mistaken 'to understand ourselves as our actions' for this is 'to live under the illusion that we can make ourselves good' (Trozzo 2019, p. 133). Dataism is a philosophy that proposes the opposite: our calculable, datafiable actions are what constitutes our being and within that ontology the good is defined; generally in terms of efficiency:

> It is only in breaking the illusion that we can become good that we are able to rest in our identity as belonging to God as God's good creation. Only in doing so can we become truly human. Being truly human entails knowing our deep embeddedness in relationships with God and with others. From this identity, actions may follow that are beneficial to others, or could be deemed good. These good actions, however, stem from accepting our theological identity first as coming from the source of being rather than as something that we create for ourselves *ex nihilo*. True humanity for Luther, then, is a matter of being possessed by God. (Trozzo 2019, p. 134)

Under the gaze of data-analytic companies and states we are defined by the observations of others, and our own gaze upon ourselves as objects. Instead, argues Trozzo, it is through the lens of our 'response to the creative Word' that we are to understand ourselves as 'more than data and more than body' (Trozzo 2019, p. 138). Transposing this into a harmonically close key we can talk of grounding our being in the divine love from which we respond with love to others, God and ourselves. An artificial intelligence approach holds a stance towards the world that sees it as a problem, or rather a series of problems, to be solved. Thomas Merton asks, 'Is the world a problem?' and concludes that it is not:

> but we are a problem to ourselves because we are alienated from ourselves, and this alienation is due precisely to an inveterate habit of division by which we break reality into pieces and then wonder why, after we have manipulated the pieces until they fall apart, we find ourselves out of touch with life, with reality, with the world and most of all with ourselves. (Merton 1980, p. 156)

Merton could be describing datafication before we come to realize that its manipulation does not actually create wholeness and order but, especially when energized by hate and othering, contributes to its falling apart. In another essay, Merton ponders the power and meaning of love where he makes the profound assertion that humanity's 'greatest dignity, [our] most essential and peculiar power, the most intimate secrets of [our] humanity is [our] capacity to love' (Merton 1976, p. 2). If, and it is as we have seen a weighty condition, there is artificial intelligence, then it has to be kept in its place under the service of love. The absurdity of positing artificial love, artificial sympathy or artificial compassion fortifies us to resist the elevation of artificial intelligence as the arbiter of our adequacy as decision-makers.

Nothing about us without us!

'Nothing about us without us!' (*Nihil de nobis, sine nobis*) is the clarion call in asserting rights when outsiders, at their own behest, purport to speak on a minority group's behalf. Decisions are made ostensibly to address an injustice but those directly affected are denied their own voice at the table. This might well occur when there is pressure to attain merely the communal good (for the most members of society) and is antithetical to aspirations of the common good. Asserting a preferential optic for those who are poor is an endeavour to take the 'Nothing about us, without us' clarion call seriously. Hacking democracy relies on substantial financial investment in data-analytic companies who are able to develop the targeting of individuals with political messages.

At a basic level people are influenced by weaponized information in ways that are considerably opaque, and those funding agencies largely eschew the limelight. To engage in politics using powerful instruments ought to go hand in hand with transparency, public accountability and regulation. Too much about us is done without us.

In a more sophisticated analysis, the power of political decision-making needs to reside among those like us; fellow citizens not AI systems. Not only ought we not to cede our responsibilities to AI, but those responsibilities ought to be borne by those like us. In most cases this will be through a form of representative democracy, but by representatives furnished by, and availing themselves of, information and technological knowledge suited to challenging the leaders of technocratic corporations.

As part of 'the crowd' it is incumbent upon us to repudiate the manipulating of an affect heuristic that appeals to fear, anger and even hate. In what is akin to an abuser 'gaslighting' a victim, making her doubt her own perception of events and agency, political micro-targeting as it is being currently deployed creates the false perception that other systems can make better decisions. It may be quite appropriate to develop AI for particular functions (narrow AI) and for it to make decisions about encounters with 'objects' in unstructured environments. However, if politicians, corporate boards or government officials defer to AI in questions of people's entitlement to resources or the governance of populations, it is a narrow and literally hope-less thinking that is privileged.

When we, 'the crowd', concede to this deference on our behalf by a tiny minority of already privileged people, we fail to assert our own dignity; we are *not* inadequate biological computers – we are human beings. It is remarkably easy for us to be manipulated, for we desire propaganda. Our democratic processes turn out to be much more fragile – and in need of 'the crowd's' protection – than we hitherto believed. In a world of political micro-targeting, 'false prophets' have acquired a powerful tool. 'False prophets' here are not so much those who disseminate disinformation but those who, for their own ends, are manipulating 'the crowd'. The 'false prophets' are the billionaire funders who make the work of data scientists in this field possible. Political decision-making is viewed, in effect, as amoral.

What haunts me in Harari's vision of AI is humans being framed as little more than spectators in the future. Spectators are in some sense not quite 'the crowd', certainly not as portrayed in the Gospels or Hebrew Bible. Silicon Valley is colonizing minds in everyday life – by its tropes rather than invading troops. They are lured by the prospect of more data; we are scratched where we have been made to itch.

4

Identity: Quantifying Yourself

Uncover your tracks

Quantified and qualified

> Mark my footsteps, good my page; Tread thou in them boldly. Thou shalt find the winter's rage freeze thy blood less coldly.

Wenceslas's page finds that this action protects him from dying, lost in the freezing storm. But this smart page spots another servant hopelessly lost. The smart page offers his hand in the almost total darkness and, shouting over the howling wind, says, 'For a penny you can take my hand and you can come behind me – who's following the king's footsteps – and you'll be safely home with us.' The smart page sells his expertise in following Wenceslas's footsteps to a needy servant in what Wenceslas does not envisage as output of his venture to provide food and fuel to that 'yonder peasant'; as a data surplus monetized by a smart page. This, however, is self-quantification linked to surveillance capitalism.

Wenceslas might be pointing to his footsteps. A twenty-first-century commuter might be handling his health care via a mobile app, locating doctors nearby or managing his prescriptions. Using the Health4Me app he might take up financial incentives of discounts at local gyms or retailers directly through a Reward Me component, 'that now makes it even more rewarding and fun to take charge of your health' (United Healthcare 2020). While Wenceslas perhaps relied on the traditional rhythms of liturgical life for his discipline of prayer, a twenty-first-century Christian might use the Echo app to set goals for her prayer sessions, setting timer notifications for how long she might wish to pray: from ten seconds in various increments to one hour (Echo app 2020). Wenceslas has maintained a level of personal fitness that enabled him to trudge through a winter storm. Were the resources of the MyFitnessPal app available he could have tracked his workout regimes and meals with the option of participating in community forums with other fit monarchs to share success stories and be mutually accountable (MyFitnessPal app 2020).

Our focus in this chapter is on the datafication of the self, what we can call the 'self-gaze'. The sharing of this data, whether with app designers only, our peers or indirectly with third-party companies purchasing metadata of an app's users, is a distinct form of surveillance. We will consider the self not merely as quantified (in the sense of keeping private track of actions or mood) but as a *qualified* self that is mediated to others (Humphreys 2018, p. 19). These practices, understood as *exploitation* of labour, occur within an economic ecosystem of surveillance capitalism. The critique of imperial luxury economics in the book of Revelation helps us gain a perspective from outside our current digital paradigm, especially when religion is involved. Bringing together Silicon Valley and the challenges for Christians in ancient Corinth opens up theological consideration of work and profit where there are possibilities of a counter-logic of gift rather than exchange. When turning to apps for self-quantifying one's spirituality we address the issue of narcissism, scrupulosity and hypocrisy, particularly attendant to the use of spirituality-tracking apps – and sharing capabilities.

Betting on our future

'Surveillance capitalism' is a recent concept deployed most prominently by Shoshana Zuboff to describe a way of doing business that 'unilaterally claims human experience as free raw material for translation into behavioural data' (Zuboff 2019, p. 8). In broad terms, surveillance capitalism is developed within an economy that is based on the production and circulation of knowledge (Caruso 2017, p. 596). The notion of 'information society' most likely originates in articles published in the early 1960s in the Japanese broadcasting journal *Hoso Asahi*, although Fritz Machlup's 1962 monograph published in the USA is also a contender (Duff et al. 1996). In 1977 Marc Porat drew further attention to the 'information economy', seeking to establish 'what share of our national wealth originates with the production, processing and distribution of information goods and services' (Porat 1977, p. 1). Manuel Castells, in a parallel with 'industry' and 'industrial society', emphasizes the role information plays in a society with the concept of informationalism, 'a specific form of social organization in which information generation, processing, and transmission become the fundamental sources of productivity and power because of new technological conditions emerging in this historical period' (Castells 2000, p. 21, fn31).

The later availability of cheap and powerful processing power decentralizes the information sector to generate what Yochai Benkler terms the 'networked information economy', particularly radical in its 'effective, large-scale cooperative efforts – peer production of information, knowledge, and culture' (Benkler 2006, p. 5). There is creativity generated by intellectual, rather than physical, labour, which cognitive capitalism seeks to exploit (Boutang 2011, p. 91). These creative agents are not being creative only in their workplace, producing (in capitalist terms) by creativity that takes place in people's own time, for example in the DIY home improvement impetus that exploded in the 1970s, blurring the product and consumer; Alvin Toffler's 'prosumption' (Toffler 1980).

For examples of surveillance capitalism, we can turn to the slogans or straplines of some major data-brokering companies. Acxiom says that 'by understanding [your customer] through data and technology, you can *deliver experiences that matter*' (Acxiom 2020, emphasis added). Nielsen, more familiar to the public perhaps as the TV viewing figures company, has split part of its business into Nielsen Global Connect, which, in providing data for business decisions, offers itself for 'Shaping a Smarter Market™' (Nielsen Global Connect 2020). 'Smarter' here means informed by more and better data. In effect, data is currency, as they claim in their strapline for their media arm, Nielsen Global Media: 'One Media Truth™. See what's commanding attention today and what will resonate tomorrow. Our unbiased metrics are the currency advertisers, agencies and media owners need to run their businesses' (Nielsen Global Media 2020). Experian uses its own data and buys in other data on consumers' credit worthiness; to which individuals can buy access to know what companies know about them. In Experian's pitch, 'We unlock the power of data to create opportunities for people, business and society' (Experian 2020). Equifax also deploys the 'power' trope in its advertising: 'Powering the Decisions that Move People Forward' (Equifax 2020a). When seeking to attract individuals rather than businesses to use its resources, Equifax foregrounds the link between one's credit worthiness and one's identity: 'Stay in control with our individual and family plans' (Equifax 2020b). In its property market business, Corelogic too likes to promote itself in terms of power: 'Powering Housing Through Data, Analytics and Connectivity' (Corelogic 2020).

These are not self-quantification corporations but are indicative of the wider context of the information economy to gather and analyse data, very clearly with the intention of shaping people's behaviour. When we bring this back to surveillance capital, we will need to consider quite what is traded and how we are moulded as consumers within these systems. It is not simply data about what we are doing *now* or have done *in the past*. Rather, as Zuboff argues, 'Google discovered that we are less valuable than others' bets on our future behaviour' (Zuboff 2019, p. 93).

'It's the act that counts'

Hooking the self

Looking at the ways in which self-quantification apps present themselves to prospective users offers us insight into what those companies consider to be hooks in our sense of self to which they can readily attach. (Although an examination of the visual representations used in promotional pages would be fascinating – not least in terms of the body images – our focus will be on the language.)

If we take Strava, a major exercise app, as an example, the company wants us to think: 'Track & Analyse', 'Share & Connect', 'Explore & Compete' (Strava 2020). Granted, the app is designed for all levels and the language of 'measure your performance' is redolent of the training regimes of serious athletes. The attempt appears to be to incorporate those of us who might be casual exercisers into a social imaginary of sporting achievement. It is more than the number of steps or speed that matters; I am encouraged to think of myself as 'athletic' (to be honest, this is closer to fantasy than imagination). Those who are part of organized clubs will be familiar with the value of exercising together. Strava, like other apps, dissolves time and space. I can cycle a route and share that with friends who might do that same route but at a different time on another day. For Strava, exercising includes 'shar[ing] your adventure'; redefining the activity as akin to a voyage of self-discovery. The community is not confined to one's friends but one is encouraged to 'compete with a global community' of strangers who relate on this singular aspect of their lives. Friends and strangers can (dependent upon your privacy settings) 'give kudos' to your performance, in the form of 'like'-type icons. Interestingly, the Strava site does not mention the importance of *receiving* kudos. The philosophical question, 'If a tree falls in a forest and there is no one around to hear it, does it make a sound?' takes a new form: 'If I share a run on Strava and there is no one around to give me a kudos click, did I exercise?' In other words, exercise may be a social construction requiring acknowledgement by another person. This is not to deny the physiological benefits but to recognize that something shifts in the identity of being 'one who exercises'.

Strava is a useful example also in terms of its monetizing of exercise. Strava Metro is the arm of the company that sells data to urban planners. The strapline is 'Better data, better cities', which means: 'Understand[ing] patterns. Know when and where people are moving on your network. Improve Safety. Identify high-risk corridors and uncover factors that contribute. Evaluate Projects. Compare before and after infrastructure projects' (Strava Metro 2020).

On this site Strava uses an endorsement from a planner in Victoria who says, 'It's like having thousands of counters set up all across the city.' The data is 'aggregated and deidentified' and does not include information from those users who have opted out – this is the case for both free and premium (paying) users. There are clearly sufficient users willing to share their data in this way to make a viable contribution to the revenue stream of premium 'Strava Summit' users.

One of the benefits of paid membership is the beacon:

> Peace of mind for athletes and their loved ones. Turn on Beacon and you can share your location in real time with your friend, partner, parent, coach, butler, therapist, highly intelligent dog – anyone cool enough to have your back in an emergency. (Strava 2020)

Here, Strava hooks into safety concerns. Pre-digital runners (or walkers) might tell a member of the family, 'I'm going for a walk. I'll be about an hour.' After 90 minutes the family might become concerned at the runner's failure to return. After a couple of hours, significant alarm would be raised. But with Beacon, the family can know exactly where the runner is, moment by moment. Mugging, accident or illness can be immediately alerted (unless of course the mugger steals the runner's mobile device and it is not one that requires a passcode if removed and reattached to a different wrist). The runner who chooses not to avail herself of Beacon is constructing her self-identity as an exerciser rather differently from the one who wants to be under constant surveillance.

'I count, therefore I am'

Identity work

Whether counting steps, weights lifted, blood-sugar level, mood, calories or any of the myriad of quantifiable actions or bodily states, in quantifying users are engaging in 'a practice of selfhood' (Lupton 2016, p. 68). Users are 'performing identity work' (Humphreys 2018, p. 51), or, in acts of interpreting the self, 'users are stimulated to engage with and to relate to the bodily self through the access to, and interpretation of, data' (Kristensen and Prigge 2018, p. 46). Recording data might be episodic or continual; an app might require to be invoked, for example, at the start of a workout, but other apps run continuously in the background after an initial invocation. The self is the first, but by no means the only, audience. A user does not discover that she has been self-quantifying;

rather, in an act of self-awareness (Lupton 2016, p. 68) she chooses to make herself more heedful of one or more aspects of her lived experience. Stephen Crites argues that there is an inherently narrative quality to experience, for although the ways in which people express their culture are culturally particular and at least partly conditioned by time and place, the forms of cultural expression are not historical accidents but rather are the 'necessary mark of being human, i.e. being capable of having a history' (Crites 1989, p. 65). Crites talks of people inhabiting stories and thus making sense of their self and world – both through weighty sacred stories and through lighter personal narratives. We are in tension, says Crites, as we seek to sense for ourselves an integrated single story, for we 'awaken to consciousness in a society, with the inner story of experience and its enveloping musicality already infused with cultural forms' (Crites 1989, p. 80). A history of the self is, as Dan McAdams argues, a 'history' in being 'an account of the past that seeks to explain how and why events transpired as they actually did' (McAdams 1993, p. 102). The therapist Anton Boisen coined the term 'living human document' as the interpreted experience of an individual (Boisen 1960, 1971 [1936]). The living human *database* of the quantifying self does not replace but supplements the wider effort of us each composing our own 'document'.

The self is one audience, the devices that run the self-quantifying apps is a second. Jill Rettberg, following in the footsteps of Marshall McLuhan (McLuhan 2001 [1964]), identifies some users' anthropomorphizing wearable technologies or smartphones: 'we are the narrators, and they are the narratees, the audience for our words or our data' (Rettberg 2018, p. 31). Rettberg's important point here is that such devices offer us visualizations of our data. Tables of daily comparisons, graphs of elevations or biometric data, rings to be completed or maps of routes covered are a form of audience feedback, in the light of which we further develop our narrative. It might be possible to extend Rettberg's insight further and refer to a 'statistical soliloquy'.

There is a third (and highly variegated) audience: those with whom users share their data. In this respect Lee Humphreys' theory of the qualified, rather than merely quantified, self is particularly important:

> To qualify can mean to describe or to designate in a particular way. The qualified self is therefore a described self, a characterized self. The aggregation of descriptions, of our media traces, and the media traces of others which feature us, convey a particular version of who we are, a qualified version. However, to qualify also means to modify or moderate. In this way, the qualified self is a modified version of the self. (Humphreys 2018, p. 19)

The self is thus *qualified* in a number of senses. It is a selected or partial version of the self; users choose, to a large but not total extent, which aspects of their everyday life to share and which to keep to themselves. This is no less true of other forms of self-narration. Neither do we know ourselves completely (our subconscious is indeed below our consciousness), nor do we disclose *every* element of our story. To adapt the phrase traditionally associated with Queen Elizabeth I, we fit frosted glass in the window into our souls. The self is qualified in a second sense: we modify the self we convey, putting it into a broader context, better to be understood in a more nuanced manner. Helen Nissenbaum contends for the 'contextual integrity' of data in order to restore consideration of all information (not merely that which is designated 'private') in its relationship to its surrounding social landscape (Nissenbaum 2010). This second sense of the qualified self is contextual integrity in constructing the self, as well as this being an approach to others' personal information. It is not merely that specific data only makes sense in a broader context but the qualified self is an assertion that *there is* a bigger picture, whether or not this is disclosed. To put this another way, others should acknowledge *that* a particular self is qualified, without necessarily being entitled to know *how* that self is qualified.

There is a third sense of qualified: meeting the criteria set by others for inclusion within a domain. The domain, for example, might be recognition as an athlete at a high level of achievement, inclusion in a social category of well-being (both physical and mental) or scientifically delineated state of health. When self-quantifying, the user is also self-categorizing; a digital expression of time-honoured processes of social identity (Tajfel 1981).

Humphreys perceives many, even most, users of self-tracking devices shifting from a primarily inwards to an outwards gaze: 'a shift in prioritization from the processes of datafication to mediation' (Humphreys 2018, p. 22). Just as there are still diarists (writing only for themselves), bloggers and vloggers proliferate. In the sometimes overlapping domain of self-quantification, 'audience and sharing are default to the qualified self rather than the exception' (Humphreys 2018, p. 23). The mediated/ qualified self is doing more than performance and presentation of the self: he or she is *representing* the self through 'the production of a textual object, such as a Facebook post' (Humphreys 2018, p. 52).

While there is, rightly, much attention paid to the quantified/qualified *self*, users' representation is not only of themselves but of others (Humphreys 2018, p. 53). Acts of comparison – like those many of us used to do when inflicting our holiday snaps on family or neighbours – not only reveal something about the photographer (Humphreys 2018, p. 54) but also provoke a reaction in others. The tolerant neighbour might once have been bored to tears at 72 (or, if three rolls of film, 108) 35mm slides but their perception of Lanzarote was shaped by what they remained awake long enough to see. The relationship between these neighbours too was moulded by this and other social interactions. Similarly, the overzealous slide-projectionist (if sufficiently self-aware) learned how to moderate his enthusiasm in order not only to be a good photographer but a better neighbour. A similar principle is in play with digital self-qualification, for, as Humphreys recognizes, 'People engage in identity work through the media of others' (Humphreys 2018, p. 70).

The quantified/qualified self is also engaged in the practice of *remembrancing*, 'the creation or use of media traces as part of our memory work regarding ourselves, the people in our lives, and the world around us' (Humphreys 2018, p. 73). So at the same time as often being focused on goals of self-improvement ahead, the user is building a stash of memories. A younger generation (to whom, on the whole, self-tracking apps are marketed) value monitoring progress towards goals. However, older users may become aware of a decline in fitness, health or mood. Regardless of age, a user can be surprised by stumbling across or receiving an algorithmically driven notification of the achievement of a fellow self-tracker who has since died. On a lighter note, it is not difficult to imagine fierce competitions among aged self-trackers who continue the practice into their life in a care home. Strava already includes an option for recording activities undertaken in a wheelchair and we can expect the market to reflect the lifecycle of its current users as they reach advanced old age.

Memory is not perfect and our understanding of events is always partial. The quantified/qualified self can face a discrepancy and, in drawing upon accounting practices, Humphreys notes a 'reconciliation process' (Humphreys 2018, p. 102). This is not so much at the level of, say, misremembering which route one took on a ramble through the nearby hills on a summer's day. Rather, the need for reconciliation may arise when the user sees trends (Humphreys 2018, p. 99). It might be that a user is fitter than she feels or that the evidence of one day suggests. Of course, she may believe herself to be fitter than she turns out to be when she examines her aggregated data.

A governed self

In what Btihaj Ajana refers to as a 'metric culture', there is growing cultural interest in numbers, as well as a culture that is increasingly shaped and populated with numbers (Ajana 2018, loc. 27.5). One of the consequences, and indeed challenges, is the 'highly "over-examined"' life

(Ajana 2018, loc. 24.8). We can view this problem by way of a number of comparisons. There is a difference between the need to monitor a nuclear reactor and the condition of one's footwear. The consequences of failure in the two systems is catastrophic for the former and mildly inconveniencing for the latter. We would have few qualms regarding repeatedly testing life-support equipment but not offer a corresponding regimen of intensive MIR scanning to otherwise healthy and careful people; the systems have different degrees of fragility. Tolerance ranges are also significant, just as they are in the attention one needs to give in making a stew and baking a soufflé. The food intake of a professional athlete may need to be within toleration limits that are simply unnecessary at that level of granularity for the lifestyle of a sedentary academic. Quantification of the well-being and fitness of astronauts or Navy Seals is necessary, but if identical thoroughness were applied to monitoring by a hobby cyclist there would be a lack of proportionality.

There is more at stake than the overzealous wasting their time and money on disproportionate self-tracking. Luciano Floridi argues that the gaze modifies the self towards which it is turned: 'the hyperconscious self never really stops trying to understand how it is seen by the other' (Floridi 2014, p. 74). Heading out for a party, one partner might ask the other, 'Does this outfit make my bum look big?' Were the enquirer to spend the evening asking each of the other guests the same question, most would be concerned about the wearer's mental health. Floridi makes a further point about fixating on the others' gazing:

> through the digital gaze, the self sees itself from a third-person perspective through the observation of itself in a proxy constrained by the nature of the digital medium, one that provides only a partial and specific reflection. It would be like being constrained to look at oneself from a distorting mirror that can provide no access to other images of oneself. (Floridi 2014, p. 74)

What we have here is a fool's errand: the very third parties the self-quantifier attends to so fervently are also qualified selves (in the senses we have already discussed). This is not to say that all third parties are self-quantifiers but to press the point that in our digitally mediated metric culture *all* representations of the self are distorted to one degree or another. The situation of the quantified/qualified self is more problematic still, for, as Floridi goes on to argue, 'digital gaze may become mesmerizing: one may be lost in one's own perception of oneself as attributed by others in the infosphere' (Floridi 2014, p. 74). This is a matter of degree rather than being a form of hypnotic trance or not. Being aware of how one comports oneself in a professional setting can be crucial to instilling confidence in nervous patients or students. Similarly, being careful about one's digital persona may avoid unnecessary embarrassment at a job interview. There may be some performers for whom constant self-quantification and management of online presence is integral to their success: here we might think of drag artists or some professional musicians – but they form a tiny proportion of the population as a whole. Nevertheless, Floridi's point is acutely relevant when someone is not only seeking to present themselves in a positive way but when theirs is a battle to avoid being perceived by others in a negative light. Young women and girls can find themselves in the spotlight for cyberbullying, particularly when one online mistake in what they reveal of themselves might expose them to permanent reputational harm (J. Bailey 2015). Returning more specifically to self-quantification apps, Humphreys makes the important observation that in sharing the everyday details of life a user 'blurs the public and private', for although the 'details of life may be very mundane ... their intimacy cannot be overlooked' (Humphreys 2018, p. 48).

Here is both governing self and a self that is governed in the light of prescriptions of what is normal and acceptable. Referring to fitness apps in particular, Aristea Fotopoulou and Kate O'Riordan disclose their political dimension:

> The promotional media and the interface of the consumer device constitute biopedagogies about how to prevent the pathologised body and reproduce dominant discourses about the 'fit' and healthy body. Our attention is directed to the tensions between media representations, user experience, and knowledge-making about health promotion wearables, against the backdrop of economic cuts, austerity and the reshaping of the health sector throughout Europe. In this context, the rhetoric of crisis in the healthcare sectors, and fears that care may become unavailable to many, invite new modes of control over the body and health. (Fotopoulou and O'Riordan 2017, p. 56)

Public health promotion is one thing; encouraging people to give up smoking, to drink alcohol in moderation or to exercise are laudable campaigns not only because of the individual benefits but also for reducing demand on health services. A biopedagogy that legitimates ideologically driven austerity cuts is another matter altogether. Lupton makes this link between self-optimization and the ideal citizen to highlight what we might call a version of the magician's sleight of hand. Attention is diverted to the quantifying self (the 'responsible' citizen) away from systemic issues of social injustice:

In the discourses that champion the ideal of the rational neoliberal citizen, social structural factors that influence people's living conditions and life chances – such as social class, gender, geographical location, race and ethnicity – are discounted in favour of the notion that people are self-made. (Lupton 2016, p. 50)

It is, however, important to remember that social media, in general, 'are not inherently an expression of neoliberal culture' because, as Christian Fuchs argues, 'at the same time movements that want to foreground the logic of the commons and the public have challenged these [neoliberal] developments' (Fuchs 2017, p. 128). Nevertheless, self-quantification largely depends on relatively expensive technology and data packages, and thereby the digital divide (Norris 2001) is reinforced to the detriment of those who may be able to afford a pay-as-you-go phone but not attain to the economically privileged status of being a self-quantifier.

The improving self, although governed, is an agent within the broader context of surveillance capitalism.

Surveillance capitalism

Behavioural surpluses

Zuboff identifies three principal components of surveillance capitalism: 'behavioural surplus', 'prediction products' and 'behavioural futures markets' (Zuboff 2019, p. 8). 'Behavioural surplus' comprises the foot-prints we leave behind or, to use a different metaphor, the exhaust we emit from our digital activities; the datafication of the exceptional and the everyday. We are connected to fellow employees, to family and friends, to shops, government and health-care systems, and, in Zuboff's view, 'digital connection is now a means to others' commercial ends' (Zuboff 2019, p. 9). Although we derive some advantage (not least in the development of data infrastructures that enable home working and family videoconferencing), Zuboff is correct to point to the imbalance in the marketing of personal information, for corporations 'accumulate vast domains of new knowledge *from* us, but not *for us*' (Zuboff 2019, p. 11). Whereas capitalism once sought to dominate nature and its resources, its target is now *human* nature, particularly our everyday lived experience (Zuboff 2019, p. 515).

The future is no longer unknowable (and therefore the justification for freedom of markets) but with sufficient knowledge (data) and suitably sophisticated analytical systems profit can be made from data. Yet at the same time, claims Zuboff, surveillance capitalism (epitomized for her in Google – in both its parent and subsidiary forms) claims 'unfettered freedom' of the traditional market (Zuboff 2019, p. 495). 'Organic reciprocities with people' (Zuboff 2019, p. 495) are set aside in new relationships with users and in drawing a small number of employees (relative to the vast revenues and profits generated) not from societies within which corporations operate but outsourced and from a thin stratum, namely data scientists. Zuboff describes life under surveillance capitalism as 'the new collectivism' or 'hive' in which, 'from their high perch in the division of learning, a privileged priesthood of "tuners" fuels the connected hive, cultivating it as a source of continuous raw-material supply' (Zuboff 2019, p. 505). Her language is hyperbolic but serves to remind us, lest we forget, that data gathering and analysis is rarely philanthropic; despite advertising copy that emphasizes control of our own lives and the safety of our own and loved ones, surveillance is a capitalist system.

As our behaviour (and inner drives) are monetized, our 'right to the future tense' is challenged; 'the right to act free of the influence of illegitimate forces that operate outside our awareness to influence, modify, and condition our behavior' (Zuboff 2019, p. 195). We are not at the stage where we might argue 'Google made me do it' in quite the same way as some of our forebears might have blamed the devil. However, it is easy to forget what life was like before the arrival of Google over our horizon, approaching our shores and, at least in a Foucauldian sense, getting inside our head to discipline us in this invader's culture. As Zuboff aptly reminds us, there was a significant point when Google turned from improving its service for users to reading users' minds in order to place ads in front of us that match our (modified) interests (Zuboff 2019, p. 78). There is, for Zuboff, a crucial point in the logic of surveillance capitalism:

> This new market form declares that serving the genuine needs of people is less lucrative, and therefore less important, than selling predictions of their behavior. Google discovered that *we are less valuable than others' bets on our future behavior*. This changed everything. (Zuboff 2019, p. 93, emphasis in original)

We might express this by way of a familiar tale:

> Luke 10.29–33: But wanting to justify himself, he asked Jesus, 'And who is my neighbour?' Jesus replied, 'A man was going down from Jerusalem to Jericho, and fell into the hands of robbers, who stripped him, beat him, and went away, leaving him half dead. Now by chance a priest was going down that road; and when he saw him, he passed by

on the other side. So likewise a Levite, when he came to the place and saw him, passed by on the other side. But a Samaritan while travelling came near him; and when he saw him …'

… caught a glimpse of the priest and the Levite just before the road turned a sharp corner and took them out of view. The Samaritan rushed to them and he was moved with curiosity. He first asked the priest, 'How frightened were you when you saw the robbers' victim; on a scale of 1–10; 1 being nonplussed to 10 being terrified out of your wits?' 'A definite 8', replied the priest. 'All right', replied the Samaritan. 'How many times a year do you make this trip?' 'About once a month', the priest responded. The Levite overheard and was ready with his answers. Not wanting to appear as afraid as the priest, the Levite answered, 'I'm only a 5 on the fear scale, but I need to make this journey every week.' The Samaritan thanked them both and continued on the road up to Jerusalem, where he set up a stall at the southern gate. Above his bench he pinned a sign, 'Priest-protection service – 4 denarii a trip. Levitical discount: 3 trips for the price of 2.'

We are dispossessed of our behaviour in a cycle of colonialist conquest comprising: incursion, habituation, adaptation, redirection (Zuboff 2019, pp. 139–50). (Zuboff likens surveillance capitalism to the 'conquest' declaration by the Spanish in America (Zuboff 2019, p. 179).) Incursion carries its military connotations of raids into our physical as well as mental spaces, such as our smartphone by way of ads or our street in the form of CCTV. Zuboff is correct to identify 'some combination of agreement, helplessness, and resignation' (Zuboff 2019, p. 140) in becoming accustomed to this normality (what we have seen Lyon account for in his concept of a culture of surveillance). A colonizing power finds constant confrontation tiresome and resource-sapping so will modify its response. Allowing regular festivals but perhaps replacing the local deity with the colonizer's was largely how the Christian world acquired Christmas. Zuboff recognizes this tactic – albeit with regard to regulatory bodies and public opinion – in Google's tweaking of its practices (Zuboff 2019, p. 140). But, she argues, such redirection of data-supply operation is 'just enough so that they appear to be compliant with social and legal demands' (Zuboff 2019, p. 140).

Dispossession occurs despite appearances to the contrary; this Zuboff terms 'the problem of two texts' (Zuboff 2019, p. 186). The texts we can all read are those advertising straplines exemplified by those of Strava that we have already noted: 'Track & Analyse', 'Share & Connect', 'Explore & Compete' (Strava 2020). This is the freedom and control that the colonizing power comes offering. But what Zuboff calls 'the shadow text' is available only to surveillance capitalists, for it contains what has been extracted from our engagement with the first text: 'This unprecedented concentration of knowledge produces an equally unprecedented concentration of power: asymmetries that must be understood as the unauthorized privatization of the division of learning in society' (Zuboff 2019, p. 192).

Zuboff's is a compelling analogy of colonial conquest of the workplaces of many of us, but more widely of this manifestation of technologized culture. Writing from a Scottish context, I get the idea that a colonizing system might be welcomed and readily embraced, partly but not wholly in ignorance. The construction of 'Britishness', particularly in the aftermath of the defeat of the Jacobite rising of 1745, was about forging more than a constitutional arrangement – a new nationality to which all subjects of the Crown in the British Isles might pledge, but crucially also feel, an allegiance.

Had we known in advance how Google or Facebook developed, how keen would we have been to cooperate? We sometimes give our older generations a hard time (as do they towards themselves) about being 'unable to download the internet'. However, the tech-savvy among us might alternatively be framed as collaborators with the colonial invader, and our wise elders those who, from their collective memory, sense something is wrong but cannot quite put their finger on it. Zuboff, it seems to me, distils this dispossession down to its most crucial in the example of the smartphone. Our human experience is datafied and claimed as the raw material of surveillance capitalism in a process of rendition (Zuboff 2019, p. 233). This is, as we have seen, the core of the theory; the smartphone is its ubiquitous device. But to attach the epithet 'smart' to a person meant crediting them with a higher than average degree of mental ability. Bringing this over into describing the capabilities of a device meant that having a *smart*phone seems only advantageous. '"Smart" is a euphemism for rendition', claims Zuboff (Zuboff 2019, p. 238). Had we talked of a data-rendition-phone it is possible that our acquiescence to surveillance capitalism might have carried a more critical, if not even resistance, dimension. Language, in any colonialist venture, is crucial.

Prosuming

The self-quantifier/qualifier is the latest incarnation of the prosumer. Alvin Toffler lays out this economic agent in describing a pre-Industrial Revolution 'first wave' of prosumption in which 'most people consumed what they themselves produced' (Toffler 1980, p. 283). (The qualification 'most' admits the production of goods for consumption by elites, whether imperial or feudal.) The Industrial Revolution separated producers from consumers in a 'second wave'. Now, in a 'third wave', the prosumer arises once more as some production is shifted from 'the visible economy that the economists monitor to the phantom economy they have forgotten' (Toffler 1980, p. 285). The contemporary prosumer is the consumer put to work in such ways as self-service filling stations, ATM bank facilities, self-scanning in the supermarket and, significantly for our discussion, DIY medical technologies such as blood glucose monitors (Ritzer and Jurgenson 2010, p. 18).

Toffler recognizes that consumers are willingly seduced into production (Toffler 1980, p. 292). Seduction in self-quantification/qualification appeals to our instinct to reach out to others with something of ourselves. Our propensity in this direction is commodified by the likes of Facebook, which in another magician's sleight of hand 'euphemistically describes this commodification process as "sharing"' (Fuchs 2012, p. 35). Naturally, not all self-quantifying is for sharing; most women will be unlikely to disseminate the details of their menstrual cycle on social media. However, I recall a quandary when I bumped into an acquaintance in the street who had been blogging the results of his and his wife's fertility tests. Despite having read these on a public blog I was unsure of the etiquette in mentioning them in casual conversation. Such extremes aside, the message of social media platforms is much more ambiguous than it at first appears: '"The world will be better if you share more" – but a better world for whom is the real question?' (Fuchs 2012, p. 36).

Seduction also entices with its siren call of 'convenience', which comprises at least two harmonic lines: consumer empowerment over our transactions and 'the recalibration of knowledge asymmetries among the consumer, the worker, and the company' (Stark and Levy 2018, p. 1211). These digital Sirens sing of the power offered to us in being autonomous as consumers, but the rocks to which we are lured are the benefits carried to corporate management, often, as Luke Stark and Karen Levy rightly observe, also to the detriment of those working in poor employment conditions servicing the consumer (Stark and Levy 2018, p. 1211).

There is, however, a more positive angle in self-tracking: scientific research projects, not least in the Covid-19 pandemic, that rely on subjects contributing their data – whether from self-optimizing apps or other monitoring devices. In such cases it is more appropriate to position the knowledge production 'in-between prosumption and citizen science' (Heyen 2016, p. 298). It is useful to think of prosumption in contextual, rather than abstract, terms because of the diversity of motivations and goals in which these actions circulate. There is certainly an exploitative dimension, but we ought not to neglect the possibilities of empowerment too. When prosuming, we might well gain the benefits of enjoyment and satisfaction, perhaps through increased social connectedness (Yamamoto et al. 2019, p. 1888).

The context is *informational capitalism*, 'the alignment of capitalism as a mode of production with informationalism as a mode of development' (J. E. Cohen 2019, p. 5). We could, it might be argued, simply accept that groups of people share similar life chances and so benefit through earning income or possessing valuable goods in the market of data (a Weberian model of class), or, as does Fuchs in his Marxian analysis, aim 'at the abolition of exploitation and the establishment of a participatory democracy' (Fuchs 2010, p. 179). Self-quantification apps are marketed as lifestyle enhancements that appear quite individual even when data is shared with others in avowedly social self-qualification. By positioning the apps within informational or surveillance capitalism we are confronted with the political dimensions: the argument for the abolition of exploitation as a normative principle. To put this another way, we can question the extent to which self-quantification/self-qualification has to be a capitalist venture – and if so, whether this can be a capitalism that is for the common good – or we can push further in contending for information or surveillance socialism.

Fuchs makes a claim for knowledge forming 'part of the commons of society' because knowledge is 'a social product produced and consumed by all' (Fuchs 2010, p. 193). Fuchs expands the Marxist designation of 'class' to include 'the multitude' who prosume the digital commons (Fuchs 2010, p. 193). However, producing informational capital (at least in self-qualification) is not quite like manual labour where 40 hours of labour creates value. A runner is not running *for* Strava or generating data *for* the company. The value is, as Adam Arvidsson and Elanor Colleoni argue (following Cova et al.), 'ever more related to the ability to create and reaffirm affective bonds, like the ties that bind consumers into a community of interest or "tribe," or the link structure that underpins the network centrality of valuable "influencers"' (Arvidsson and Colleoni 2012, p. 136). I think we can recognize the value of the generated data *and* the 'labour' involved in the affective bonds in which the data is constructed. We could talk perhaps of *molecules of data* – by analogy with atoms (data) and chemical bonds (affective bonds). However, we ought not to lose sight of the fact that affective bonds in self-qualification are themselves datafied (rendered in data points).

Fuchs's vision is radical:

In a communist Internet age, programmers, administrators and users control Internet platforms by participatory self-management. Network access is provided free to all. There are no corporate Internet service providers ... On the commons-based Internet: 1) humans co-create and share knowledge, 2) humans are equal participants in the decision-making processes that concern the platforms and technologies they use, 3) the free access to and sharing of knowledge, the remixing of knowledge, and the co-creation of new knowledge help to create well-rounded individuals. (Fuchs 2017, p. 324)

Technology and the media are not the main aspect, but a part of society. Therefore all humans should be able to truly participate and benefit from media and technology, which is not the case today. Capitalism is a class society. The capitalist Internet is a class-structured Internet: corporations and other central actors dominate attention and symbolic, social and material benefits. A just society is a classless society. A just Internet is a classless Internet. (Fuchs 2017, p. 345)

At the very least, there would need to be transparency as to who in particular is benefiting from enclosing what could well be information for the common good behind the fences of digital platforms (Jordan 2015, p. 204). In his proposal for an economics of the common good, Jean Tirole states what it is easy to forget, that 'the market economy is not an end in itself' (Tirole 2017, p. 3). The Common Good Capitalism Movement aims to reorientate a free market economy so that 'individuals and organizations freely choose to give priority to the common good and second priority to profit or mission' (CGCM 2020). Christian Felber draws attention to ways of doing business that are built on values that often feature in political constitutions: 'building of trust, mutual appreciation, cooperation, connectedness with nature, solidarity and sharing' (Felber 2019, p. xxix). This means assessing the *goals* rather than singularly focusing on the *means* of business, for: 'What happens in the real world if the utmost goal of human beings is to pursue their own advantage and to act against others is that they learn to take advantage of others and deem this to be right and normal' (Felber 2019, p. 3).

There are those who argue that markets contribute to the common good by enabling creativity and enterprise (Griffiths 2015, p. 141). Yet although markets may 'coordinate the different interests of people engaging in voluntary transactions' (Griffiths 2015, p. 144), there are other parties who are not involved in this two-party transaction. Third parties may be significantly disadvantaged if they are not part of this exchange for systemic injustice that has locked them out. This becomes acute when we think about just how voluntary is people's involvement in surveillance capitalism. It is more voluntary for some than for others; in the case of much self-quantification/qualification it is indeed voluntary and possible for an already privileged sector of society.

Surreptitious data-sharing

Even for voluntary self-quantifiers, the use of their data is far from transparent and this hides the value each person is generating by their exercising, dieting or health reporting. There is surreptitious data sharing, not so much in terms of privacy breaches but in data from users being marketable to third (and even fourth) parties.

There were reports in 2015 of health apps sending 'searches including words such as "herpes" and "interferon" to no fewer than five domains with no notification that it was happening' (Chang 2015). In a study of 110 popular, free Android and iOS apps, also published in 2015, Jinyan Zang and colleagues demonstrate that 'a significant proportion' of apps were sharing user inputs with third parties without requiring a notification to users (Zang et al. 2015). There have been problems with some diabetes tracking apps sharing data without advising users, as in a 2014 study, published in 2016:

> In the transmission analysis, sensitive health information from diabetes apps (e.g. insulin and blood glucose levels) was routinely collected and shared with third parties, with 56 of 65 apps (86.2%) placing tracking cookies; 31 of the 41 apps (76%) without privacy policies, and 19 of 24 apps (79%) with privacy policies shared user information, which was not statistically significantly different (N = 65; $\chi21$ = 0.11, P > .25). Of the 19 apps with privacy policies that shared data with third parties, 11 apps disclosed this fact, whereas 8 apps did not. (Blenner et al. 2016, p. 1052)

A study running from January 2016 to August 2017 concludes:

> A large portion of the assessed apps has been found to jeopardize user's privacy and security by violating sensitive data protection regulations set to prevent the inappropriate and uncontrollable usage, processing and disclosure of health data to third parties. According to our analysis, a relevant number of popular m-health apps could violate users' privacy by revealing sensitive information such as health conditions, medical symptoms, photos, location, e-mails and passwords. (Papageorgiou et al. 2018, p. 9400)

Of course, apps will analyse the usage data to monitor and develop their technical functioning. However, there is neither a global data protection regulation nor, in some cases such as the USA, a national framework.

Users also need to be aware of 'cross-device tracking', where they are tracked both via an app on their mobile device and on particular websites, building a more substantial profile than they might expect. Narseo Vallina-Rodriguez and Srikanth Sundarsan note how individual tracking sites may be owned by the same corporate entity and warn of extension of this as a result of future mergers (Vallina-Rodriguez and Sundarsan 2017). Where data protection regulations are loose or inadequately enforced, there are can be particular issues for minors:

> we have observed trackers in apps targeted to children. By testing 111 kids' apps in our lab, we observed that 11 of them leaked a unique identifier, the MAC address, of the Wi-Fi router it was connected to. This is a problem, because it is easy to search online for physical locations associated with particular MAC addresses. Collecting private information about children, including their location, accounts and other unique identifiers, potentially violates the Federal Trade Commission's rules protecting children's privacy. (Vallina-Rodriguez and Sundarsan 2017)

In an indication of the possible value of self-quantifiers' data, the market for 'femtech', technology-based products and services focused on women's health, is estimated to reach US$50 billion by 2025 (Rosato 2020). The self-quantifier is a target therefore of marketers whose interest is in not only securing a share of the existing business but shaping users' self-perception of the personal benefit of self-quantification in order to extend the market. It is not quite the case that every breath you take generates money for app developers, but every move you make being revenue generating is approaching.

'I count, I matter'

When Grandma sent a home-knitted pullover, somewhat misshapen, with arms too long and in a garish colour, all but the most ungracious grandchild would conclude that 'It's the thought that counts.' So too would be the attitude when our friend botches an attempt to hold a surprise birthday party for us. In the world of self-quantification and information capitalism it is very much the *act* that counts. Descartes' motto, 'I think, therefore I am', begins to be replaced by 'I count, therefore I am'. Two meanings are here: 'I count' in the sense of quantifying and digitizing everyday life, and 'I matter', my value lying in the extent to which my quantifying secures me attention from my network of relationships.

There is a process underway in which self-quantification not only shapes our achievements but our personhood. We are not quite at the point of a new ontology but the paradigm of a living human database is coalescing. Our audience gazes on us standing on stage speaking our statistical soliloquy. Yes, we manage our self-presentation but the frosted glass in the window of our soul is not always as opaque as we might prefer. Anyone who has used one of those public toilets installed with switchable glass will likely share a similar discombobulation. Closing the door applies a voltage for electro-chromatic technology that changes the glass from clear to frosted. The disconcerting approach to a stall with a clear glass door and nervously trusting the technology over an old-fashioned mechanical lock is a parable for our self-quantifying times. Just when might we be revealed in our indignity?

As we fixate on others' gaze, our governed and governing self deposits our behavioural surplus; our prosumption eagerly encouraged by information capitalists. We might not yet be fully colonized by the values of Silicon Valley but the degree to which we are being shaped is far from obvious. There might well be a good few digital gangsters out there making us an offer we cannot refuse in terms of our digital emissions. The more worrying are those who 'come in peace' offering us a better life in exchange for produce, which for them is significantly more valuable than we realize it to be. Avoiding direct conflict with us, the colonizers mould our self-perception with new rituals and stories; we come to desire what they offer, in this case digitization of our everyday lives. In many respects our lives as colonized people improve, but those advances are not for all, nor are all the changes we embrace unequivocally positive. We have resources in our old traditions and tales that help us with a standpoint that is not that of the colonizers; here, not that of surveillance capitalists. But what if our faith traditions are themselves colonized by Silicon Valley? A Christian spirituality might be enhanced, but how sharp can its critical cutting edge remain?

The rich not yet sent away empty

Roman imperial luxury

In the eyes of New Testament writers, being a trader or merchant is neither morally neutral nor spiritually inert. Commercial transactions occur against a broader horizon and in relation to particular systems of power. There is no blanket condemnation of trading. The parable of the kingdom of heaven being like treasure hidden in a field (Matt. 13.44) assumes an economic system of trade that makes it possible for the one finding and hiding treasure in a field to liquidize his material assets in order to buy that field. In another saying, Jesus likens the kingdom of heaven to a merchant who is in search of fine pearls (Matt. 13.45). Here again, selling all he has enables the merchant to buy that pearl of great price. In the parable of the talents there are plaudits and no sign of even implied criticism of trading with five talents to make five more (Matt. 25.21). On the other hand, as we have already seen, the rich are sent away empty in the overturning envisaged in the Magnificat (Luke 1.53).

> 'Fallen, fallen is Babylon the great! It has become a dwelling-place of demons, a haunt of every foul spirit, a haunt of every foul bird, a haunt of every foul and hateful beast. For all the nations have drunk of the wine of the wrath of her fornication, and the kings of the earth have committed fornication with her, and the merchants of the earth have grown rich from the power of her luxury.' ...
>
> And the kings of the earth, who committed fornication and lived in luxury with her, will weep and wail over her when they see the smoke of her burning; they will stand far off, in fear of her torment, and say, 'Alas, alas, the great city, Babylon, the mighty city! For in one hour your judgement has come.'
>
> And the merchants of the earth weep and mourn for her, since no one buys their cargo any more. (Rev. 18.2-3, 9-11)

In the focal text of our concern in this chapter (Rev. 18) we find the merchants of the Roman Empire making themselves rich 'from the power of her [Babylon's] luxury' (Rev. 18.3). Rome, the epicentre of iniquities and commerce, has 'glorified herself and lived luxuriously' (Rev. 18.7). John the Seer delivers his economic analysis: the merchants of the known world are reliant on Babylon/Rome's business and trading networks; when these are lost in the apocalyptic catastrophe, traders across the world 'weep and mourn' for this commercial centre (Rev. 18.11).

In visionary time, it takes but one hour for all Rome's wealth to be laid waste (Rev. 18.17); just as in Jesus' asserting that Satan's kingdom, divided against itself, is laid waste (Matt. 12.25; Luke 11.17). It is not only land-based merchants who suffer loss, but 'all shipmasters, and seafarers [and] sailors' (Rev. 18.17). Mercantile trade had developed a symbiotic relationship that tied its fortunes to the city and, in the view of John the Seer, entangled merchants in the moral and spiritual degradation of the Roman Empire.

For N. T. Wright, Revelation discloses how 'idolatrous worship [is] worked out through ... aggressive economic exploitation' (Wright 2012, p. 117). Rome is, for Richard Bauckham, a 'corrupting influence on the peoples of the Empire' (Bauckham 1993b, p. 343). While there might be a *Pax Romana* it is, in effect, 'a system of economic exploitation' (Bauckham 1993b, p. 347) and 'much more pacification than peace' (Kraybill 1996, p. 147). Rome is a symbol – as well as an instantiation – of the confluence of economic affluence, idolizing self-deification and military and political brutality (Bauckham 1993b, p. 349). It is wealthy families, in local sites of power, who embody and are integral to the functioning of a system of intertwined political, religious and economic activities (Collins 1984, p. 82; Friesen 2003, p. 62).

Wes Howard-Brook and Anthony Gwyther compare Roman and recent empires with a focus on global capital (Howard-Brook and Gwyther 1999). Against the backdrop of GATT (General Agreement on Tariffs and Trade), in which corporations are able to sue governments to have laws invalidated, global capital is facilitated to the advantage of the powerful in 'the transfer of wealth from the poor and middle class to the wealthy' (Howard-Brook and Gwyther 1999, p. 242). Using the symbolic themes of Revelation, Howard-Brook and Gwyther identify the illusory power of marketing and media to create false realities, the seductive immorality of what global capital offers, the place of death (and murder) as an instrument of these institutions that seek (in what can be likened to idol worship) to unite diverse peoples as loyal imperial subjects (Howard-Brook and Gwyther 1999, pp. 252–9).

Allen Callahan's conclusion regarding Revelation's critique encapsulates the approach to reading this text that we are taking here:

> The maritime luxury of Roman imperialism has retarded virtue, burdened faith, bound the spirit, and hindered the soul. John's visionary critique insists that we cannot separate political and moral economies, that political economy and moral economy are intimately bound together, that justice is the tie that binds the public square to our private lives. (Callahan 1999, p. 65)

This reading as economic critique is on much more solid hermeneutical ground than that which seeks to decode Revelation. As Bauckham observes, 'Revelation does not predict a sequence of events, as though it were history written in advance ... The kaleidoscope of images with which John depicts [the final period of history] are concerned with its nature and meaning' (Bauckham 1993a, p. 150).

The chip of the beast?

Christopher Rowland aptly observes that 'reading Revelation is much like reading a good and pungent political cartoon' (Rowland 1993, p. 33). Therefore, when we look at the 'mark of the beast' (Rev. 13.16; 14.9, 11; 16.2; 20.4) we are *not* seeking to identify technologies that might be the fulfilment of any prophetic (in the sense of futuristic) pointer to what is, for many Christians, the cause célèbre of surveillance in Revelation:

> Christians should prepare for the time when the prophesied beast forces everyone, small and great, rich and poor, free and slave, to receive a mark ... if we allow everything on planet earth to be implanted with spychips and permit a system in which people must identify themselves in order to enter stores, the antichrist will be able to step into a ready-made system in which every morsel of food can be monitored and controlled. (Albrecht and McIntyre 2006, p. 220)

So contrary to Katherine Albrecht, Liz McIntyre and, writing separately, Grant Jeffrey (Jeffrey 2000, pp. 153–67), prophetic references to implanted RFID chips or electronic tattoos are a distraction from the more profound critique of empire that Revelation inspires its readers to continue. Instead, the 'mark of the beast', according to Elizabeth Schüssler Fiorenza, 'functions as a counterimage to the sealing to the 144,000' and could well be a reference to the currency of the time that had the image either of the emperor or the goddess Roma imprinted on it (Schüssler Fiorenza 1991, p. 86). For Schüssler Fiorenza, our concern should be to pick up Revelation's challenge to any economic and political oppression as 'systemic evil and structural sin' (Schüssler Fiorenza 1991, p. 87).

The 'mark of the beast' impacts people's (in)visibility. It is the *refusal* that makes the faithful follower of Jesus hyper-visible. *Not* bearing a very visible sign is a figurative means of inspiring and sustaining Christians' challenge to the imperial cult and all that flows from it. Here Rowland is again helpful: 'in the present age those marked with the Beast have freedom to go about their activities, whereas those who refuse to be so marked and side with God and the Lamb are persecuted and their deaths are greeted with glee by the inhabitants of the earth' (Rowland 1993, p. 13). If the 'mark' is indeed imperial currency, then it is not merely a means of trade but it exerts – or at least attempts to exert – a shaping of the users' perceptions. Coins in the Roman Empire are, suggests Bruce Metzger, a means of impressing sovereignty 'vividly in the minds of [the Emperor's] subjects' (Metzger 1993, p. 76).

Whether or not the allusion in Revelation is to actual currency is a side issue in comparison to what is at stake economically, socially and, for the followers of Jesus most importantly, spiritually. (Not that these – economics, social relations and spirituality – can really be separated out.) The more pressing matter is participation in the imperial cult in local temple worship. While there might be occasions when attendance is commanded, the more run-of-the-mill, day-to-day benefits of going with the flow of the cult lay, for the elite, in the opportunity of being fully part of a patronage social system. Taking their place in the cult 'enhanced their reputation and status' (Howard-Brook and Gwyther 1999, p. 104). Those ordinary members of the community, not part of the elite, would still find it advantageous to be seen doing their religious duty: 'the remainder of the population benefited ... by the sense of social inclusion it gave through being part of trade guilds or other organizations that took part in the civic activities' (Howard-Brook and Gwyther 1999, p. 105). This web of relationships is obvious in the silversmith's riot described by Luke in Acts 19.

It is within a particular political economy – of Rome's exploitation of its empire to the advantage of the imperial family, its military and its wealthy families distributed throughout the known world – that Christians find acute challenges, but share disadvantage and exploitation in common with most other imperial subjects. Christians' bodies are at stake, not only in the sense of persecution but in their enculturation into prevailing spiritual, economic and political mores; interwoven as those inseparably are.

Trading in Corinth

The challenges of living in the Roman Empire even when it is accommodating Christian communities is exemplified in Corinth. Crucial for maritime trade traversing the isthmus (from Lechaeum in the west to Cenchreae in the east), this colony, among minor temples, supports a major temple of Apollo and, significantly, to the imperial family at the temple of Octavia. With its unsavoury reputation like any port, Corinth's ruined temple to Aphrodite does not mean that the activities of its cult prostitutes have ceased as business continues to be brisk. What John the Seer renders in apocalyptic visions, the apostle Paul articulates in epistolary pastoral exhortations:

> Do you not know that wrongdoers will not inherit the kingdom of God? Do not be deceived! Fornicators, idolaters, adulterers, male prostitutes, sodomites, thieves, the greedy, drunkards, revilers, robbers – none of

these will inherit the kingdom of God. And this is what some of you used to be. But you were washed, you were sanctified, you were justified in the name of the Lord Jesus Christ and in the Spirit of our God. (1 Cor. 6.9–11)

Immorality is a component of the local economy, which is itself entangled with civic responsibilities to maintain the cults, particularly as a demonstration of loyalty to the imperial family. For Paul, fornication and prostitution are spiritual, not only social or economic, issues for Christians in Corinth. The danger is being united in the body, for 'the two shall be one flesh' (1 Cor. 6.16). Such union is a violation of the temple of the Holy Spirit, namely the body of a Corinthian Christian. Paul clarifies and extends his antipathy to mismatched partnerships in 2 Corinthians:

Do not be mismatched with unbelievers. For what partnership is there between righteousness and lawlessness? Or what fellowship is there between light and darkness? What agreement does Christ have with Beliar? Or what does a believer share with an unbeliever? What agreement has the temple of God with idols? (2 Cor. 6.14–16a)

The conjunction of civic life, trade, social relations and spirituality poses acute problems in Paul's view for Corinthian Christians. However, despite the unequivocal language of separation as purity, Paul does not eschew involvement in Corinth's economy. On arrival from Athens he finds two refugees from Italy, Aquila and Priscilla, when he lands in Corinth. Paul lives with them and they ply their trade as trained tentmakers (Acts 18.3). It is reasonable to assume that their clients were from across the diverse population of this mercantile and maritime city and not limited to the Christian community. So Paul is making tents to be bought by travellers, traders and sailors (possibly also by soldiers); pagans and most likely among them those condemned for their greed, brutality and lasciviousness.

Christian participation in the political economy of the Roman Empire is evidently complex but here the key ethical principle for Paul is that Christians' bodies are temples of the living God (1 Cor. 6.19; 2 Cor. 6.16). The question, then, for us is how scraping data from a temple of the Holy Spirit is justifiable within a political economy of information capitalism. How, in other words, do the critiques of Revelation and the Corinthian correspondence address surrendering data from everyday life, lived for God, in the process of self-quantification?

What does Silicon Valley have to do with Corinth?

So far in this chapter we have considered self-quantification and its place within informational capitalism. We have drawn out the critique of the political economy of imperial Rome from the apocalyptic visions of John the Seer, anchoring those to the particular context of the Roman colony of Corinth. Revelation portrays an economy in the service of the imperial family and elites, reliant on military brutality, legitimated by a cultic system – by which allegiance could be demonstrated and judged. It is not just a matter of Christians being faithful by accepting martyrdom rather than apostasy. There is more at stake than direct collusion or surrender to idolatry. There is a form of apostasy articulated as surrender to the particular political economy of this empire. The clear and present danger is of being shaped by the values of the imperial economy if one is a buyer, trainer, slave owner, slave, rich, military, or ordinary person with opportunities for sexual immorality (e.g. in Corinth); broadly speaking, an ethics of social relations is at stake. On a bigger canvas, John the Seer is striking against idolatry, and social and cultural mores – instead presenting the path of victory as the way of the slain Lamb; power confronted by suffering and service.

To move from surrender to the particular values of the imperial Roman economy to questions arising in the twenty-first century around self-quantifiers being complicit with informational capitalism means posing two principal questions: to what extent is self-quantification 'work' within this economic system, and, subsequently, what challenges does a Christian theological outlook bring to capitalism (informational or otherwise)? We will focus on two encyclicals of Roman Catholic Social Teaching to engage with both questions: *Laborem exercens*, John Paul II's 1981 discourse on work, and his 1991 reflection on a post-communist world in *Centesimus annus*. From there we will explore the positive possibilities of reconceiving self-quantification as gift (rather than exchange), before raising a challenge to the use of apps specifically in the realm of Christian spirituality.

Valley capitalism

Behavioural surplus as work?

Work and dignity

Although *Laborem exercens* pays particular attention to paid employment, as befits its contemporary context, it does not neglect pre-industrial or even pre-agrarian work:

> The Church is convinced that work is a fundamental dimension of man's existence on earth ... Work understood as a 'transitive' activity, that is to say an activity beginning in the human subject and directed towards an external object, presupposes a specific dominion by man over 'the earth', and in its turn it confirms and develops this dominion. (John Paul II 1981, §4)

Such transitive activity surely includes subsistence farming and, I suggest, the activities of hunter-gatherers. (This will give us, a little later, a possible link to self-quantification as a form of work.) John Paul uses this transitive notion to refine his theory of work when, in either mechanical or digital systems, a person appears to be supervising equipment more than doing what is commonly perceived as 'work'. The work of the street cleaner is no more intrinsically valuable than that of a software engineer; their respective market value and social status is not what is of primary concern. Rather, it is the subjective sense that is primary:

> As a person he (*sic*) works, he performs various actions belonging to the work process; independently of their objective content, these actions must all serve to realize his humanity, to fulfil the calling to be a person that is his by reason of his very humanity. (John Paul II 1981, §6)

In the 'gospel of work', dignity in being able to fulfil one's humanity can only be secured when work exists for people, not people for work (John Paul II 1981, §6). This has implications for those who seek to found their identity in their work (those commonly termed 'workaholics') and for employers, managers and politicians who might be tempted to value people on the basis of the work they are able to do. As we will see later, work and the market are not ends in themselves but *for* attaining a good society comprising people who achieve fulfilment as human beings and, 'in a sense' as John Paul qualifies this assertion, become 'more a human being' (John Paul II 1981, §9).

Because we are created in the image of God we share by our work 'in the activity of the Creator' (John Paul II 1981, §25). This is hard to perceive if we make the error of taking the objective, rather than subjective, standpoint and therefore baulk at the notion of a repetitive, unskilled task being 'creative'. It is working, rather than the work, that has priority. Of course, this does not mean that there is spiritual value in work that is immoral, for example deforestation of crucial ecosystems or unjust war. It is, as John Paul quotes *Gaudium et spes*, not merely the subjective that matters:

the norm of human activity is this: that in accord with the divine plan and will, it harmonize with the genuine good of the human race, and that it allow men as individuals and as members of society to pursue their total vocation and fulfil it. (Second Vatican Council 1965, §35)

As well as co-creativity with God, a person might understand their mundane, repetitive or demeaned work as activity they undertake as love for God – as did the seventeenth-century Brother Lawrence (Brother Lawrence 1981).

For John Paul, placing work in the light of the cross and resurrection means that the effort exerted in work is also significant. Toil 'marks the way of human life on earth and constitutes an announcement of death' (John Paul II 1981, §27). Just as human decision-making takes place against a horizon of contingency and mortality so too does work.

How much, then, of the production of behavioural surplus as valuable data might be considered work? Such surplus is a product of value within an economic system, so it is a commodity but not like flour or oil, for example. It is not quite the same as an intellectual endeavour or a development based on skills. Nor is behavioural surplus the same as a skill – although some advanced actions that are self-quantified do require skill, for example sports and fitness training. Collecting digital emissions from everyday life is somewhat like putting up a solar panel by which you sell the surplus energy to the national grid. In some cases you might in effect be renting your roof surface to the solar-panel supplier and you get only a cut of the income.

You would not normally pay your children a wage for what they do around the home. But one might incentivize or reward with pocket money. Indirectly their effort contributes to the operation of the family unit from which other family members are better able to contribute to *their* employment from which they make a living. An amateur musician does not make a living from her art, yet she contributes to the cultural economy, albeit indirectly. Voluntary work, on the other hand, does not provide an analogy because it is generally for a not-for-profit organization. There is some similarity with outsourcing of data generation; it is unpaid but the app is given for free in exchange. The user gains enjoyment, satisfaction and so on in being able to track his behaviour. Working for an employer beyond contracted hours could be an equivalent of behavioural surplus. We therefore come to the question of the extent to which self-quantification and its profit-generating capacity can contribute to a person's dignity.

Profit and dignity

We turn to John Paul II's encyclical, *Centesimus annus*, written not only to commemorate the one hundredth anniversary of *Rerum novarum*, but to mark the collapse of the Soviet Union and claims of the supremacy of particularly neoliberal capitalism. He identifies errors in socialism, arising at least in part because of its atheism, by which 'the good of the individual is completely subordinated to the functioning of the socio-economic mechanism' (John Paul II 1991, §13). Autonomy is dissolved, even forbidden, for the sake of the social order; humans are 'reduced to a series of social relationships' (John Paul II 1991, §13). John Paul is convinced that, whether by socialists or capitalists, 'it is not possible to understand man on the basis of economics alone' (John Paul II 1991, §24). The market is not therefore an end in itself, nor is it an instrument for the profit of a few. Rather, the market should be 'appropriately controlled by the forces of society and by the State, so as to guarantee that the basic needs of the whole of society are satisfied' (John Paul II 1991, §35). In other words, the universal destination of material goods is the flourishing of all humanity.

There are further limits of the market, for while, admits John Paul, it would appear that 'the free market is the most efficient instrument for utilizing resources and effectively responding to need ... there are many human needs which find no place on the market' (John Paul II 1991, §34). This would be the case for providing basic necessities in developing countries but also true for aspects of all countries' cultural life and, arguably, health care and education. John Paul argues not for abolishing markets but constraining markets *and* enabling those currently outside capitalist systems to develop the skills and resources to 'enter the circle of exchange' (John Paul II 1991, §34). He appreciates that profit is *one*, but not the sole, indicator or regulator of a flourishing business, for 'It is possible for the financial accounts to be in order, and yet for the people – who make up the firm's most valuable asset – to be humiliated and their dignity offended' (John Paul II 1991, §35). A theological, and indeed a humanist, perspective is vital as a standpoint outside, and sometimes against, economism because, 'Of itself, an economic system does not possess criteria for correctly distinguishing new and higher forms of satisfying human needs from artificial new needs which hinder the formation of a mature personality' (John Paul II 1991, §36).

John Paul affirms business, markets, private property and creativity as positive dimensions of capitalism but is highly critical of the unequivocal valorizing of choice and thereby the absolute freedom of the market. Rather, there ought to be 'a strong juridical framework which places [capitalism] at the service of human freedom in its totality' (John Paul II 1991, §42).

Where, then, does self-quantification fit into this regulated market directed towards the human flourishing of all? It will be useful to consider a number of possible parallels to self-quantification being behavioural surplus monetized by informational capitalism in order to see more clearly what is at stake. A first parallel might be with owning (or renting) a less-well-insulated home. You contribute a benefit to your neighbour of the surplus heat through your shared walls and/or shared ceiling/floor. A second parallel might be with contributing to the atmosphere of a concert you are attending or to the vibe in a tourist area. This makes it more attractive so generating something valuable to a concert promoter or local businesses in the tourist area. A third parallel to a behavioural surplus could be a musician practising at home, whom her neighbour hears and enjoys. There is a benefit of surplus to the neighbour. However, we might view this situation rather differently if the neighbour then charges for tickets to enter his home so that an audience can listen to the musician practising next door. The musician would surely expect a cut of the profits. A further refining of this parallel might be if the neighbour sells an instrument to the musician; this would be closer to the self-quantifier purchasing or downloading an app – but that might be more akin to the neighbour *lending* an instrument to the musician.

The first parallel might make a small difference to one's neighbours' heating bills but is scarcely part of a market exchange. Similarly, an attentive audience in an almost full auditorium is welcome for financial reasons, but the component of 'contributing to the atmosphere' is not quantifiable, largely because it is about individual perceptions and it would strike most people as strange to attempt to monetize. The third parallel opens intriguing questions around opportunity (the skill of playing well) and being taken advantage of for another's material benefit. Is it then a matter of grudgingly accepting that this is competition in the market, and claiming one's cut? Catholic Social Teaching suggests that there are alternatives.

The selfish self-quantifier?

Competition and love

Keri Day takes a similar approach to John Paul II in arguing that 'competition must not be the organizing principle of all of social life, as it impedes visions of human flourishing' (Day 2016, p. 13). This has gone hand in glove with a mode 'that defines human meaning based on the material things one can acquire' (Day 2016, p. 47); what we might call a leakage into social relations so that trust and love are defined according to market practices. Such a 'commodification of the human subject ... dehumanizes social bonds and privileges economic profit-maximization as a primary social value' (Day 2016, p. 48). Day proceeds, by way of Eric Fromm, to argue that owners become 'possessed by' property, as what one owns comes to constitute one's self and identity (Day 2016, p. 50). The challenge, as Day articulates it, comes in becoming, in Kierkegaardian terms, 'a united self' that 'enables one to live for something (i.e., for a cause, for God, for neighbor, etc.) that permeates all one does, which does not change on an hourly or daily basis due to popular opinion, expedient circumstances, or material reward' (Day 2016, pp. 66–7). The counter-practice to this neoliberal colonization of our mind can, Day suggests, be seen in black feminist and womanist religious perspectives of love as a practice of self-actualization (Day 2016, p. 105). These are social bonds of a particular quality, with an emphasis on the communal, for 'this cooperative way of being then holds promise in influencing social, political, and economic systems' (Day 2016, p. 157).

Adam Kotsko contends that neoliberalism is not content to sit back, but 'it must force us to be selfish in the particular way it demands, which means seeking open-ended material gain' (Kotsko 2018, p. 84). In market competition (rather than exchange) there must be winners and losers; the system 'necessarily entails inequality' (Kotsko 2018, p. 92). Such inequality is manifest and utilized on a wide canvas:

> Neoliberalism is a social order, which means that it is an order of family and sexuality and an order of racial hierarchy and subordination. It is a political order, which means that it is an order of law and punishment and an order of war and international relations. (Kotsko 2018, p. 94)

This is not to say that self-quantifiers are somehow guilty by association with the worst aspects of neoliberal informational capitalism. Selfishness is a defensive posture towards those who are perceived as a threat; it is more than 'I want that', it has a dimension of 'You cannot have that'. It might seem that were everyone to self-quantify, everyone would be more self-optimized. More data would offer more accurate predictive models. But in a world of finite and inequitably distributed resources, those who are more self-optimized could have an advantage to acquire limited resources because they have used aggregated data to anticipate their needs (or perhaps more correctly put, they will have been told their needs ahead of others). This is not to deny the potential for some forms of self-quantification to form users who are more aware of their excesses of consumption and become more attuned to global (or local) inequities and injustice, but it seems to me that one consequence of self-quantification lies in getting some people to the front of the queue for resources. These might be health care – when the self-quantifier identifies earlier than others when a medical condition might be arising. Similarly, being at the front of the queue (or in the consulting room before a queue even starts) could be an advantage of self-quantifying one's mental health. Early intervention might be economically advantageous to health and social care systems, but might it not be, once again, the already privileged who benefit from early intervention at the expense of others? If not actually selfish, the self-quantifier is colluding with a system that encourages selfishness. So the issue is more than the extent to which self-quantification is at work within informational capitalism. Rather, the question is how much and what sort of self-quantification is a practice of *love*, particularly when the qualification of the self takes place within modes of competition and acquisition?

Sacrifice and love

Jung Mo Sung helps us see the contrast between love and selfishness when these play out under neoliberal economics. Sung makes a crucial distinction between being called to sacrifice and being inspired to love. Demands for the sacrifice of human lives come from the market, state, political party or the Church, but these 'are made in the name of a sacralized institution which presents itself as the only way to building paradise' (Sung 2007, p. 27). Such claims are idolatry in Sung's view because no institution bears this capacity, so cannot make claims of necessary sacrifices. It is only the kingdom of God that carries paradise and does so in God's grace and mercy, 'not [in the] work of our hands and, even less the fruit of our sacrifices in obeying the laws of the market' (Sung 2007, p. 27). The kingdom of God is a vision, always on our horizon, that gives meaning to our struggles against injustice.

In Sung's analysis, 'We know that the absolute ruling of the market's logic means cuts in social expenditure and exclusion of the "incompetent" (the poor) and of those who are not necessary any more in the current process of accumulation of capital' (Sung 2007, p. 18). The sacrifice of others on the altar of austerity economics is supposedly 'for the greater good', or, through having transcendentalized the market, 'economic redemption' (Sung 2007, p. 91). Making sacrifices along the way of self-optimization, identified as these might be through self-quantification, is another form of the greater good, this time one's own greater good. However, Sung challenges us to ask instead about love:

Whoever, for love, is freely in the struggle as a gift of oneself, never feels that it was not worthwhile or that it was a bitter experience because it did not lead to victory. For the main motivation for the struggle was not the promise of victory but rather solidarity and affirmation of human dignity. But for those who undertake anything as sacrifice and obligation the only compensation for the bitterness of the struggle and even life is victory or reward. (Sung 2007, pp. 27–8)

Sung is touching a crucial critique of capitalism, informational or any other form; a quantifiable beneficial output is not what love is about. Quantifiable benefit is not what legitimates care for others. It is not what constitutes loving one's self. Again, this is not to deny benefits from self-quantification but to disclose the way taking care of oneself is being redefined in neoliberal, or even simply capitalist, terms.

Perhaps self-quantification is predominately, if not uniquely, a middle-class problem of those with the possibility to emulate social media influencers or heroes and heroines of athleticism. Competition has leaked from the market into everyday life, competing also against oneself. To try and look from the vantage point of the social location of the poor is fraught with difficulties of paternalism, naivety and plain ignorance. Nevertheless, a different light can be shed on otherwise accepted economic logic. Miguel De La Torre remarks on the parable of the workers in the vineyard (Matt. 20.1–16), who stand hoping that a patron will offer them a few hours' work. If we read this parable through our capitalist glasses we are affronted at the notion that those working different numbers of hours receive the same pay. However, argues De La Torre, when we read with those living precarious lives in this way today, we learn that:

the lesson is that those who are economically privileged, like the factory owner, must remain responsible for those who are not. For those who live under an economic system that commodifies the workers' time, justice is defined as a set pay for a set number of hours worked. Yet Jesús here defines justice as ensuring that each worker obtains a living wage, regardless of the hours worked, so that all can share in the abundant life. (De La Torre 2015, p. 107)

This is a logic of mercy in which the universal destination of material goods is indeed the flourishing of all – even if this has sometimes to mean just meeting the minimum upon which flourishing in greater capacity is yet to be built. If commodification is not the only game in town, a subversive notion in the current ethos of capitalism, we can draw further on Catholic Social Teaching to explore the twin logics of gift and solidarity.

Corinthian benefaction

The logic of gift

Gift is fundamental to Benedict XVI's thesis where in *Caritas in veritate* (Benedict XVI 2009) he refers back to Paul VI's encyclical of March 1967 – *Populorum progressio* (the progressive development of peoples). Over 40 years later, Benedict wants to return to the issue of development and asks, in a fresh way, what love in truth means in a world that he sees is 'becoming progressively and pervasively globalized' (Benedict XVI 2009 §9). Paul VI proposed that the *purpose* of development should be but one aim: 'to serve human nature' (Paul VI 1967, §34). The question is, as we saw when discussing AI, not just 'development' but *authentic* development (Benedict XVI 2009, §18). Benedict ponders what, in the gospel, God has said, at the most fundamental level, about humanity. God has given 'a resounding "yes" to humanity' (Benedict XVI 2009, §18). The consequence of this divine affirmation is that development, if it is to be authentic, has to be about the *whole* person and include *everyone* – not only a select few.

Benedict is troubled by the dominance of competition in globalized economies (Benedict XVI 2009, §37). He recognizes the importance of contracts and of political attempts to require justice and redistribution of wealth by law. However, he claims that in addition to a logic of contractual exchange and a political logic there is a need for 'the logic of the unconditional gift' (Benedict XVI 2009, §37). When the logic of the market and the logic of the state dominate the landscape – each with their respective monopolies – much, argues Benedict, is lost; namely, 'solidarity in relations between citizens, participation and adherence, actions of gratuitousness' (Benedict XVI 2009, §39). It is in civil society that economic relations of solidarity find the most fertile soil to develop, which makes the cultivation of civil society of crucial importance to authentic human development. However, Benedict's is a call for the logic of gift not to be sequestered in the civic sphere but for gift to shape also the domains of market and state:

> on the one hand ... the logic of gift does not exclude justice, nor does it merely sit alongside it as a second element added from without; on the other hand, economic, social and political development, if it is to be authentically human, needs to make room for the *principle of gratuitousness* as an expression of fraternity. (Benedict XVI 2009, §34, emphasis in original)

In other words, humans are neither to be defined as, nor primarily formed by, economic, political or cultural trends, ideologies or propaganda as *homo oeconomicus* or *homo collectivus*, but in every sphere of life, as *homo reciprocans* (Grassl 2011, p. 114). Benedict challenges the prevailing dichotomous model that situates for-profit, hybrid and non-profit business in relation to profit (along one axis) and social mission (on a second axis). Instead, Benedict proposes a triadic model. Civil society, market and state each sit at a corner of an equilateral triangle. Each brings its respective logic to bear upon the social system: market brings efficiency in its commercial logic, state brings equity in its logic of justice, and civil society brings reciprocity in its logic of gift. But it is the logic of gift and thus reciprocity, because it reflects the most fundamental metaphysics of being human, which ought to be given its primary (although not paramount) place.

The logic of solidarity

In parallel with an ontology of gift, Benedict argues from an ontology of relationality. It is, he argues, in true openness to others that we are authentically individual. This, as we would expect, is a theological claim based on Benedict's understanding that God, as Trinity, is relational in God's being. Be that as it may, the implications of humanity understood relationally are socially and politically profound in this framework. One such is the response of solidarity as a cornerstone of authentic human development (and to the notion of surveillance from the cross that underlies our approach). While there is a divinely gifted 'innate yearning to "be more"' (Benedict XVI 2009, §29), development cannot be at the expense of others. So solidarity invokes restraint (to avoid exploitation of others) *and* extension (in advocacy and support of those who are unjustly constrained). A parallel moral responsibility, rather unhelpfully termed 'fraternity' by Benedict, complements solidarity. It is not that solidarity is abstract; for identification with others is always in material disadvantages in particular contexts. However, in coupling solidarity to fraternity Benedict seems to touch upon the potential for solidarity being too readily associated with homogeneity that suppresses distinctives for the sake of the whole. The enforced 'solidarity' of 'the workers' (under communism) or 'the nation' (under fascism) are the shadow side of mutual and allied action of movements for civil rights. As Stefano Zamagni observes, 'a society based on solidarity and not on fraternity would be a society that everyone would try to escape' (Zamagni 2012, p. 76). Solidarity, argues Zamagni, 'enables *unequals* to become equals' whereas fraternity 'allows equals to be different' (Zamagni 2012, p. 76).

As I will discuss below, the combination of solidarity and fraternity is crucial given the propensity of contemporary surveillance to sort populations with a view to protecting the 'normal' from risky outliers. There are, as Daniel Finn notes, considerable difficulties with the word 'fraternity', not least around its associations with stereotypically immature behaviour by US males in college and the word's gendered etymology and history (Finn 2012, p. 79). Fellowship (although carrying some vestigial gendering) might better capture the counterbalance to solidarity than 'fraternity'. 'Communion' is an alternative candidate but its heavy associations with Christianity weigh against it for its use in wider public discussion.

This logic of gift drives Benedict's evaluation of technology. If humanity understands itself as 'gift' we cannot therefore make the presumption that the wonders of either technology or finance can deliver authentic development. It is incumbent upon us to ask not only 'how' but 'why' particular human activity – here technological advancement – is pursued. Moral responsibility is woven into technological development, even (perhaps we might add especially) 'when we work through satellites or through remote electronic impulses, our actions always remain human, an expression of our responsible freedom' (Benedict XVI 2009, §70). Benedict is not against technological developments. In fact he views such endeavours against the backdrop of God's command in the Genesis myth that humans are to cultivate land. Again, Benedict's attention is towards those who are engaging in technological advancement. Technologists, and all those involved directly or indirectly in the development, regulation, marketing and deploying of technologies, are moral agents: 'development is impossible without upright men and women, without financiers and politicians whose consciences are finely attuned to the requirements of the common good' (Benedict XVI 2009, §71).

The problem with gift

Gift is, in practice, vulnerable to the action of opportunists (Zamagni 2012, p. 75). Reciprocity cannot be demanded, otherwise we move outside the concept of 'gift'. The widespread commercialization of traditional seasons and occasions for gift-giving is an easy target for any critic, but it does seem that those who eschew the logic of exchange (enforceable by law) are acting counterculturally. Conventions of civility are difficult to nurture and sustain in complex societies of strangers. Our turn to surveillance in everyday life to negotiate our relationships as strangers is a response to the loss of conventions and connectedness upon which we might previously have relied to a greater extent. In such contexts, it is unsurprising that there are problematic associations with the term 'gift', most notably connotations of paternalism and the enacting of a status of power over another (as in 'donation'). Similarly, gift is easily framed as a 'handout' or 'freebie', with pejorative implications that the recipient ought to have worked to be rewarded but instead is getting something for nothing. Gift construed as 'charity' holds negative associations with imbalances of power in which recipients are deemed unable to reciprocate, even in kind; being passive, even indolent. We could add further troublesome connections between 'gift' and 'largesse' (from the particularly wealthy to those with less), or alms and offerings (often closely linked to religious duties).

The complex relationships of power within 'gift' are those that are integral to the much wider critique of development that Benedict and his predecessors have sought to address with their notion of *authentic* development. Whenever we read 'the logic of gift' we must do so in the light of the underpinning discussions of human dignity and solidarity. Benedict encapsulates the refutation of paternalism and other negative connotations: 'I cannot "give" what is mine to the other, without first giving him what pertains to him in justice' (Benedict XVI 2009, §6).

More problematic is the way that Benedict discusses gift as if it is acontextual. It matters, I believe, if one is talking about gift within a feudal or honour system of patronage. Assumptions of social order influence one's understanding of 'gift', just as in societies where neoliberal economics are taken to be the only game in town. My point is not simply that 'gift' is understood differently across time and cultures but that any *theological* perspectives on 'gift' are also shaped. Appeals to theological framing of 'gift' need to acknowledge how sacred texts and traditions of dogmatic reasoning are themselves contextual. To gloss over context is not to make one's argument immune from contextual dimensions but risks universalizing one's context. We just need to think of the 'gifting' of lives for others that has framed the deaths of combatants in the First World War, which has been incorporated into many memorials within churches. More recent appeals to patriotism by exclusive forms of nationalism similarly shape theological perspectives on what 'true citizens' will gift to the state by way of loyalty and service.

Self-quantification in an economy of grace

Solidarity-fellowship arises from the fundamental relationality of being human. This logic of gift that Benedict pleads to be foregrounded in economic and political life can be similarly brought to bear on contemporary systems of surveillance. The solidarity-fellowship dynamic is crucial to appreciating what surveillance is for. This might be a strange question to keep asking when the needs of national security, service delivery, retail, policing and advertising abound. Neither is the question of the purpose of surveillance answered by recourse to definitions. Benedict's logic of gift, set within his broader probing of the ultimate destination of material goods, instead prompts us to position self-quantification practices (technologies, systems and dispositions) under the larger, more fundamental goal of authentic development of people.

Benedict observes that love is both received as well as given (Benedict XVI 2009, §5). This strikes a chord about people being able to *receive* a gift as well as being able to *give*. If so, we can extend our analytical framework to consider how we are able to receive information or data concerning others when 'we' are the public. Instead of focusing on data-processing corporations or state systems as the recipients of data, we can usefully ponder what it means for *us* to receive the data of our fellow citizens (and, in some cases, non-citizens). If we are to engage critically with the first part (what sort of relationships we desire) we need to articulate, and critically consider, our understanding of what it means to be human. I am not advocating everyone need adopt Benedict's take on the nature of being human, but rather that we use his perspective to prompt, and perhaps enhance, discussion. If, for the sake of argument, we accept Benedict's view that gift is the frame within which we understand life, then this is deeply confrontational. This ontology strikes against humanity's self-definition and requires us to look beyond (or behind) political, social and economic definition. It may well be that our struggles to receive our own life as gift, and those of others as gift, arise from unspoken and pre-reflective assumptions.

If we think of gifting our self-quantifying data we are certainly opening ourselves to the opportunism such as that of the neighbour (from our earlier analogy) who sells tickets to listen to a musician practising in the next house. This monetized eavesdropping strikes us as unfair. Here we may require a different framing of the issue: what if we do consider our personal data as not belonging to us, but to God? This is what Paul's appeal to the Corinthians to treat their bodies as temples of the Holy Spirit might well suggest. Kathryn Tanner's *Economy of Grace* can help us here. Drawing on Locke's view of property rights being, at root, common, Tanner asserts:

> All private property is on loan or held in tenancy from God, who retains full possession (in some significant sense) and whose purposes – the good of all – must therefore be served if one is to maintain rightful possession ... Therefore what looks like a sale in a capitalist sense of free disposal or transfer of ownership is not really that but the transfer of rights of use with strings attached. (Tanner 2005, p. 41)

What we are expressing in the language of being a temple of the Holy Spirit, and work as co-creating, Tanner expounds in terms of responsibility to co-tend: 'One cannot give someone free disposal over oneself (or others) without contravening this sort of obligation to maintain and care for God's property; granting someone rights of free disposal simply means not holding him or her to such an obligation' (Tanner 2005, p. 42). This does not jettison one's responsibilities but relativizes claims to be able to dispose of, or otherwise dispense with – by application to our discussion – the data that is one's behavioural surplus.

Tanner's is a problematic proposal given the exigencies and ubiquity of the market, besides its mutation into neoliberal economics. However, by pointing us towards gift exchange she helps us reconsider self-quantification. Tanner's contribution is to disclose the importance of the social relations that are organized by, and organize, gift exchange. There can be 'the impersonal fashion of capitalist exchange or the more person-specific mode of gift exchange' (Tanner 2005, p. 52), although these are, as she notes, not without their own challenges.

So it is not a matter of side-stepping the monetizing of behavioural surplus within informational capitalism but rather questioning the social relations such a system relies upon, reinforces or perhaps invents: withholding one's data when that is an option within a particular app; favouring those apps that draw a tighter boundary around the monetizing of data is another possible route. Such responses, and others, might well be different when apps are being used to self-quantify spirituality. It is to this we must now turn to consider additional challenges that arise in the light of Jesus' injunctions in Matthew 6 and reflection on some wider aspects of pastoral theology.

(Ac)count your blessings

Self-quantifying spirituality apps

There is a multiplicity of apps for Bible study, general spiritual growth or church life in general. These have been developed within a digital eco-system that is more complex in some theological traditions than others. For example, liturgically high Catholic, Anglo-Catholic and Orthodox services of worship may well make little, if any, use of digital projection. Mega-churches, perhaps simultaneously broadcasting to multiple sites, operate within a denser digital jungle. The financial resources and/or inclinations of Christian communities to digitize are not equally distributed. Some regions within a country will be more digital than others; likewise, variations between countries can be significant. For example, a rural Appalachian congregation in the USA may be non-digital, just like one in rural Malawi. However, large, urban churches in both countries might well be highly digital – perhaps even connected by shared financial resourcing or content.

Our focus is on self-quantification apps, a component within the digital ecosystem. Pray As You Go, produced by Jesuit Media Initiatives, offers a basic daily framework of prayer sessions combining music, Scripture and questions for reflection (Jesuit Media Initiatives 2020). PrayerMate lets users create personal (private) prayer lists. It is self-quantifying at a very basic level; the user keeping track of her engagement. iDisciple pulls in feeds of the user's choice of Christian authors (including some that are recommended) (iDisciple 2020). An iDisciple can create growth plans. Echo Prayer encourages users to maintain a 'prayer streak' to 'build a healthy prayer discipline' (Echo app 2020). 'Pray now' on the Echo app takes the user to a feed of prayer needs from a particular church or organization. Prayer Timer settings will generate notifications (reminders) to pray, and the length of such a prayer session can be set in various increments from ten seconds to one hour. Should a user be new to the app or not be diligent in recording, she can encounter the wry notification: 'You currently have no answered prayers.'

YouVersion Bible lets users retrieve reading plans and, for a while in 2018, showed a graphic of people sharing verses by locations around the world (YouVersion 2018). The Bible verse 'shared, booked, and highlighted most often by the global YouVersion Community during 2019' was Philippians 4.6: 'Don't worry about anything, instead pray about everything. Tell God what you need, and thank him for all he has done' (translation not specified; YouVersion 2020). Some apps, such as She Reads Truth, offer subscription plans for study books (She Reads Truth 2020). Of course, Bible reading or prayer apps are not theologically neutral but represent a range of stables. Just as has been the case in Christian literature through the ages, doctrinal concerns mean X will recommend Y, but not recommend Z (because Z endorses commentator W).

Christian apps are but one corner of the wider spirituality self-tracking business. There are apps to shift a user's mindset regarding money, to utilize 'law of attraction' or brain focus principles, to meditate, to practise kindness (with suggested kindness challenges), or to get good news fed to the user to help with mood (Good News Network 2020). Self-quantification of spirituality is partly in continuity with previous ages. For example, sixteenth-century Jesuits had guidelines for how to narrate their spiritual lives and, in the seventeenth century, guides on recording mercies and deliverances were available as a method of self-improvement in, as Rettberg notes, John Beadles's 1656 *A Journal or Diary of a Thankful Christian* (Rettberg 2018, p. 34). The discontinuity lies in self-quantification within an ecosystem of information capitalism; colonizing minds with a particular economic perspective on technologized spirituality.

The spiritual accountant

The datafied hypocrite?

What does Jesus' injunction to discrete spiritual discipline mean for twenty-first-century self-quantifiers? At first sight self-quantifying – understood more accurately, as we have seen, as self-qualification – looks to be contradicting that warning: 'Beware of practising your piety before others in order to be seen by them; for then you have no reward from your Father in heaven' (Matt. 6.1). Granted, there are those for whom self-quantification is intended as a private matter, but when is this 'in order to be seen' by others – even if these are close friends or family? Arguably, sharing one's reading plan with a database, with possibly quite limited artificial intelligence, puts one at a distance from human operators. But sharing spiritual discipline, as we have seen with apps for other activities, generates a reward of sorts, especially if identity construction is important for the user. To be seen, by even a few, to be the 'right sort of' Christian comes perilously close to the spirit, if not the letter, of Jesus' warning.

In the same set of sayings, Jesus uses 'hypocrites' as the figures from whom the disciple is to be different: 'whenever you pray, do not be like the hypocrites; for they love to stand and pray in the synagogues and at the street corners, so that they may be seen by others' (Matt. 6.5). The 'hypocrite' here is not to be understood as one who says one thing but does another. In twenty-first-century usage, a hypocrite would extol the virtue of secret almsgiving but advertise his own generosity. Similarly, a modern hypocrite might preach marital faithfulness but engage in adultery. This meaning does not capture the import of the first-century term. Michael Brown draws our attention to the term appearing here in a 'thread of performatives' (Brown 2008, p. 116). Instead of an action being true or false, the comparison is between action that is or is not achieving the aims of the passage as a whole. The writer is concerned with building and maintaining distinctively Christian community. There are actions that undermine community and social partnership and there are actions that promote such aims. Dissonance can occur between what an act is supposed to accomplish and what it actually accomplishes. In specific terms, hypocrites understood in this way 'promote alienation rather than salvation' (Brown 2008, p. 118). Practising one's spirituality has its own form of 'performance anxiety'. In another context we may have encountered the paralysis of 'stage fright' in which, when faced with an audience, we are unable to recall or speak the words we have prepared. Academics can be afflicted with 'imposter syndrome' – another form of performance anxiety in which we lack confidence in our (genuine) abilities so that we live in the fear of someday being exposed as ignorant or foolish in our arguments. Brown suggests that the writer of this Gospel wants to confront his community with the possibility that their actions are not achieving what they intend to achieve. It is a *lack* of performance anxiety that afflicts hypocrites. They are insufficiently critical of their pious actions and require Jesus' challenge. If Christians draw attention to their almsgiving, prayer and fasting they are promoting a 'negative form of relationality' (Brown 2008, p. 131). 'What makes the performance of the hypocrites an alienated one is that it places self-importance at the centre of the disciple's concern, neglecting the social reality that is the very nature of life itself' (Brown 2008, p. 133).

For Christians living in Greco-Roman society, honour is what oils the gears of social, political and economic relationships. One honours those of superior social status and one derives honour from others. An individual could gain honour through advertising their giving to projects for the benefits of citizens (such as paying for the construction of a synagogue or temple). This is a complex world for the Christian seeking to be faithful to Jesus, who advocates giving in secret. To give to a public project and at the same time seek to acquire honour is not what is expected of the Christian. Furthermore, to advertise one's giving can be a way of keeping hold of that 'gift', for, as Brown puts it, the almsgiver is a hypocrite 'if she intends to use her gift as a means of transforming the world into her vision of what should be rather than the divine aim as expressed through the teachings of Jesus' (Brown 2008, p. 124).

The nudged disciple?

Although spirituality apps can contribute to a negative form of relationality, Jason Pridmore and Yijing Wang conclude that a number of such apps have an important and positive *nudging* function (Pridmore and Wang 2018, p. 504). This is about using technology to prompt oneself in the direction of spiritual development even if, as Pridmore and Wang observed from their empirical study, users 'do not use or see more "tallying" features within these applications as valuable' (Pridmore and Wang 2018, p. 512). Nudges or prompts rather than 'continual or comparative self-monitoring' is, in Pridmore and Wang's terms, 'self-paternalism'; a willing response to features provided by the app (Pridmore and Wang 2018, p. 504). This is illustrated well in an extract from Abby's voice memo diary when she was participating in Victoria Bellar's empirical study:

> I am thinking that this app is really helping me keep track of reading. For the first time, I'm actually reading almost every day. I have missed a day here and there, but for the most part, I'm keeping on track. I feel that the app is important to me because it shows my progress and that helps me keep going. (Bellar 2017, p. 120)

In Bellar's cohort of 20 participants only one person made use of the social networking elements on their chosen religious app. Paula, another participant, admitted to feeling vulnerable when strangers commented on her post about a particular Bible verse, although she had felt it valuable to relate to others' interpretations of that verse (Bellar 2017, p. 121). However, it is important to note that 'the rest of the participants indicated interest in having the option of posting on social media sites, but they never really got around to using the feature' (Bellar 2017, p. 121). It may be that most Christians are quite coy or sensitive, knowing the reputation for trolling that some social media functions can attract.

Bex Lewis proposes that we interpret Christian social media activities as communities of faithful practice with opportunities for liberating mission and encouragement (and restrictions for some users) (Lewis 2018). Given the proclivity of Christian spirituality apps to carry advertisements – in keeping with the ethos and values of the developers or owners – I do wonder if there are not some rather too blurred boundaries in play. When is Christian 'encouragement' to grow really advertising a new product, whether an app, book, conference or music download? Spiritual apps (and other products) are commercial, even if given away free, except for in-app purchases to unlock additional features. When so many adverts for Christian products feature well-groomed people generally considered to be physically attractive, you have to wonder what sort of messages are sent. Assumptions might be being made about someone's spirituality based (to some extent) on wholly irrelevant factors such as their looks, and perhaps there is a subtle temptation to envy their good looks, not only their spirituality.

If spirituality apps are entangled with advertising, Christian users have to be conscious of how they might be shaped by those advertisers under the guise of 'encouraging' them to spiritual development. This not to say Christians should avoid spirituality apps but that they ought never to treat the apps and their digital ecosystem as neutral.

The scrupulous self-evaluator?

There is a difference between a person's perception of well-being and their objective level of well-being. In biblical terms, the warnings to the churches in the letters of the book of Revelation are a reminder of the possibility of overconfidence. For example, the Seer writes to Sardis, 'you have a name for being alive, but you are dead' (Rev. 3.1) because he believes they put too much weight on the reputation attributed to them by others. The church at Laodicea are held to account: 'For you say, "I am rich, I have prospered, and I need nothing." You do not realize that you are wretched, pitiable, poor, blind, and naked' (Rev. 3.17). Other Christians, in the Matthean community, have a contrasting attitude of innocent blindness to their righteous acts: 'Then the righteous will answer him, "Lord, when was it that we saw you hungry and gave you food, or thirsty and gave you something to drink? And when was it that we saw you a stranger and welcomed you, or naked and gave you clothing?"' (Matt. 25.37–38). I am not sure that a spirituality app developed by the Laodiceans would be of much value – although I could imagine it selling very well because of the positive message its self-evaluation generates. On the other hand, it is impossible to envisage the 'righteous' of Jesus' parable being the sort of people who self-track or who even carry smartphones that leave digital footprints to which they could later refer. Rather, it is action remembered only by the Lord that matters.

It is possible to overquantify the self: 'An obsession with self-quantification and self-monitoring has the potential for individuals to become hypochondriacs, or more likely, hyper anxious' (Combs and Barham 2016, p. 70). Any notion of *perfect* health is a misnomer, for there is always something wrong with or inadequate about one's body or indeed one's spiritual life. It is, however, only some forms and/or degrees of abnormality that should be of concern. As the professor of medicine Gilbert Welch has warned, if we monitor ourselves closely enough we are bound to find something 'wrong' with us; 'abnormality is normal' (quoted in Bowden 2012).

There are indeed long-standing Christian traditions of self-examination from, among others, Ignatius of Loyola or the Wesleys, founders of Methodism. However, while there is value in monitoring one's spiritual life, this can degrade: 'An unhealthy use of religion can deflect a troubled individual away from the authentic source of their distress into a whirlwind of "religiosity" that defends and reinforces the pathology' (Watts et al. 2002, p. 61). This may develop into 'religious addiction' in which there is a negative impact on people's social relations: 'The person becomes obsessed and single minded. The religiosity is negative and depressing'

(T. Doyle, quoted in C. Z. Taylor 2002, p. 294). In order to avoid pain, a person might feel better by constructing an identity that they esteem, but do so by adhering to rigid and closely self-monitored practices (Vander-heyden 1999, p. 294).

The vain prayer?

Pope Francis makes a crucial distinction between vigilance and vanity towards one's spiritual condition. Checking oneself about being diligent to end the day before the Lord in reflection is to be diligent. Similarly, being sufficiently self-aware to recognize one's need of help when struggling is important. Francis retells a warning from the early centuries of Christianity:

> The Desert Monks say that vanity is like an onion: when you pick up an onion, and begin to peel it; and you feel vain, you begin to peel away your vanity. And you go, and go, to another layer, and another, and another, and another … and ultimately you arrive at … nothing. 'Ah, thank God, I've peeled the onion, I've peeled away my vanity.' Do this, and you'll smell like an onion! (Francis 2014)

It is appreciating the nature of the qualified (rather than just quantified) self that assumes importance here. Following Aquinas, John-Mark Miravelle notes how 'Vanity, like every sin, flows from pride, but vanity is specified by being directed to the praise or good estimation of others' (Miravelle 2017, p. 170). In a twenty-first-century world of banal self-promotion via social networking platforms, Miravelle poses the challenge acutely: 'The virtuous evaluation of an act or a resolution does not involve asking, "Will I be admired for this?" but instead "Is this admirable?"' (Miravelle 2017, p. 172).

The common self-gaze

Uncovering tracks is a dimension of the common good when data is being used for environmental protection, health care and other benefits such as traffic management. The common good does not operate apart from the market but is not to be subsumed under economic relations. Civil society is important and some behavioural surplus contributes to the common good. A difficulty arises where self-quantification is so shaped by social imaginaries that individuals and whole communities of users are badly distorted in their expectations of self, and of others. An ideal vision of activity, health, body and spirituality can be projected and absorbed uncritically. This is a negative form of a collective gaze, whereas the common gaze attends to the flourishing of all, giving primary attention to those marginalized or disadvantaged.

Betting on our future is problematic when it is not clear who 'our' is in each case. Whose future is surveillance capitalism betting on at any given time? Is it for all or for the already privileged? Such questions will return in the next chapter when we consider algorithmic oppression. The ideal optimized self may not be obtainable by those on limited incomes and so they are excluded. Furthermore, the ideal self might simply be a projection by businesses of the ideal consumer against which others are judged and found wanting; the inadequate or 'flawed' consumer (Bauman 1990). A governed self within the common good is arguably prone to self-obsession and distorting self-image in the light of others' self-quantifying. How does this affect one's sense of community beyond those in whom one sees one's reflection? Looking outwards may be the case, but only to see oneself reflected, rather than looking at others for their needs. One looks through others at oneself in a culture of competition rather than love.

When it is the act that counts, quantifying may incentivize participation in social activities but it may be that self-quantification deflects action from the common good in favour of individual self-optimization. In other words, poor health indicators or unachieved professional or social goals are taken to be the result of bad individual choices perhaps related to non-aspirational cultural values. Self-quantification serves an ideological function in deflecting attention from systemic inequalities. On the other hand, building communities of shared self-quantification identities may well enhance the common good because people need a local sense of engagement with others. The general common good is too distant a concept to motivate easily.

The common gaze contributes to problematizing the monetizing of all behaviour whenever possible. It challenges the construction of the 'common' as co-prosumers in a frantic seduction into informational capitalism. Minds are being colonized by surveillance capitalists who redefine who matters and gets to quantify. This raises the significant question from Revelation about entangling in luxury, imperial power and religious cults and commitments. These are antithetical to the common good – but do not necessitate sectarian withdrawal given the positive evaluation of merchants in other biblical texts. Nevertheless, there remains a question over the cult of self-optimization when it turns attention away from the common good and the value of sacrificing for others.

To protect the logic of gift requires a degree of self-assurance and strong identity not to fear the giving of oneself. The microcosm of Christian spiritual apps, and their tendencies good and bad, highlights broader cultural trends. Solidarity and grace might be personal aims but end up hindered by scrupulosity in the midst of being nudged to do the good thing; the ambiguity and ambivalence of the process of motivation being themselves a challenge to solidarity. We are left with the question of how being cultivated in vanity can advance the common good when what is required is authentic validation in order to contribute to the common good. While gift calls for self-sacrifice, this is not self-abnegation. Self-quantification has the potential to improve the well-being of those who choose to give of themselves for others. Wenceslas, we should remember, was fit enough to be out in freezing temperatures caring for his subjects.

5

Identification: Algorithms of Oppression and Liberation

Traced, tracked, delivered, I'm yours

Around 1 million Muslim Uyghurs have been identified as a threat and detained by the Chinese state. The Integrated Joint Operations Platform draws data from multiple digital sources as well as reports from local officials who spot unusual activity during home visits (Human Rights Watch 2018). Residents in the Xinjiang region, in which the Uyghurs are the largest ethnic group, outnumbering the national-majority Han Chinese (Toops 2016), are required to install software that scans for Islamic key-words and images, and sharing this material may well result in detention (Lucas and Feng 2018). According to one Uyghur woman who was held in a detention centre in Hotan in 2016, attending a mosque on a day other than a Friday identifies one as a religious extremist (Roberts 2018, p. 245). 'Visitors' management systems' operate in access-controlled communities in conjunction with the tracking of car licence plates and citizen ID card numbers (Human Rights Watch 2018). The state, here, claims liberation from internal terrorist threat and the freedom provided for those re-educated from extremist religion. This comes at the cost to the Uyghurs, who are to accept oppression.

Automated facial recognition within the UK passport system proves disproportionately challenging for people with either very dark or very light skin as the photo checking technology, although acknowledged to be problematic in this regard, was nevertheless deemed sufficiently well performing to be deployed (Vaughan 2019). Two of the latest algorithms from a company whose facial recognition software is in use by police in the USA, Australia and France was found by the National Institute of Standards and Technology in 2017 to be 'significantly more likely to mix up black women's faces than those of white women, or black or white men'; it was defended by the company as a step in the development of a yet-to-be commercially released product (Simonite 2019). Being correctly identified on a non-biased basis is crucial not only for public confidence in security systems but as a matter of justice, lest existing social prejudices are reinforced under the guise of technical objectivity. If biometric data from an insufficiently diverse cross-section of society is used in training algorithms then disparities in performance come as little of a surprise (Fussey and Murray 2019, p. 22). Citizens are liberated in moving across international borders, kept safer from actors intent on harm. At the same time, innocent travellers, including some citizens, are discriminated against, finding their passage disrupted.

The 'sharing economy' relies on data to match offers and requests, to monitor behaviour (of good and bad participants) and to monetize not only the sharers' offers but the platform on which these can be disseminated. Giana Eckhardt and Fleura Bardhi argue convincingly that this popular term, sharing, is a misnomer because when a company is an intermediary between people who do not know one another this is not sharing as hitherto understood. Instead we ought to talk about 'an access economy' (Eckhardt and Bardhi 2015). Discrimination in the formal housing rental market may be illegal but is found to be present in this corner of the sharing economy, namely in users of Airbnb. As a host I can accept or reject a guest – but before I make that decision I can see their name and perhaps a photograph (as at June 2020 guests are expected but not required to upload a photograph as a step in their booking process (Airbnb 2020)). Built into the platform is the option for me to get some sense of who this person seems to be, and if I am content to admit them to my property. In a July 2015 study of Airbnb in the USA (focused on Baltimore, Dallas, Los Angeles, St Louis and Washington DC), researchers found discrimination against distinctively African American names:

> African American guests received a positive response roughly 42 percent of the time, compared to roughly 50 percent for white guests. This 8 percentage point (roughly 16 percent) penalty for African American guests is particularly noteworthy when compared to the discrimination-free setting of competing short-term accommodation platforms such as Expedia. The penalty is consistent with the racial gap found in contexts ranging from labour markets to online lending to classified ads to taxi-cabs. (Edelman et al. 2017, p. 2)

This is not to be interpreted as simply white landlords discriminating against African Americans because African American hosts also discriminate against African Americans. As the researchers note, their findings cannot isolate the discrimination as based on race, socio-economic status or a combination of these two (Edelman et al. 2017, p. 17). The study did, however, find that discrimination was concentrated among hosts who, according to their review history on the Airbnb platform, had not had any African American guests before. The sharing economy liberates hosts to raise money from their property and feel relatively safe by filtering their guests in advance. Guests are liberated from paying higher charges for hotel accommodation but with the hidden cost of possible discrimination.

A judge preparing to sentence a convicted felon may have more than guidance notes and her years of experience on the bench to rely upon. She may be able to draw on software that assesses the risk of recidivism by the individual in the dock. But the judge may be wary if the risk factors comprising the algorithm are not disclosed because of commercial sensitivities around a proprietary product. Furthermore, if this software is found to be little better than guesswork, as is claimed to be the case for one particular US system (Dressel and Farid 2018), it is difficult to shake off concerns around inherent gender and/or racial biases. By way of contrast, an open approach to disclosing the algorithm's risk factors is taken in other systems, such as PSA-Court (PSA 2020). Yet finding a way of reducing the number of people entering the judicial system, and time and again re-entering it, would go some way towards neutralizing the effect of prison as a college in which to learn criminality. In the UK, the Durham Constabulary developed a Harm Assessment Risk Tool in 2015/16 to help custody officers make the often difficult call on whether or not to charge individuals at moderate risk of recidivism. But as the Law Society reported in 2019:

> algorithmic systems need not be heavily biased in order to have a problematic effect. Even systems containing small biases are likely to result in cumulative disadvantage as their impact is compounded by the number of times and junctures where an individual or a community is impacted by one or more problematic systems. (Law Society 2019, p. 18)

To put this another way, one very slightly out-of-tune instrument in a large orchestra may have minimal effect on all but a very few of the members of the audience. Should many instruments go out of tune (even just by a little), the later part of the performance will be seriously marred. Someone in the criminal justice system might also be receiving welfare benefits, perhaps being considered for a local council house allocation, and perhaps appear in school disciplinary records or attainment monitoring processes. Any even small bias in those systems could fall below their respective thresholds but cumulatively amount to considerable injustice for a specific individual. People caught up in the criminal justice system might be offered liberation from the biases of individual custody officers and judges only to find that prejudices (minor as some might be when considered within separate processes) are coded (perhaps unconsciously) into software purporting to be objective.

Mapping cases of cholera in early nineteenth-century London was a major breakthrough in public health, which identified not only existing sufferers but those seemingly most at risk and, significantly, the reason why. In this case it was a contaminated street water pump in Broad Street in 1854. In the event of a contagious disease, such as Covid-19 and the pandemic that commenced in 2020, extensive mining of multiple sources of data is integral both to identifying those who are carriers and developing vaccines and treatments. 'Contact tracing' enters the everyday polite vocabulary of nations across the globe, whereas it was previously associated with sexually transmitted diseases and stigmatization. To poorly informed and already racially prejudiced individuals, 'appearing Asian' is a proxy for being contagious and, in some people's eyes, guilty by association for the appearance of the virus in the first place. The identification of a virus and the identification of a person carrying the virus are two overlapping but distinct discourses, neither occurring separately from broader social attitudes. To be designated a spreader or even a super-spreader is a social, not merely a medical, diagnosis. The process that can save lives can also blight lives.

Identification occurs not only in relation to social but also political attitudes. It would seem uncontroversial to work through a check list on an Indicator of Relative Need (as is used by Public Health Scotland) that identifies people requiring assistance with eating, cooking, their mobility, toileting and dressing, in conjunction with questions about someone's mental well-being (Public Health Scotland 2020). However, thresholds of relative need are judgements. Assessments by the UK Department for Work and Pensions have proved highly controversial, especially when undertaken on sick and emotionally vulnerable people. For example, advice from Citizens Advice about how to answer questions in an Employment and Support Allowance assessment points to a system stacked against the client:

> They might ask if you go shopping in a supermarket. Make it clear if you can't or need help doing this – otherwise they might assume you can walk around the supermarket on your own.
>
> They might ask how long you've been sitting in the waiting room before the assessment. If you say 'Half an hour', they'll make a note that you can sit on an ordinary chair for at least 30 minutes. Tell them if you found it uncomfortable or needed to get up and walk around because you couldn't sit for that long. (Citizens Advice 2020)

Answering honestly is insufficient for justice; providing unsought-for clarifications to ensure a just interpretation demands a high level of knowledge of the system as well as considerable mental acuity during a stressful interview. Standardized questions might give the appearance of equity but be anything but equitable. To be identified as being in need – or in less need – takes place in a political context:

> The turn to scoring systems and predictive analytics is being fuelled by an austerity context in which local councils have faced substantial cuts. While these technologies are being implemented as 'smart' and effective solutions for better service provision, they are introduced in the context of service reduction. (Dencik et al. 2019, p. 19)

Liberation from disease and unmet care needs is offered, as is freedom for the public purse from false claimants. Yet the system bears down upon some of the most vulnerable of honest claimants.

In this chapter we explore the discrimination that arises when identification is achieved by means of algorithmic classification and sorting. The empirical work of Safiya Umoja Noble and Virginia Eubanks raises concerns over significant bias against some groups of people that requires surveillance of surveillance if there is to be any likelihood of fair outcomes. Our theological critique takes the boundary-challenging impetus of radical biblical hermeneutics as a starting point to draw a functional parallel between ancient religious notions of ritual and twenty-first-century classifications, both seeking to impose order on a threatening environment. Jesus' reframing of holiness as compassion, proposed by Marcus Borg, offers possibilities of probing for what purpose current digital classifications, often using proxy values to infer characteristics, might be liberated. Relying on the concept of a compassionate gaze is confronted by the failure of the divine gaze of care and covenantal commitment to Jews during their persecution by the Nazis. This requires us to explore how a compassionate gaze might be a theologically informed awareness of the brutalities and lives taken in the Holocaust. Melissa Raphael's Jewish feminist theology of Shekhinah moves us forward, along with Mayra Rivera's Christian post-colonial theology of relational transcendence. We are then able to refine both the divine gaze and the common gaze as a wounded gaze.

Algorithmic oppression

To be made readable in order that one can be sorted into classifications is a prerequisite of admission to particular spaces as well as reception of benefits. Being searched *for* within ranking systems reveals how these are non-innocent, and one can find oneself dismissed as, in effect, collateral damage. Algorithms can oppress, but there may be ways they have a liberative potential too.

Legible identification

Identification and identity are related but distinct concepts, loosely so in common usage. ID cards are not 'identity cards' but 'identification cards'. Few people ever experience 'identity theft' but many have the identifying credentials used to operate their bank account or use their credit card stolen and used for fraudulent withdrawals or purchases. Some usage is so embedded in everyday language that it takes precedent over tighter definitions. It is futile to contend against the use of the term 'mistaken identity' when it properly ought to be referred to as 'mistaken identification'. Identity is both defined by self and by others, with a dimension of commonality and individuation (Raab 2009, p. 227). I know who I am and others know me because I have characteristics that I share with various categories of people, and it is within those relationships that I come to a sense of self, almost certainly unique among the 108,760,543,791 who have ever been born (the Population Research Bureau's astonishingly precise figure is, as they readily admit, part science and part art calculation; Kaneda and Haub 2020). It would take more than the mere loss of an ID card from me to experience what in popular parlance we might call 'a loss of my sense of identity'.

   'Identification' is readily to be understood as a means of establishing that *this* is the person for whom we are looking: 'the process that separates out and reliably marks a single, unique, individual' (Gandy Jr 2012, p. 126). Hence, what the police hold is strictly speaking an *identification* and not an *identity* parade. However, even that process is not yet complete because it will be necessary to ascertain who the identified suspect is in terms of their unique criminal record, as well as any parenting, financial and other legal responsibilities. So the question moves from, 'Did this person commit this crime?' to include '*Who* is this person?'

   Identification is necessary for determining someone's eligibility and is closely connected to a person's legibility (Lyon 2009, pp. 46–7). To be legible is to be readable, meaning in this context machine-readable by the state or other authorities. It is not enough to ascertain that a citizen is aged over 65 years and therefore entitled to a particular concessionary rate on, for example, public transport. In an effort to anticipate demand for council services, public authorities seek to know each person's broader needs and possibly their patterns of behaviour; the benefit to the client is a more personalized, citizen-centred range of services (Raab 2009, p. 234). It is all well and good to identify the individual needs of a category of people when this is based on their actual characteristics. Those lacking fluency in spoken and written English require information leaflets in an accessible language. In such a case this distributive collective property pertains to all the members of this category. If a need or trait is inferred on statistical probability calculated across a variety of characteristics, then such non-distributive collective properties carry the possibilities of unfair and inequitable actions for particular individuals (Raab 2009, p. 240, citing Vedder 1995, pp. 9–11). It is non-distributive collective properties that are the particular focus of critics such as Cathy O'Neil, to whom we shortly turn our attention.

Such algorithmic social sorting is not so much about *identification* as it is *classification*. If identification is to know who you are, classification is interested in *what* you are by means of 'the simultaneous maximization of similarities and differences within and between analytically determined groups' (Gandy Jr 2012, p. 126). When we considered the use of algorithms to influence or hack democracy we saw the intention to shape a sufficient number of people's behaviour in favour of one candidate rather than another. In this chapter our interest is the angle of identifying those who are, or are not, entitled to access particular services or locations. As deeply manipulated as they may or may not be, it is influence that is brought to bear upon citizens and within which they need to make their democratic decision. Hacking democracy, in the facets we explored, has not been about denying an individual their vote, although voter suppression, gerrymandering of electoral district/ward boundaries and tampering with electronic voting equipment are not inconsequential matters. When we turn attention to identification this is the realm of determining access or exclusion from state (but also in some cases commercial) provision. It is the world of statistical discrimination, 'a decision to exclude or deny opportunity to an individual on the basis of the attributes of the group to which he or she is assumed to belong' (Gandy Jr 2012, p. 126).

The issue becomes acute when someone seeks to cross a border – which for some will be an international border, but for many more, and much more frequently, will be a boundary that delimits access to, for example, a particular welfare service, parts of a city or preferential commercial discounts. In the overlapping of multiple domains of actual and potential discrimination, individuals can experience harsh consequences of their intersectionality. Gloria Anzaldúa's notion of borderlands becomes particularly important in this respect. She takes the US–Mexico border as a metaphor for diverse forms of crossings and, significantly, broadens our perspective to include what it can mean to live in borderlands, and not only what the challenges of actually crossing a border entail. So it is important to attend to the experience of statistical discrimination as it moves to and fro between identification and classification at the crossing points where entitlement is granted or denied, but also to what it means to live in the borderlands (metaphorical and material) of these systems. For, as Anzaldúa asserts:

> living in the borderlands produces knowledge by being within a system whilst also retaining the knowledge of an outsider who comes from outside the system ... Because Borderlands Theory allows for the articulation of multiple oppressions and forms of resistance to these oppressions, it has produced rich and unique analyses in various academic fields. (Anzaldúa 2012, p. 7)

Classification often returns to identification; being assigned to a group can then require someone to prove that it is indeed they and not another person who is making a request for access to what they have been deemed to be entitled. Ms Jane Smith may be eligible for an income support benefit, but sitting across from an assessor, Jane must still be able to show that she is this woman. Having that name will scarcely be adequate, so Jane may have to rely on digital forms of identification in order to lay claim on what she has been classified to receive. The challenge facing her may be greater should she have to identify herself in a wholly digital environment. Jane's whole life is mired in bureaucratic surveillance.

Googled discrimination

In her book *Algorithms of Oppression*, Safiya Umoja Noble looks deeply into search engines and finds systemic discrimination of marginalized groups, 'who are problematically represented in erroneous, stereotypical, or even pornographic ways in search engines and who have also struggled for nonstereotypical or nonracist and nonsexist depictions in the media and in libraries' (Noble 2018, p. 10). A Google search is not, even after refinements of algorithms in recent years, according to Noble, an innocent action that somehow lifts the users out of biases and misrepresentations. Black girls searching for information about themselves can receive results heavily skewed towards sexual objectification or assumptions of a criminal history despite not entering those or associated terms in the Google search box (Noble 2018, pp. 80–1). Such misrepresentation and hyper-sexualization reflects contemporary life in America and its history of racial discrimination. As part of her research in April 2016, Noble finds that Google was returning images of women, and mostly of white women, in response to the search term 'nurse' (Noble 2018, p. 83).

In the early days of our use of the internet many of us likely rather naively assumed that we were being presented with a straightforward index of pages of content that matched the term we had entered into the 'search' box. That might have been the case when I recall my first forays into cyberspace within the closed world of CompuServe in 1993 or thereabouts. One or two magazine publishers had constructed pages of content hosted within the CompuServe system. Accessing these did not initially involve access to the World Wide Web. The day when CompuServe opened up access to the internet as a whole was exciting, with the prospect that the world of knowledge was now my oyster. At first, I perceived this as being admitted to a library that provided a catalogue of items that I could instantly retrieve (although given the limitations of a dial-up 512k modem, it was much less than 'instant').

It took a little while to appreciate that a search engine was not presenting a mere index but a *ranked* index. This difference was to become increasingly significant as the dominance of Google generated the verb 'to google'. Although 'to google' is used in common speech to mean 'to search the internet', this is more than a little misleading. To google is to request a ranked list of results. An oversimplistic analogy will make the point.

My favourite Edinburgh gelato shop has eight ice-cream-making bowls in its counter-top display. A few regular flavours are available each Sunday when I visit: vanilla and dark chocolate. Other flavours are rotated on what seems to me to be a random basis. Whisky, Ferrero Rocher and pineapple sorbet are some that make an irregular appearance. Just inside the door is a small chalkboard listing the day's flavours. I am presented with an index in no particular order. A ranked index of gelato would be rather different and appear on a digital board. The supplier of strawberries might have paid to have her flavour at the top of the list. The scrupulous gelato maker would put a little pound sign against 'strawberry (£)' to alert me to this sponsored flavour. Next on the list might be the day's favourite flavour based on the sales that morning. Being a regular customer (I will admit to weekly), the staff know what I have liked in the past and a bit about my typically Scottish sweet tooth.

So to help me choose the flavours at numbers 3 and 4 on the list, the servers are nudging me towards mint or Ferrero Rocher. Am I going to go with today's most bought? Even if I do not, I am still influenced by knowing what is most popular.

Of course, the flavour that is 'most bought' might be tripe and onions; a bizarre flavour that might have appealed to a flurry of adventurous gelato-lovers that morning – but which they all concluded they would never, ever choose again. What is the most selected over a specific period of time may not be in any sense the 'favourite' flavour – at least in the sense in which we typically mean favourite.

I make my choice – two scoops: one of lemon cheesecake and one of vanilla. The next customer sees a different ranked list of the eight options. The sponsored one, 'strawberry (£)', is still at the top but he has made different choices in the past so sees banana sorbet as number 3.

This frivolous and partly fictitious example points to a deeper and more serious issue of ranked indices:

> information monopolies such as Google have the ability to prioritize web search results on the basis of a variety of topics, such as promoting their own business interests over those of competitors or smaller companies that are less profitable advertising clients than larger multinational cooperations are. (Noble 2018, p. 24)

When this overlies historical misrepresentations of race and gender, the challenges become those of ownership over identity markers and possibilities of reclamation at both individual and community level (Noble 2018, p. 131). Such redress and reorientation are acutely difficult in the USA because 'information practices are situated under the auspices of free speech and protected corporate speech, rather than being posited as an information resource that is working in the public domain, much like a library' (Noble 2018, p. 143). This is the politics of librarianship for, as has been the case in analogue classification systems, 'bibliographic and naming controls are central to making knowledge discoverable' (Noble 2018, p. 144). Noble's call is for 'public search engine alternatives, united with public-interest journalism and librarianship, to ensure that the public has access to the highest quality information available' (Noble 2018, p. 152); what we might call searching for the common good.

Sorted entitlement

What if the situation is not my being nudged towards a particular flavour in a gelato shop but access to a place on a waiting list for housing? The social work department might be making decisions about child protection cases, using algorithms in an automated or semi-automated system. Allocating welfare and medical aid involves weighing up complex factors. Being able to reduce staff costs at the same time as claiming impartiality is attractive to some politicians. Algorithmic decision-making systems might be an attractive proposition, especially if marketed astutely by the private companies developing them. From her ethnographic study of the USA, Virginia Eubanks publishes her *Automating Inequality* (Eubanks 2017).

Looking at public assistance programmes, such as Medicaid in Indiana, homeless services in Los Angeles and child welfare in Allegheny County, Pennsylvania, Eubanks finds people facing 'life-threatening consequences' of digital poverty management at the same time as many being discouraged by automated eligibility systems from claiming what they need not just to thrive but to survive (Eubanks 2017, p. 11). She finds continuity with historical practices of governing people in poverty in the political choices made in deploying digital systems:

> The advocates of automated and algorithmic approaches to public services often describe the new generation of digital tools as 'disruptive.' They tell us that big data shakes up hidebound bureaucracies, stimulates innovative solutions, and increases transparency. But when we focus on programs specifically targeted at poor and working-class people, the new regime of data analytics is more evolution than revolution. It is simply an expansion and continuation of moralistic and punitive poverty management strategies that have been with us since the 1820s. (Eubanks 2017, p. 37)

This is by no means a phenomenon limited to the USA. The Poor Law reforms of 1834 in the UK established residence in workhouses as a mandatory condition of receiving support. Control of the bodies of people in poverty was deemed crucial to responding to industrialization and urbanization as these impacted upon those at the bottom of the socio-economic ladder. Eubanks's point is that political rhetoric to 'shake up' the welfare system is highly disruptive to recipients, to whom little regard is paid. Identification and classification issues became critical in Indiana's 2007 shift to an automated welfare eligibility system. Documents, such as drivers' licences, social security cards and other supporting evidence, had to be faxed to a central document processing centre and in December 2007 'just over 11,000 documents were unindexed. By February 2009, nearly 283,000 documents had disappeared' (Eubanks 2017, p. 50). Teething problems with any new system might be expected but Eubanks's case study sounds remarkably familiar to those who have followed the saga of the UK's Department of Welfare and Pensions assessment 'scandals' (Butler 2018). A switch to automation often involves inflexible rules that interpret 'any deviation from the newly rigid application process, no matter how inconsequential or inadvertent, as an active refusal to cooperate' (Eubanks 2017, p. 51).

In her study of how homeless people in downtown Los Angeles were allocated homes in an initiative in 2013, Eubanks finds that although the intention was to address a mismatch between what was done for the chronically (rather than crisis) homeless it became not so much a want of data but a collision with political obstacles that compounded people's problems. The county used VI-SPDAT (Vulnerability Index – Service Prioritization Decision Assistance Tool) to gather information from clients. This tool included very intimate questions, such as, 'Do you ever do things that may be considered to be risky like exchange sex for money, run drugs for someone, have unprotected sex with someone you don't know, share a needle or anything like that?' (Eubanks 2017, p. 93). Even if California is ramping up its data protection regulations (not so for many other US states), the deeper issue is the collection of such information that readily 'equates poverty and homelessness with criminality' (Eubanks 2017, p. 116). Such an equation rests upon some fundamental political assumptions about the causes of homelessness:

> If homelessness is inevitable – like a disease or a natural disaster – then it is perfectly reasonable to use triage-oriented solutions that prioritize in-house people for a chance at limited house resources. But if homelessness is a human tragedy created by policy decision and professional middle-class apathy, coordinated entry allows us to distance ourselves from the human impacts of our choice to not act decisively. As a system of moral valuation, coordinated entry is a machine for producing rationalization, for helping us convince ourselves that only the most deserving people are getting help. Those judged 'too risky' are coded for criminalization. Those who fall through the cracks face prisons, institutions, or death. (Eubanks 2017, p. 123)

This is not to deny that some individuals act irresponsibly; the point is that how we frame a social issue such as homelessness legitimates (at least among those not immediately affected) a deeply intrusive gaze. It is as if a flood is heard approaching a village. The wealthy have transport by which to quickly evacuate and implement a triage system to grab a few others deemed most worthy of rescue. But this flood has come because of negligence by the owners of a dam miles up the valley who took short-term decisions at the expense of maintenance of the dam wall. How we understand social injustice determines the algorithmic sorting we rationalize as our requirement of those in most need; a preferential optic for those who are poor, or not, confronts everyone.

Collateral damage

Frank Pasquale is exercised about the privileging of the 'privacy' of corporations as to the coding of algorithmic decision-making in contrast to those companies' relative lack of attention to the privacy of the public: 'The law, so aggressively protective of secrecy in the world of commerce, is increasingly silent when it comes to the privacy of persons' (Pasquale 2015, p. 3). This would be concerning enough but considerable (often poorly considered) power resides in the hands of the proprietors of black-boxed decision-making systems. There are, according to Pasquale, secret judgements made by software: 'It matters because authority is increasingly expressed algorithmically. Decisions that used to be based on human reflection are now made automatically' (Pasquale 2015, p. 8). How people are perceived by others, their trustworthiness, probity, in effect their character, is at stake because 'reputation is determined by secret algorithms processing inaccessible data' (Pasquale 2015, p. 14).

Pasquale's principal point is the lack of accountability in how algorithmic decision-making systems are constructed. While once we might have been riled at decisions made in board rooms 'behind closed doors' or perhaps on the fairways of prestigious and exclusive golf courses, 'Black boxes embody a paradox of the so-called information age: Data is becoming staggering in its breadth and depth, yet often the information most important to us is out of our reach, available only to insiders' (Pasquale 2015, p. 191). Pasquale turns to Pope Francis's reminder, in *Evangelii gaudium*, of the purpose of material goods: 'Rather than contort ourselves to fit "an impersonal economy lacking a truly human purpose," we might ask how institutions could be reshaped to meet higher ends than shareholder value' (Pasquale 2015, p. 218, quoting Francis 2013, §55).

Where data protection is weak (in failing to limit the use of data to the purpose for which consent is granted), Pasquale identifies a problematic move from record to reputation (Pasquale 2015, p. 27). Using a passing reference in a news report, he observes a potential, hidden penalty:

we already know that at least one credit card company pays attention to certain mental health events, like going to marriage counseling. When statistics imply that couples in counseling are more likely to divorce than couples who aren't, counseling becomes a 'signal' that that marital discord may be about to spill over into financial distress. (Pasquale 2015, p. 31)

Pasquale's point here is particularly apposite because being categorized is performative (if not actually going as far as being a self-fulfilling prophecy): 'Unlike the engineer, whose studies do nothing to the bridges she examines, a credit scoring system *increases the chance* of a consumer defaulting once it labels him a risk and prices a loan accordingly' (Pasquale 2015, p. 41). The performativity of algorithmic identification makes the need for transparent and accountable modelling all the more important despite industry claims for commercial secrecy.

Cathy O'Neil has coined the term 'weapons of math destruction' to refer to algorithmic sorting that often has devastating effects on actual (rather than statistically modelled) people, leaving them as 'collateral damage' (O'Neil 2016, p. 146). Her opening example demonstrates the key points of her argument. In 2009, Washington DC implements an assessment tool (IMPACT), ostensibly to weed out low-performing teachers (O'Neil 2016, pp. 5–11). The challenge is to quantify the value each teacher contributes to the raising or lowering of students' progress. At the heart of such a model lies the assumption that if a student is not learning enough it is because their teachers are not doing a good enough job. Given that the factors influencing a student's learning are multiple and many of those not quantifiable, this seems like a fool's errand. The district fired 206 teachers at the end of the school year 2009–10. O'Neil's contention is that some of those fired are not bad teachers but victims of the poor use of a statistical data-analysis tool. To begin with, making a deduction based on the results of a class of 25 or so students in one year is a fundamental error akin to believing that because there might be 10 per cent of the population who enjoy curried avocado, then in your social group of 20, two of your friends must like that dish. Such probabilities apply only to very large numbers, not small groups.

Significant, in O'Neil's view, is the failure of the school district to escape a feedback loop in which reality is defined and results used to support that prior definition: 'instead of search for the truth, the score comes to embody it' (O'Neil 2016, p. 7). Other injustices, argues O'Neil, arise when people are assigned to a wrong category by mistake, with little if any opportunity for this to be corrected. This can be devastating when it is one's credit score that, derived partly from proxy values, impacts on borrowing rates. The choice of which values to use as proxies is fraught with complex, but unacknowledged, difficulties; educational excellence is one of those important to institutions seeking national reputation. Happiness, confidence and friendship are not reducible to numerical values (despite some attempts) and proxies such as acceptance and graduation rates or alumni giving are poor substitutes. However, as O'Neil observes, it is easier to game the model 'because proxies are easier to manipulate than the complicated reality they represent' (O'Neil 2016, p. 55).

If we consider graduate income levels a few years after leaving a university course in theology compared to those of alumni of another humanities degree, there might be considerable disparity. Many more theology students might make vocational choices to serve religious communities or charitable agencies that pay significantly less than other sectors. Where this outcome is part of a proxy for the department's 'value for money', theology is disadvantaged precisely because it is forming people by advocating values of self-sacrifice. It becomes a matter of how institutions – particularly public bodies – view those people who are the outliers in statistical modelling. Is being out of place on a graph tantamount to being collateral damage in probabilistic reasoning?

Surveillance of categorization

David Lyon talks about surveillance strategies having two faces – good and bad – at the same time (Lyon 2001, p. 3). This is highly apposite for considering identification via classification because, as we have seen so far, it is not difficult to find examples that not only limit people's life chances but do so in unfair and inequitable ways. Even under the most positive of circumstances the world is not our oyster, as if we can get anything we want from life. In Shakespeare's *The Merry Wives of Windsor* (from which the saying is usually misquoted), Falstaff refuses to lend Pistol money, so Pistol's retort is to see the abundant possibilities of life ahead of him that his skills (and his sword) will enable him to prise open.

As attractive as it might be to view the obstacles preventing us from achieving our ambitions as wholly external, even systemic, this is far from the case. We have aptitudes and dispositions as well as physical constitutions that vary considerably. None but a few can develop the artistry and skill to be a concert pianist or top-level athlete. Not everyone has the same intellectual capacity. My not being a concert pianist does not mark me out as being oppressed.

There are classifications into which we might be placed that are quite accurate in their account of *what* we are. However, it might be a relationship between this and other classifications that unfairly limits a person's choices. Noble's analysis alerts us to the need not only to have control over our classification – or least to be able to hold this classifying to account – but also to the positioning of an accurate classification *in relation* to other classifications. If a broader category privileges one or two sub-categories over others, this is entering the territory of oppression. Leaving a profession to be represented in a databank disproportionately by one ethnic group is to be complicit with a feedback loop that implicitly (if not always deliberately) shapes the broad category. (This is what probably lies behind Noble's discovery of Google Images returning pictures mostly of white women in a search for 'nurse' (Noble 2018, p. 81).) Liberation here means not only proportionate representation of categories but turning misrepresentation into consciousness-raising in which those advantaged and disadvantaged re-examine not only expectations but material outcomes. Surveillance *of* categorization becomes thereby a tool for liberation from the oppression that is instantiated in that very categorization.

This requires reframing categorization and identification not merely as data-protection or privacy issues but as social justice and civil rights matters. To be coded for criminalization or any other form of failure is a systemic injustice, not excused as collateral damage from an otherwise valuable apparatus. It is not a question of how to be liberated *from* the performativity of algorithms but how to be freed from the ways horizons are lowered. We might not be able to be whatever we want to be but the aim can be to free ourselves – and others – from having our sights and options inequitably and unjustly restricted. So in there being good and bad faces of algorithmic sorting, it is important to establish *for whom* it is good and bad; it will not be universal. It is ironic that categorization enables the identification of those for whom a system proves to be oppressive. How then do the biblical text and theological concerns help us to frame this issue of categorization from outside the technological paradigm that so engulfs us?

Identifying the righteous

A major challenge for a religion is how to identify who is 'doing it right', who is in the 'right place', and who are therefore the 'right' or 'righteous' ones. This becomes acute at boundaries, whether these are of tribes, communities or nowadays often groups sharing urban spaces. Who can move over a boundary that marks a special, sacred space is troublesome, and no less so when the boundaries are around moral and social norms. What happens at the edges of communities as they manage membership and entitlement to their religion's privileges can be reassuring for those firmly on the inside but deeply discomfiting for those whose status is marginal. Some people held at the margins choose, on the basis of their faith, to contest what insiders deem incontestable.

Defending and transgressing boundaries

Constructing and policing boundaries in religious life is problematic in the power this gives to leadership groups who are in a position to name the borders and doing so by claiming divine authority. Questions as to whose advantage and to whose detriment these boundaries are maintained are less often addressed – at least from *within* the borders. It is vital to recognize the value of challenging religious boundaries, especially when these are assigned divine sanction in Scripture. A hermeneutics of suspicion directs attention to boundaries and has been integral to liberation theologies. In terms of our preferential optic for those disadvantaged by digital classifications, it is important before moving into particular biblical passages, that we draw on models of interpretation that cast a suspicious gaze on how boundaries function not only for liberation but for oppression. Their contribution to destabilizing religious boundary maintenance helps underpin the challenge of the common gaze.

Black double-consciousness

The pioneering black Christian theologian W. E. B. Du Bois recognized, in 1926, a crucial step in liberation that remains crucial when slavery, post-slavery denial of many civil and economic rights, and enduring institutionalized white superiority are the context in which black Christians (and black people more widely in white-majority contexts) often continue to live. He describes being mentally subject to the categories imposed by others:

> this sense of always looking at one's self through the eyes of others, of measuring one's soul by the tape of a world that looks on in amused content and pity. One ever feels his two-ness, – an American, a Negro; two souls, two thoughts, two unreconciled strivings; two warring ideals in one dark body, whose dogged strength alone keeps it from being torn asunder. (Du Bois 1926, p. 3)

Anthony Reddie helpfully explains double-consciousness in more contemporary terms:

In the first instance there is the internalized vision held by Black people themselves, in which they see themselves in largely positive terms, as they attempt to construct an image for their self-determination in the world. This internalized vision is placed alongside the external world of White power and influence in which Black people have to deal with issues of degradation, demonization and dispossession. These two 'unreconciled strivings' have continued to fight their tumultuous struggle within the battlefield of the Black mind. (Reddie 2012, p. 36)

For Vincent Wimbush, placing African American experience in the foreground makes a difference to reading in three specific, interrelated ways. It means intentionally attending to how texts function for readers in the present. Interpreting a biblical text when one's day-to-day experience of life is that of 'struggle, conflict, resistance and hurt' generates interest less in a supposedly settled and universal meaning of a text than in its significance for one's circumstances (Wimbush 2000, p. 14).

James Cone founded black liberation theology with his *Black Theology and Black Power* (Cone 1969), followed by *A Black Theology of Liberation* (Cone 1990 [1970]) and *God of the Oppressed* (Cone 1977). For Cone, the sources and norms of black theology lie in black experience, history and culture together, in which God's self-revelation is manifested. Cone's paradigm is inseparable from his (and his black community's) interpreting of the biblical witness to the God of the Exodus and of Jesus Christ. For Cone, '*revelation is a black event* – it is what blacks are doing about their liberation' (Cone 1990 [1970], p. 30, emphasis in original). His work confronts the failure of the dominant, white theology to speak to the black struggle. Cone is aiming to expunge black Christians' internalized subservience to a Saviour who had been made in the image of whites and their control of the levers of political power. For Cone, 'black theology must realize that the white Jesus has no place in the black community, and it is our task to destroy him' (Cone 1990 [1970], p. 38). Such iconoclasm is necessary, in Cone's view, because the white God is 'an idol created by racists' (Cone 1990 [1970], p. 59). A necessary further step is black self-determination; black people speaking for black people because 'too many whites think they know how we feel about them' (Cone 1990 [1970], p. 62).

Kelly Brown Douglas, in her 2015 book *Stand Your Ground: Black Bodies and the Justice of God*, unpacks the construction of blackness itself as sin (K. B. Douglas 2015, p. 66). In her view this is a racialized version of natural law, which provides 'the sacred canopy for white mistreatment of black bodies' (K. B. Douglas 2015, p. 50). The black body is chattel. The way things are is falsely taken to be the way things are supposed to be, which is a fatal problem of natural law reasoning of this form. Black bodies are therefore constructed and perceived as a threat, not just as inferior (K. B. Douglas 2015, p. 68). Black people are thus guilty of trespassing into what is, in effect, white space – a space often heavily subject to surveillance by police, neighbourhood watch groups and armed vigilantes (K. B. Douglas 2015, p. 86).

Queerying abomination

Queer hermeneutics are also oppositional as an identitarian hermeneutic focusing on constructing and reconstructing gays' sense of self. This takes place particularly in the face of a hermeneutic of abomination, the interpretation of the biblical texts that have traditionally been deployed against homosexual people (e.g. Gen. 19.1–11; Lev. 18.22; Lev. 20.13). Robert Goss, in his groundbreaking book of 1993, tackles what for gay people are deemed to be 'texts of terror' and argues for 'deconstructing biblical terrorism' (Goss 1993, p. 97). In a parallel reconstructive move, Goss offers a queer reading that 'transforms texts into narratives of resistance, releasing powerful motivational elements in our struggle against homophobic oppression' (Goss 1993, p. 106). Here we have, in Jeremy Punt's terms, a hermeneutics of marginality (Punt 2008, p. 24.6). To be marginalized is to be acted upon by others, from the outside. On the other hand, marginality points to how a person may embrace this condition of being marginalized, exploiting it in creative ways, 'redrawing the boundaries, shifting centre and periphery' (Punt 2008, p. 24.6).

In his *Practicing Safer Texts*, Ken Stone links the function of rules about both sex and food in setting boundaries for a community. He pays particular attention to 'boundary anxiety' as the policing of boundaries by which a community constructs its identity, particularly as 'not-someone else'. Stone is against binary categorizations in general and how such strategies produce and reproduce inside and outside distinctions: 'the tendency to define an "inside" and an "outside" of identity by defining the Other on the basis of the Other's supposed negative practices – and, in the process, defining oneself by way of contrast – has extremely troubling consequences' (Stone 2005, p. 61). Not only is Stone interested, as we might expect, in Levitical laws but in a parallel strategy of the early Church as it deals with food laws as boundary-marking.

Bringing this insight into the modern world, Stone argues that the binary of public/private plays out in managing social relationships in which religion colludes by privatizing sexual relations, thereby contributing to domestic violence often hidden and excluded from public (i.e. legal) oversight. Stone makes the important point that boundaries operate rhetorically. If one can cast the other community in a particular light (as being in some specific way depraved) this is on the terms of one's own existing boundary and is a means of legitimating the strengthening of that boundary (see Stone 2005, p. 52). This might be alternatively framed as a form of arms race in which proliferation of weapons is deemed necessary in a cycle of ever-intensifying action-response. In reading queer hermeneutics we are looking for the ways it destabilizes boundaries or binary categorizations.

Unmasking colonial power

Being required to be legible at rhetorical boundaries is a demand to submit to surveillance according to categories, arguably made binary in order to ease identification and to quell the fears of those who sense losing their power to define. Post-colonial reading is another challenge to categorization by the powerful for their advantage and to the advantages of 'the natives'; 'need' and 'benefit' being decided by the colonialists, particularly (but by no means exclusively) of the nineteenth and early twentieth centuries. Neocolonialists in the form of global corporations and superpowers in the twenty-first century – those with their hands firmly on the levers of surveillance technology – understand the importance of imposing their own sense of superiority. Post-colonial reading confronts centuries of oppression, questioning how the 'benefits' of empire have been set by imperial actors:

> Colonial reading can be summed up as informed by theories concerning the innate superiority of Western culture, the Western male as subject, and the natives, heathens, women, blacks, indigenous people, as the Other, needing to be controlled and subjugated. It is based on the desire for power/domination. (Sugirtharajah 1998, p. 15)

People who are once-colonized take their place as those who craft their own history, tell their own story and resist criticism by the West of how they are constructing their own new identities. People in previously colonized areas of the world are 'unmasking the link between ideas and power which lies behind Western texts, theories, and learning' (Sugirtharajah 1999, p. 17). This may well take place in the face of *neo*colonialism in which economic, cultural or political power (rather than direct military intervention) is used by significantly larger states to maintain (or exert) influence over much smaller states. Sugirtharajah identifies three modes of interpretation with origins in the colonial era, to which post-colonialism stands as a contemporary response. Phase 1 in the nineteenth century was an 'orientalist' policy 'promoting and reviving India's ancient linguistic, philosophical and religious heritage' (Sugirtharajah 1999, p. 4). The result was a limited and ideological construction of the Indian tradition that 'equated India with Hindu-Aryan, privileged Sanskrit texts over vernacular, and negated the Indian native and folk traditions' (Sugirtharajah 1999, p. 8). Pioneered in the latter half of the nineteenth century, continuing into the 1950s and even appearing in the 1980s, a second, Anglicist, mode introduced Western intellectual and analytical tools to describe and shape the 'other'. The Anglicist mode is 'a strategic attempt to replace indigenous texts and learning with Western science and Western modes of thinking and to integrate the colonial into the culture of the colonizer' (Sugirtharajah 1999, p. 8).

Post-colonial studies place significant importance on reading (as well as writing and action) by subalterns. The interest is in how history might be written 'outside the historically dominant frameworks' that might be, in some post-colonial contexts, the framework not only of colonizers but of later nationalists who are the elite of their community post-colonialization (Gopal 2004, p. 139). Subalterns are 'the small voice of history', subordinates within the social and political system (Gopal 2004, p. 141). However, subalterns are not simply *any* oppressed other. Rather, as Homi Bhabha observes, the subaltern is in some ways necessary to her oppressor because it is in distancing himself from, and oppressing, the subaltern that the oppressor forms his self-identity (Bhabha 1995, p. 17).

This is important for confronting with the preferential option for those who are poor because it is to recognize that accepting categorization as 'poor' has the side effect of benefiting the powerful, who are thus able to distance themselves, claiming, '*we* are not like *them*'. Of course, being poor is not merely a categorization but an everyday experience of poverty – whether this is acknowledged by the rich or not. On the one hand, Elsa Tamez helpfully complicates the notion of oppressor/oppressed by drawing attention to the practice of despoliation. It is not simply that the poor are oppressed. Rather, through theft, oppressors impoverish others: 'the oppressed are therefore *those who have been impoverished*, for while the oppressor oppresses the poor because they are poor and powerless, the poor have become poor in the first place because they have been oppressed' (Tamez 1982, p. 7, emphasis in original). On the other hand, categorizing people as poor and expecting them to adopt this definition takes place in a complex matrix of power relations in which self-definition may be overridden by assigned-definition. It is a danger inherent in using such a hermeneutic – but a danger of which to be aware without dismissing the value of a preferential optic for those who are digitally poor.

Knowing your place

Actual places are where double-consciousness, like refusing to be subject to a hermeneutics of abomination, has to be practised. Intellectual and psychological effort is most certainly required but it is in terms of access to institutional buildings and their resources that the rubber hits the ground. The subaltern voice is not one reserved to public discussion but is engaged in public action. The 2020 #BlackLivesMatter destruction of statues of figures representing slavery and other racial oppression is a recent example. Identification is a process crucial for access to particular places. One can be found to be in the wrong place. One can be denied entry legitimately to a place to which one is not entitled access. One can be refused access illegitimately to a place that ought to be yours to enter. Identification is required to prove eligibility and appropriate presence as one of the 'right ones' in the 'right place'.

Identification is crucial in the birth narratives of both Moses and Jesus. Pharaoh orders the death of Hebrew male newborns but wily midwives subvert Moses' infanticide. Mary and Joseph flee with the infant Jesus to avoid the murderous threats of Herod, escaping his killing of male children in the vicinity of Bethlehem under the age of two years. Moses is recognized as the murderer of an Egyptian (Exod. 2.11–15) despite his thinking his attack had gone unnoticed. Crowds start to recognize Jesus, identifying him with various degrees of accuracy as a promised figure of salvation. Jesus is identified in the garden by Judas' kiss (Matt. 26.49; Mark 14.45; Luke 22.47–48). Jacob betrays his brother Esau by duplicitously manipulating their blind father into mis-identifying the one who rightly ought to receive the eldest son's blessing (Gen. 27).

The prophet Samuel conducts an identification parade, finally hearing the Lord's voice instructing him to anoint David as king in place of the rejected Saul (1 Sam. 16.1–13). Matthias, the replacement for Judas among the apostles, was identified by the casting of lots (Acts 1.26). Mundane and extraordinary techniques of identification operate side by side.

'Out of place' in Leviticus

As much as the narrative is driven by the exploits of key figures, the structuring of the cultic life of the people of the covenant is around a different form of identification. It was crucial to know what was clean and unclean and how to negotiate life around these categories. Classification, we might say, was integral to holiness.

Any animal that has divided hoofs and is cleft-footed and chews the cud – such you may eat. But among those that chew the cud or have divided hoofs, you shall not eat the following: the camel, for even though it chews the cud, it does not have divided hoofs; it is unclean for you. (Lev. 11.3–4)

The priest shall examine the disease on the skin of his body, and if the hair in the diseased area has turned white and the disease appears to be deeper than the skin of his body, it is a leprous disease; after the priest has examined him he shall pronounce him ceremonially unclean. (Lev. 13.3)

You shall not approach a woman to uncover her nakedness while she is in her menstrual uncleanness. You shall not have sexual relations with your kinsman's wife, and defile yourself with her. You shall not give any of your offspring to sacrifice them to Molech, and so profane the name of your God: I am the LORD. You shall not lie with a male as with a woman; it is an abomination. You shall not have sexual relations with any animal and defile yourself with it, nor shall any woman give herself to an animal to have sexual relations with it: it is perversion.

Do not defile yourselves in any of these ways, for by all these practices the nations I am casting out before you have defiled themselves. Thus the land became defiled; and I punished it for its iniquity, and the land vomited out its inhabitants. (Lev. 18.19–25)

In Leviticus, animals are classified according to their being clean or unclean. Certain skin conditions are classified as unclean or only requiring quarantine. Particular behaviours fall into a category of defilement beyond even the parameters of the covenant relationship. This classification legitimates the expropriation of the land of Israel's defeated enemies, who are vomited out of the land. We are interested in how not only human identification within classification is performed but how the divine gaze might be envisaged as involved in these processes.

The anthropologist Mary Douglas argued that purification should be seen as 'a positive effort to organise the environment' (M. Douglas 1966, p. 2). In countering that which 'offends against order' a community is 'reordering [its] environment, making it conform to an idea' (M. Douglas 1966, p. 2). In an observation that has strong resonances with our interest in categorization, Douglas proposed the further idea of holiness as completeness: 'holiness requires that individuals shall conform to the class to which they belong. And holiness requires that different classes of things shall not be confused' (M. Douglas 1966, p. 53). Douglas proposed that what we see in categorization of purity/defilement is an analogical mode of thought rather than the rational-instrumental mode that is generally more familiar to us in twenty-first-century paradigms (M. Douglas 2000, pp. 15–16).

The bodies of animals and humans, and the constructions in which sacred rituals are performed, are governed by rules that, as well as ordering the environment, are one of the principal forms in which thought about God and the world is undertaken: 'Leviticus presents its philosophical doctrines in the form of rules of behaviour. Its paradigm lesson about God and existence is enacted on the body of a sacrificial animal, or on the altar, or on the body of human person' (M. Douglas 2000, p. 39). It is not a matter of *how* sacrificing the correct animal in the proper way re-establishes or reinforces a community's relationship with God; that is the scientific rational-instrumental mode of enquiry. Rather, it is vital to know and be diligent in placing something in proper relation to other things. Otherwise there is the danger of contagion; sacred uncleanness is spread from one object to another.

This is dirt 'as matter out of place' (M. Douglas 2002 [1966], p. 44), and thus uncleanness must be treated as a matter of order (M. Douglas 2002 [1966], p. 50). To maintain or restore order one must know the classifications that are proper and against which an animal, bodily fluid or practice is out of place. When encountering an anomaly, one can ignore it, perceive it and condemn, or confront it and work it into a 'new pattern of reality' (M. Douglas 2002 [1966], p. 48). Douglas identifies a number of provisions in analogical thinking for dealing with what is identified as being out of place: (1) settle for one or other interpretation and thereby reduce ambiguity; (2) physically control it; (3) let the anomalies strengthen the definitions to which they do not conform; (4) label it dangerous; or (5) use it in ritual as a symbol to enrich meaning (M. Douglas 2002 [1966], pp. 48–9).

So from the examples we quoted from Leviticus we find the priest examining a skin condition to categorize it, requiring different responses (a better term than 'treatment' in this context). Clear control is attempted over the sexual practices of the community. Differentiating Israel from her neighbours' worship of Molech strengthens Israel's communal identity. Taboo sexual relationships are described as dangerous with reference to their consequences for the previous inhabitants of the land. It becomes the duty of the later prophets to incorporate the language of uncleanness to frame broader appeals for loyalty to the covenant.

Douglas's views change over her career and she makes considerable corrections to her earlier interpretation of Leviticus. In her preface to the 2002 edition of her classic *Purity and Danger*, she admits three mistakes:

(1) circularity 'supposing that a species must be anomalous before it was forbidden, and then setting up a search for its anomalous features' (M. Douglas 2002 [1966], p. xiv); (2) absence of any positive implications for the social system of those for whom the rules were made; (3) 'to have accepted unquestioningly that the rational, just, compassionate God of the Bible would ever be so inconsistent as to make abominable creatures' (M. Douglas 2002 [1966], p. xv). However, Douglas holds to her view that everyone finds dirt offensive, 'but what counts as dirt? It depends on the classifications in use' (M. Douglas 2002 [1966], p. xviii). The notion of contagion and dirt from her earlier work still stands, especially as our interest is not in establishing why particular animals (for example) are considered anomalous and others not. What is significant for our argument is the concept of things being in their proper place – in relation to other things – so that what is out of place is identified and dealt with. The cognitive practice of categorization imposes (a measure) of more order on a chaotic and threatening universe. This approach takes on particular significance at boundaries – instantiated in the design of the Temple envisaged in Ezekiel.

Mapping the place in Ezekiel

Then he brought me by way of the north gate to the front of the temple; and I looked, and lo! the glory of the LORD filled the temple of the LORD; and I fell upon my face. The LORD said to me: Mortal, mark well, look closely, and listen attentively to all that I shall tell you concerning all the ordinances of the temple of the LORD and all its laws; and mark well those who may be admitted to the temple and all those who are to be excluded from the sanctuary ...

Thus says the Lord GOD: No foreigner, uncircumcised in heart and flesh, of all the foreigners who are among the people of Israel, shall enter my sanctuary. But the Levites who went far from me, going astray from me after their idols when Israel went astray, shall bear their punishment. They shall be ministers in my sanctuary, having oversight at the gates of the temple, and serving in the temple; they shall slaughter the burnt-offering and the sacrifice for the people, and they shall attend on them and serve them ...

But the levitical priests, the descendants of Zadok, who kept the charge of my sanctuary when the people of Israel went astray from me, shall come near to me to minister to me; and they shall attend me to offer me the fat and the blood, says the Lord GOD. It is they who shall enter my sanctuary, it is they who shall approach my table, to minister to me, and they shall keep my charge. (Ezek. 44.4–5, 9–11, 15–16)

In a twenty-first-century workshop we would likely find an organizational structure presented in a chart looking somewhat like a family tree. Were we to attend induction training for a new job at our local airport it would not surprise us to see floor plans with sectors marked up in colours to distinguish who is permitted to enter various areas. The architects will have worked with various authorities to ensure that the flows of people through the building conform to security and general safety regulations. However, maps need not always depict geographical features such as coastlines and rivers. Perceptual maps can be used to position objects, opinions or attitudes in relation to an x- and a y-axis. For example, soft drinks could be mapped in terms of high–low in sugar (x-axis) and high–low in caffeine (y-axis). Other variations might not use defined axes but product attributes (high in sugar), and perceptions of product offerings (popular) can be scattered over the map; the relative closeness of associations is what is conveyed. Around the sixth century BC a somewhat similar presentation is effected to convey relative sacredness and function through describing a vision of the Jerusalem Temple by the prophet Ezekiel.

In the temple of Ezekiel 40—48 we are presented with an ideational social map of cultic space (Smith 1987, pp. 48–9). Through a language of 'gates' and 'entering', Ezekiel offers a conceptual, imaginary construction of the proper flows and sectors for different categories of worshippers; some to be excluded altogether. In Smith's terms, Ezekiel presents a series of maps that delineate different hierarchies. Map 1 is a 'hierarchy of power' based on the dichotomy of sacred/profane (40.1—44.3), while map 2 proffers a dichotomy of pure/impure and this time a 'hierarchy of status' (44.4–31). The third map (45.1–8 and 47.13—48.35) presents a 'civic and territorial' scheme, and the fourth (46) is 'orientational' (Smith 1987, p. 56). (I discuss these in relation to surveillance being used to manage flows through airports in Stoddart 2018.) Categories of people are admitted to areas of the Temple associated with the relative sacral and power positions. For example, Zadokite priests are in charge of the altar; other priests are responsible for the Temple, but without privileges of access to this most holy space. Further out still, in relation to the holiest space, is the sphere of the people. There are gates on the south and north sides through which the people pass, but the gate*house* (of a shut gate) on the east is reserved to the prince. There is no gate on the western side because this is closest to the holy place. When the paradigm is that of pure/impure, as in the second map, foreigners 'defile' the Temple (44.7, 9) and in an 'innovation' (Smith 1987, p. 62) are to be excluded, although they had previously been employed as servants within this pure place. Ezekiel's social map offers a hierarchy in terms of purity:

the people, Levites and Zadokites, to whom detailed instructions about how theirs, the highest level of purity, is to be maintained (44.15–31) (Smith 1987, p. 63).

It is important to reiterate that Ezekiel's is an ideational social mapping and is not to be conflated with the layout of the Herodian reconstruction of the first century BC, the Temple of the New Testament narratives. Nevertheless, restrictions of access depending on religion, gender and lineage applied to the respective Courts of the Gentiles, Women, Israelites and Priests. Gates, while also defensive, manage the flows of people into and through sacred spaces. In Ezekiel we have a mapping of relative sacredness by which a category of persons might be identified as being out of place. In a form of what we might call 'ritual security' the designated proper areas for each category of worshipper are laid out – not unlike a colour-coded floor plan in an airport. To be holy means keeping to one's proper place, not transgressing cultic boundaries and, equally importantly, fulfilling the cultic obligations appropriate to one's category. Holiness as purity – in terms of avoiding uncleanness, restoring from uncleanness and observing ritual cleanliness including appropriate cultic duties – is foundational (albeit interpreted differently by various groups) to the Judaism into which Jesus is born, and to the paradigm he goes on to radically realign.

Being 'a place'

The compassion code

'But I say to you that listen, Love your enemies, do good to those who hate you, bless those who curse you, pray for those who abuse you. If anyone strikes you on the cheek, offer the other also; and from anyone who takes away your coat do not withhold even your shirt. Give to everyone who begs from you; and if anyone takes away your goods, do not ask for them again. Do to others as you would have them do to you.

If you love those who love you, what credit is that to you? For even sinners love those who love them. If you do good to those who do good to you, what credit is that to you? For even sinners do the same. If you lend to those from whom you hope to receive, what credit is that to you? Even sinners lend to sinners, to receive as much again. But love your enemies, do good, and lend, expecting nothing in return. Your reward will be great, and you will be children of the Most High; for he is kind to the ungrateful and the wicked. Be merciful, just as your Father is merciful.' (Luke 6.27–36)

Jesus reframes what it means to be a community who imitate God. The narrowness of purity is replaced by the expansiveness of compassion as the manner in which God's approach to the world is to be mirrored by Israel. The Holiness Code of Leviticus 19 is echoed and modified in turning the other cheek, loving of enemies and generally reflecting God's disposition of giving the gifts of sun and rain to both the just and the unjust (Borg 1998, pp. 139–40). To love one's neighbour is extended from an injunction regarding fellow members of the covenanted community to include all.

The 'compassion code', argues Marcus Borg, replaces holiness as the content of the *imitatio Dei* with compassion (Borg 1998, p. 139). The traditionally named Holiness Code delivered a paradigm as 'You shall be holy, for I the LORD your God am holy' (Lev. 19.2). The compassion code renders a revised paradigm: 'Be *compassionate* as God is *compassionate*.' Borg justifies the change in translation from 'mercy' and 'merciful' to 'compassion' and 'compassionate': 'because of connotations in English of being merciful to one who does wrong, and its presumption of a "power relationship of superior to inferior" ... The word "compassion" avoids these connotations ... To be compassionate is to feel for somebody as a mother feels for the children of her womb' (Borg 1998, p. 16).

Crucially, not only is holiness framed as compassion rather than as cultural purity, the scope is extended beyond the injunction to show compassion to those within the covenant: 'God's compassion is seen in the fact that the sun and the rain come to both the just and the unjust, i.e., to everybody, and not just to those with whom a special relationship exists' (Borg 1998, p. 141). While earlier editions of his work argue that loving enemies encapsulated a challenge to particular resistance movements against Roman rule, Borg later revises his outlook and steers away from this specific clash to understand Jesus engaging in conflict about politics and justice, 'about whether compassion or purity was to be the core value shaping Israel's collective life. To use different language, the conflict was about whether compassion or purity was to be the core value of the kingdom of God' (Borg 1998, p. 15). Also, Borg develops a more nuanced understanding of the significance of purity in everyday life among the mass of people in Jesus' day. He sees 'purity as primarily the ideology of the ruling class, centered in the Temple' (Borg 1998, p. 10).

Borg posits Jesus contending for a new understanding of contagion. Jesus views holiness as 'transforming power' that brings wholeness, in contradistinction to the positively defiling power of uncleanness (Borg 1998, p. 147). So holiness (in the sense of compassion) does not require protecting from contagion through systems of separation; rather, compassion-holiness (akin to the work of a physician) is 'an active dynamic power that overcame uncleanness' (Borg 1998, p. 148). With this in mind, Jesus' table fellowship with 'sinners' and his love of his own enemies are indicative of the consequences of this new paradigm. Jesus is making more than a statement of social solidarity; he is reframing the religious understanding of particular categories of people and therefore of what is righteous action at the boundaries where categorization is acute.

The boundary that is thrown around those with certain skin diseases is breached by Jesus, but some he yet instructs to gain endorsement of their healing within the traditional paradigm (Luke 5.14). It is possible to see boundary issues in play in the stories of rescue from what are perceived to be demonic powers. Without apparent concerns of contagion, Jesus confronts and instructs demons to release their captives. The fear that the community directs towards those under the sway of demons is largely upended as victims are 're-presented' as ones released and made whole. Jesus' positive engagement with a Gentile Roman centurion (Matt. 8.5–13; Luke 7.1–10) destabilizes another classification of Jew–Gentile, this time at the boundary of relationship with the colonizing power. The imperial representative seeks help from a member of the colonized country, an appeal to which Jesus responds with compassion.

The replacement of the holiness code with the compassion code is not, however, total. It is important to note that the Jesus movement did not abandon the Temple, reflecting surely their understanding that Jesus was not abolishing but reinterpreting Torah (Matt. 5.17–18). Borg recognizes the twofold dynamic: of maintaining distinctive community identity and having an expansive paradigm of compassion-as-holiness; there are boundaries of the community but these are 'broad and very indistinct' (Borg 1998, p. 151). James Dunn points, on the one hand, to Jesus' association with John the Baptist and Jesus' respect for the Temple as indicative 'of the importance of purity concerns within the community' of the early Church (Dunn 2002, p. 467). On the other hand, Dunn presents Jesus' controversial table fellowship and his sitting 'loose to the purity *halakhoth* regarding clean and unclean' as pointing towards what was central to Jesus' understanding of the covenanted people of God (Dunn 2002, p. 467). Dunn maintains that 'Jesus affirmed the vital nature and necessity of purity and of dealing with impurity' and that therefore we observe a dispute over 'the emphasis to be given to the different kinds of impurity' (Dunn 2010, pp. 336–7).

Reclassification

It seems to me that we can continue to talk of compassion not only as a paradigm of holiness but in the sense also of purity. 'The pure in heart' are promised sight of God (Matt. 5.8) and this purity is not merely evidenced in acts of compassion but *is* those acts of compassion. In the famous parable of classification and boundaries, the sheep and the goats (Matt. 25.31–46), Jesus takes the compassion code a step further, for it is the unwittingly 'pure' (that is, compassionate) who are admitted to eternal life. The great boundary is one around 'the kingdom prepared for you from the foundation of the world' (Matt. 25.34) – crucially not here directly associated with death, as is so often the assumption, but the occasion when 'the Son of Man comes in his glory'. It is not for a person to unilaterally cross the boundary into the kingdom; one has to be admitted. Classification is made between sheep and goats; the unwitting sheep pose a not unexpected question to the Son of Man:

> 'Lord, when was it that we saw you hungry and gave you food, or thirsty and gave you something to drink? And when was it that we saw you a stranger and welcomed you, or naked and gave you clothing? And when was it that we saw you sick or in prison and visited you?' And the king will answer them, 'Truly I tell you, just as you did it to one of the least of these who are members of my family, you did it to me.' (Matt. 25.37–40)

Here the holiness as purity paradigm disappears and compassion dominates. Furthermore, it is compassion shorn of self-serving, instrumentalized care for others. Were one to know that being compassionate was the way of inheriting the kingdom it might be difficult to avoid feeding the hungry with that ultimate reward in mind. The danger of the naked becoming objects, clothed for the benefit of the one providing the clothes, is very real. The parable detaches compassion from religious observance in a radical reframing of the classificatory process of the kingdom of God. Breaking this parable free from its popular associations with judgement after or upon death helps read it indeed as a parable and not as a description or as akin to an advance notice of a concert. It is a parable shocking to its hearers, who might well have already been wrestling with the implications of Jesus' reframing of holiness. The characteristic of the kingdom is disclosed in a story whose setting is a great future unveiling. Compassion – for the sake of those in need – is the decisive classification; not compassion instrumentalized for one's own spiritual reward.

In some ways, in telling this parable Jesus lets the proverbial cat out of the bag. How can a compassionate person now remain ignorant of the criteria and ever ask the Son of Man the question posed in the parable? But those hearing the parable and those preserving it in the nascent community of Christian faith are likely wondering how Jesus' compassion code relates to God. Purity, framed as it is in regulatory ritual, quite readily fits within a notion of worship; purity is directed to, and is a response to, divine holiness. The same is not so directly obvious in terms of compassion, which is much more, as it were, horizontal. The 'Son of Man' figure becomes 'the king' of verse 34, who is the one to whom drink, food, hospitality, clothing and health care are offered and visits in prison are made, but indirectly and unwittingly. Acts of compassion are rendered, in effect, as acts of worship. This is not replacement in the sense that compassion is now the only true form of worship, merely that acts of compassion are elevated to worship.

A life of worship is, in this kingdom, a life of compassion. To put this another way, acting that coheres with this kingdom is compassion towards those in need. It is in this light that the highly exclusionary and retributive elements of the parable can be understood. 'Then he will answer [the goats], "Truly I tell you, just as you did not do it to one of the least of these, you did not do it to me." And these will go away into eternal punishment, but the righteous into eternal life' (Matt. 25.45–46). The contrast is drawn in vivid narrative within a parable – not, as we have noted, a press release announcing an upcoming concert.

By considering Leviticus, Ezekiel, the Sermon the Mount and the parable of the sheep and goats (at least parts thereof) we are doing what Ched Myers argues is 'the proper vocation of theology … not demythologization, but critique, creation, and redemption of socio-symbolic discourse' (Myers 1988, p. 73). The socio-symbolic discourse of classification in terms of purity enabled and sustained an ordering of an otherwise threatening contingent world. Classification remains, as does, in a sense, purity, but Jesus is constructing another set of symbols, largely by reframing the prevailing paradigm. With reference solely to the Gospel of Mark, Myers observes a Jesus who is continually transgressing or criticizing boundaries and classificatory division (Myers 1988, p. 75). Jesus is doing far more than repackaging purity classification with a softer edge; his is not purity with compassion. Rather, Jesus is pushing towards compassion *as* purity, for 'at the heart of Mark's political, social, and economic alternatives to the dominant order lies a radical new symbolic system based upon the primacy of human need' (Myers 1988, p. 443). Yes, we are classificatory creatures but this is problematic in that it shapes us at the same time as it shapes those we classify. If we are not in a position to classify but have this done to us, we are also confronted with the call to adopt a symbolic

system that is compassion. How then does this biblical perspective contribute to a critical view of identification by classification?

Liberating identification

Boundaries are commonplace in twenty-first-century cultures, as are
purity paradigms, even within rational-instrumentalist milieux. Revulsion
seems an apt term to use to describe the visceral reaction of some white
people to people of colour, particularly those white people who are in
positions of power. Purity thinking lies behind aversion to inter-ethnic
and inter-religious marriage, and in similar reactions to homosexual sex.
It is more than disapproval that can be tolerated by declining to participate in or promote these behaviours. Fear that others will be influenced to
engage in such practices is often foregrounded but even permitting them
to continue is to allow the wider community to be contaminated morally
and possibly genetically. To be 'out of place' can refer to informal zones
in a city where having the 'wrong' skin colour puts a person at high risk
of being confronted and possibly killed by vigilantes or some elements
of the police force. People with a severe facial disfigurement may know
the boundaries of their town within which they are comfortable being
visible and those within which it is an ordeal of disapproving stares. The
criteria of classification are, on the whole, quite different in first-century
AD Palestine from those operating in twenty-first-century cities across the
world; and neither are those criteria universal. The process of legitimating
such criteria and policing the boundaries of material space might include
religion, but much less so in constitutionally secular societies.

What is classification to be liberated for?

The bitter and sweet experiences of radical Christian readers from black,
queer and post-colonial standpoints chime with Noble's analysis of internet searches – but from a pre-internet standpoint. Ordering, archiving,
searching and retrieving – whether of web pages digitally or of biblical
texts by analogue print or memory – are communicative actions (Andersen 2018, p. 7). What we search for is only the tip of the iceberg. Beneath
the surface lie the culturally significant categorization and ranking of
information, and the retrieval shapes our views of ourselves and others.
Noble's demand for unbiased algorithmic classifications and thus searching being a common good, rather than a proprietary system, is affirmed
by the hermeneutical claims of those developing subaltern readings of

biblical texts on boundaries. Post-colonial, black and gay interpreters know from first-hand experience how texts can be used to preserve and enhance the status of the already privileged. We might indeed think of the centuries-long practices of reading the Bible as a form of searching. Looking for particular passages is not necessarily to be viewed cynically, as if privileged (or non-privileged) readers are merely attempting to locate texts in their favour. Nevertheless, the choice of texts for public reading (either by way of an authorized lectionary or informal local preference) is a selection that is not self-evident but deliberate. What is read *for* or indeed *at* a congregation communicates values that may energize resistance or acceptance of social or legal positions. The question is of course: To what end are readers of a text energized? Resistance might be against breaches in civil or human rights but the 'searched biblical text' read in public might be to resist others' claims on civil rights in a defence of the status quo; white Christian nationalism in the USA is one example.

Pasquale draws our attention to the performativity of algorithms; that the act of categorization changes the person who is being categorized and their life chances that result. Proxy variables distance us from ourselves and others in an informational age in a way not unlike that which occurs in an age when holiness is within a paradigm of purity. Jesus reframes purity from what was, in effect, a system of technical efficiency to be a system that prioritizes human compassion for those in need. His is a process of de-categorization that brings people closer to themselves and to others. The twenty-first century is, as Luciano Floridi argues, a digital culture 'that characterises mature information societies, [and] is now evolving from being a culture of signs and signification into a culture of proxies and interaction' (Floridi 2015, p. 487). A vicar is vicarious in the sense of being a deputy or representative of a bishop. But, says Floridi, the roots of proxy are political rather than religious: '"Vicariously" or "by proxy", both qualify actions that are possible because something represents and replaces (acts or behaves instead of) something else' (Floridi 2015, p. 488). The problem is indeed greater than us becoming what we are categorized. Algorithmic reliance on proxies to infer otherwise inaccessible characteristics puts us in danger of becoming ever more distant from reality as we engage only with the differences identified by the interaction of proxies, and even of the proxies of proxies:

This means that it is increasingly difficult to navigate in the infosphere without relying on proxies and, at the same time, that proxies are not just the solution but also part of the problem, given that they are a source of even more data, for which more proxies will be needed. The result is that the distance between us and the signified realities is quickly growing, and so is the need to shorten it through ever more signifiers with which we can interact effectively. (Floridi 2015, p. 489)

In Floridi's view we risk falling into 'some kind of occultism' (we misunderstand and think we can influence the referent by adjusting the proxy) or 'shallowism' (mistaking surrogates for proxies) (Floridi 2015, p. 490). In other words, using Floridi's example, we drink chicory coffee (containing no caffeine) as a substitute for coffee without knowing it is not actually coffee.

We are led into an 'ersatz culture', 'proxies become mere surrogates that not only hide their original references (the "real" coffee) but make it hard or even impossible to reach it because they fully replace it without any residual link to an alternative reality' (Floridi 2015, p. 490). As Floridi argues, there is not necessarily anything wrong in the creation of a surrogate, but if we only have surrogates (for example, chicory coffee) then ours is 'a worse, shallower world' (Floridi 2015, p. 490). But proxies can be helpful: 'If proxies can serve as bridges towards otherwise hard to access or even inaccessible spaces of experiences then our proxy culture will be a better, enhanced culture' (Floridi 2015, p. 490).

Jesus' critique of purity as a system resonates with the distancing and inaccessibility that Floridi discusses. Purity is a shallower world in which its rituals become surrogates that are in danger of losing their original referents of justice and mercy. Proxies are necessary – and in purity it seems that categorization of clean/unclean serves to a considerable extent as a proxy system. Order is created, and imitating God involves deploying proxies precisely because humans are not God. Maintaining or restoring cleanness is achieved by utilizing proxies for the divine otherness. What Jesus is doing in prioritizing compassion is certainly to bring in a different set of proxies – feeding the hungry, tending the sick and so on. Yet in the parable of Matthew 25 Jesus is going further and claiming encounter and engagement with 'the king' in the acts of compassion for others. The distance is not collapsed but reduced. Compassionate acts are proxies but not merely surrogates, because that to which they refer is reachable. These compassionate acts are humanizing both for the recipient and for the giver.

The Bible affirms pleas to reduce the distance that algorithmic classification generates between those with the power to run classification systems and the objects of their gaze. Floridi warns:

In a proxy culture, we may easily be *de-individualized* and treated as a type (a type of customer, a type of driver, a type of citizen, a type of patient, a type of person who lives at that postal code, who drives that type of car, who goes to that type of restaurant, etc.). Such proxies may be further used to *reidentify* us as specific consumers for customizing purposes. (Floridi 2014, p. 58, loc. 1131, emphasis in original)

Radical biblical hermeneutes from oppressed communities surely recognize this analysis of their own marginalization by the powerful – long before it was instantiated in digital forms. To be *re*-personalized – as a practitioner and recipient of compassion – is to confront those who find it to their advantage to identify by categorization. Kevin Healey and Robert Woods suggest that the quasi-religious ambition of Google (in the slogan 'information wants to be free') represents 'a techno-centric version of Christian liberation theology' (Healey and Woods Jr 2017, p. 5). The danger is that information, rather than a person, is liberated, and for the end of monetization. Radical biblical hermeneutics drives us towards not only keeping individuals and communities in the foreground but asking what liberation is *for*. If classification/purity is relegated well below compassion as holiness then we might consider the liberation of information to be *for* compassionate action. At the same time, people are liberated from oppressive algorithmic classification and identification for *compassion* and also *by* compassion. The purpose here of liberation is also a means of liberation.

Encoding compassion

Eubanks raises significant concerns around the injustices of algorithmic decision-making that identifies people and in effect codes them for criminalization or marginalization. Bringing this alongside purity as holiness we find the significance of the system: restoring purity when it has been lost. Everyday life threatened purity, for example, when someone encountered a corpse, which could well be that of a loved one. Avoidance of ritual pollution is only one side of the equation; cleansing and restoration is the other. It might even be the case that being compassionate towards a person may incur ritual uncleanness, for example in caring for those in the community who fall sick. There are processes for restoring purity, so all is not lost.

Eubanks's plea for preserving human intervention in decision-making is, in part, a plea for compassion to be maintained and injected, even as an interruption, in a classification-based identification of the needs of those in need. Being able to correct algorithmic injustice is affirmed by biblical concerns for wholeness/holiness as compassion. In his critique of algorithms, Mike Ananny builds on the important point of Bowker and Star (1999) that such processes take what does not fit (what is out of place in terms of interest to the search) and place that in a 'residual' category. This is somewhat like the moment when self-assembling furniture you are left with one unused bracket, which, rather than finding where it really ought to have gone, you quietly drop in the bin and hope for the best. However, these are people's characteristics and character that are rendered residual and marginalized. Ananny's point is that algorithmic processes are ethically problematic 'to the extent that they signal certainty, discourage alternative explorations, and create coherence among disparate objects – categorically narrowing the set of socially acceptable answers to the question of what ought to be done' (Ananny 2016, p. 103). The technological approach dismisses, or at least devalues, the residual. There is a difference between interest in an outlier that identifies a risky person – so they are flagged – and residuals that are what make people different, and even eccentric. A drive towards categorization is a drive to similarity at the expense of peculiarity. This is so even when the attempt is to categorize into quite tightly defined groups for targeted marketing. As 'personal' as it might seem, this is still allocation to a group. It is just that because we do not see that there are others in the group we experience the targeting as personal.

Even though we find the purity paradigm deficient it at least offered ways out of uncleanness. Restoration was the hope and indeed the purpose of the system; compassion surely even more so. Compassion becomes crucial as a bulwark against the false claims of accuracy that are attributed to algorithmic identification. danah boyd warns against 'apophenia: seeing patterns where none actually exist [a term that has its origins in psychiatry], simply because enormous quantities of data can offer connections that radiate in all directions' (boyd and Crawford 2012, p. 668). People's lives are blighted when correlations are given unwarranted status. Blackening the biblical text to restore occluded positive representations of Africans is but one form of that radical hermeneutical move that confronts colonialist dominance over those it deems inadequate, delinquent and recalcitrant. Compassion as a hermeneutical principle refuses to let this go unresolved. Jesus' rationale for promoting compassion as the primary paradigm for holiness contains at the very least a concern for those who are the collateral damage in the war against impurity waged by certain religious figures in his time:

> One of the lawyers answered him, 'Teacher, when you say these things, you insult us too.' And he said, 'Woe also to you lawyers! For you load people with burdens hard to bear, and you yourselves do not lift a finger to ease them.' (Luke 11.45–46)

In the twenty-first century, attempts to justify surveillance because it is proportionate to the dangers at stake do still leave some people as collateral damage, as O'Neil has rightly observed. Proportionality relies on a concept of balance but, as Lucia Zedner points out, before we can conclude that a *fair* balance has been struck we need to ask at least three questions: What has tipped the balance? In whose interests has balance been achieved? And what lies in the scale (Zedner 2006)? From his discussion of 'means and ends' legitimating algorithmic reasoning, John Kleinig concludes with the highly apposite: 'Will the means have deleterious consequences that would make their use inappropriate?' (Kleinig 2009, p. 208). Serious questions confront those making decisions about the acceptable levels of false positives and false negatives when algorithmic reasoning is deployed in developing medical technology (Kraemer et al. 2011). False negatives mean people with a disease mistakenly being given an all-clear and going untreated. The proportions of missed disease and patients' overall confidence in the system is balanced against those situations where a person is identified as having a disease when this is a misdiagnosis (a false positive). Collateral damage is another way of articulating the problem in a wider range of settings. How many people is it acceptable to falsely identify as a threat – and what is the degree of negative impact on their lives that society will accept – in order to limit the rate of false negatives? To put this another way, what extent of welfare fraud is a society willing to accommodate (users who slip through scrutiny as false negatives) in order to constrain the damage to otherwise legitimate claimants who are denied their entitlement or put under intense scrutiny (false positives)? This is a twenty-first-century form of 'burdens hard to bear', against which the biblical text affirms protest. At the same time, the text recognizes the need for boundaries, and the purity paradigm is not swept aside in its entirety.

Standing up for those who are the collateral damage of a system and advocating for systemic change is, as the outcome for Jesus portrays, itself a dangerous business. Challenging the socio-symbolic order brings conflict with powerful vested interests. On the other hand, security systems in the twenty-first century cannot be run on compassion – we expect rigorous categorization in airports in order for us not only to feel but to be relatively more safe as we travel. The biblical paradigm does not provide a solution to apply to a security system required to identify people with malicious intent to harm others. But the texts on holiness as compassion do propel us into the arena of responsibility for those who are discriminated against in the sense of being denied access to what others take as given: clothing, food, health care. Tobias Matzner urges caution in accepting that merely making the control of algorithms transparent and accountable is an adequate response to their discriminatory aspects. Without more systemic changes in society, transparency and accountability 'might increase the legitimacy of those unjust practices' (Matzner 2018, p. 41). In other words, people and systems might be seen to be unjust but this might be acceptable where the prevailing public mood and/or regulatory mechanism favours disadvantaging some people. In a very different context, we read of Jesus advocating not a more robust or even transparent purity code but a compassion code that poses more radical challenges not only to outward action but to attitudes, and practices of holiness towards those in dire need rather than more technical efficiency of ritual performance. In a sense we can say that these biblical texts affirm finding solutions that are not first and foremost technological or bureaucratic but attend to the deeper social relationships that give rise to the absence of holiness in the first place. Getting to the root of systemic injustices that are often intertwined with individually fractured relationships requires the double-consciousness of being alert to how one internalizes negative constructions in algorithmic sorting alongside the positive messages of one's own community – coming, in some instances, from those same religious traditions that oppress and liberate. A hermeneutics of abomination lives on outside biblical texts in media representations of those whom parts of society concur as being in need of exclusion from secular 'sacred' spaces (be these particular pubs and restaurants, civic memorials or public parks). The compassion code has the hallmarks of a subaltern voice, resisting being written off as unrighteous in order that others might secure their own righteousness.

When liberation comes too late

To talk of a compassion code as the imitation of God immediately raises the challenge of everyday and singular events in which expectations of the divine gaze are not met. In the light of perceived promises in the psalms it is proper that questions are asked of any understanding of God's watchful care that looks like neglect:

> The LORD is your keeper;
>   the LORD is your shade at your right hand.
> The sun shall not strike you by day,
>   nor the moon by night.
> The LORD will keep you from all evil;
>   he will keep your life.
> (Psalm 121.5–7)

When gross brutality is perpetrated against those to whom such promises have been given, the nature of the divine gaze to which imitation is expected is confronted by the Holocaust. How do we speak when the divine gaze has failed? What can be said, or rather, what sort of sight can be justified, after the events in the Nazis' concentration camps? We noted Johann-Baptist Metz's injunction to do Christian theology remembering the faces of Jewish people, not an objectified category of 'the Jews'. Irving Greenberg's still more famous declaration applies unequivocally to discussion of the common gaze, and of the divine gaze upon which it is predicated: 'no statement, theological or otherwise, should be made that would not be credible in the presence of the burning children' (I. Greenberg 1977, p. 23).

The Nazi gaze

An efficient gaze

We will limit our attention largely to the identification question: how did the Nazis know who were Jews (by the Nazis definition) and where to find them? Changes in an individual's marriage or religious status had been tracked by state registry offices since 1875–6 (Young 2017, p. 90). In April 1933, the Nazis ordered a national census for June, which would record religious affiliation and be supplemented with a special count of Jews. At this time a purge of the civil service and universities of non-Aryans commenced. On 17 August 1935, all Gestapo offices were ordered to set up a 'Jewish Register' or *Judenkartei* (Milton 1997, p. 80), and the following month the Nuremberg racial laws were enacted. This 1935 legislation deprived Jews of German citizenship, prohibited marriage between a Jew and a non-Jew and outlawed sexual relations between Jews and Germans (as now redefined). In November 1935 further legal racial categories were created of German, Jew, half-Jew (Jewish *Mischling* first degree) and quarter-Jew (Jewish *Mischling* second degree). Categorization was 'ultimately determined by birth, baptismal, marriage, and death certificates. Often stored in churches and courthouses, these records indicated what religion one adhered to or had left' (Jewish Virtual Library 2020). Of most immediate relevance to our discussion is the nature and location of the records by which a person could either prove she or he was *not* a Jew (or more likely their ambivalent, but dangerous, status as *Mischling*). Accessibility to this documentation was therefore at least one step removed from the state, drawing others into decisions over collusion with the Nuremberg laws. In the Kristallnacht directive of 10 November 1938 there was 'Summary confiscation by the police of documentary records belonging to the Jewish religious communities' (Hecht 1985, p. 49).

The notorious red 'J' stamped on ID cards (compulsory for everyone to carry) commenced from 1 January 1939 and Jews not bearing a typically Jewish name (according to Nazi perceptions) were required to include an identifier in correspondence (Israel or Sara for male and female respectively) so that the authorities would know that they were dealing with Jews (see Hecht 1985, p. 63, for an account of families living under the Nuremberg laws). Record-building and -keeping was integral to the Nazi persecution. For example, on 29 March 1941 an order was given to the Reich Association of Jews to supply details of Jewish apartments in Aryan buildings (Hecht 1985, p. 87). In occupied countries, statistical operations included requiring censuses and, in Marseille at least, opening of mail and monitoring of phone conversations to pick up any trying to avoid registering for the census (Ryan 1996, p. 40). There a particular identification point arose in connection with vital food ration cards needing to be stamped (Ryan 1996, p. 41).

It is important to note William Seltzer's caveat that although there was a heavy reliance of data gathering for operations related to the Holocaust (to establish, for example, the extent and structure of Jewish populations), 'there appears to be only one instance, namely the 1939 German census, where information permitting the identification of specific individuals may have been used operationally in the Holocaust' (Seltzer 1998, p. 515). Even if this is the case, the identification of individuals and the construction of a category (with sub-categories) of those to be persecuted are interwoven throughout the 1933–45 period. Within the camps, prisoner registration cards after 1939 at Dachau, Mauthausen and Ravensbrück were stamped *Hollerith erfasst* (registered by Hollerith), indicating, argues Milton, 'that the SS used this technology to better manage data about the vast numbers of inmates imprisoned in and transferred between concentration camps' (Milton 1997, p. 84).

The Nazi gaze was made more efficient by the use of devices available at the time, including the Hollerith machine, which processed 60–80-column punch cards on to which clerks had entered data. The complicity of a US company continues to be subject to considerable debate. In terms of legal ownership, Milton explains:

This technology, originally developed in the United States at the close of the nineteenth century, was leased in the 1920s by the Deutsche Hollerith Maschinen Gesellschaft (or Dehomag). Unable to pay license fees during the German inflation of the early 1920s, Dehomag was bought by IBM in 1922 becoming the German subsidiary of IBM. (Milton 1997, pp. 83–4)

Despite Edwin Black's claims (Black 2009, 2012), Harold James challenges inferences on how much IBM in the USA knew at the time (James 2001). In its own refutation of Black's allegations, IBM acknowledges the supply of Hollerith equipment by Dehomag (its German subsidiary during the 1930s) but asserts, 'as with hundreds of foreign-owned companies that did business in Germany at that time, Dehomag came under the control of Nazi authorities prior to and during World War II' (IBM 2001). There was a wider role of data gathering (including processing by Hollerith devices and other statistical methods) in organizing Germany's war economy (James 2001, p. 23) – but this does not need to be overstated.

Of course, the Nazis' watching, data gathering, imprisoning and executing was a deeply prejudicial gaze. But it ought not to be viewed in isolation from deeply rooted anti-Semitism in Europe that ebbed and flowed since the origins of Christianity. Whether the accusation is of spiritual myopia in failing to recognize the Messiah or full-blown deicide, Jews through the ages bear the brunt of Christian polemic that could include accusations of ritual killing of Christian children or the poisoning of wells that caused the Black Death in the Middle Ages (Brustein 2003, pp. 51–3). Theologically speaking, in such a view the Jews are held collectively and, crucially, hereditarily responsible for the murder of Jesus the Christ.

In the particular conjunction of German nationalism and anti-Semitism in the 1930s, non-Aryan pastors of Christian churches are betrayed to the Nazi regime (Bölsche 2008). Manfred Gailus documents the case of the Revd Karl Themel, who used the registry of the Lutheran Church in Berlin to hand over 2,600 names of non-Aryan Christians (Scally 2001, referring to Gailus 2008). It was often baptismal records that were so important in being able to prove one's Aryan status (Ericksen 2012, pp. 117–19). The Church, an institution with centuries of prejudice towards Jews on its own record, held the key to identification for many under this categorization regime.

God's gaze in the camps

A failed gaze

What happened to the divine gaze in the camps of Nazi persecution of the people of the covenant? Ignaz Maybaum argues that the Holocaust is providential, God making it the instrument of his will, taking Jewry out into the future of modernity, albeit by way of the sacrifice of millions of

Jews; as Jeremiah understood Nebuchadnezzar of Babylon as an awful instrument of God, so Hitler of Germany (Maybaum 1965, p. 67). God's gaze is panoramic, attending to the sweep of history rather than focused on the person caught up in its events. It may be, as in the view of Eliezer Berkovits, that God is hiding his face, not as a response to humanity but 'God's hiding himself is an attribute of the God of Israel, who is the Savior' (Berkovits 1973, p. 101). To talk of God being either present or absent in the camps is to miss the important difference between absence and silence: 'The one who is silent may be so called only because he is present' (Berkovits 1973, p. 99). This is tantamount to arguing for 'an exile of God from the human domain that was short of complete eclipse' (Sacks 1995, pp. 239–40).

If God walks away then his gaze must be elsewhere, and so, argues Emil Fackenheim, the Jew has to deal with the consequences: 'salvation once came too late; it might come too late again': 'a resurrected hope is not like a hope that never died. Murdered once, this hope could be murdered again' (Fackenheim 1990, p. 69). There is nothing meaningful and redemptive for Fackenheim in the Holocaust, but in the face of genocidal Nazism there is a new commandment (the 614th in the traditional counting): 'the authentic Jew of today is forbidden to hand Hitler yet another, posthumous victory' (Fackenheim 1967). Collective survival, instantiated in the State of Israel, is the overriding moral imperative of the 'commanding Voice which speaks from Auschwitz' (Fackenheim 1970, p. 84). The gaze is to be one of resolute and penetrating human attention towards any attempt to threaten the survival of the Jews.

In the view of Arthur Cohen, God is not one who interrupts human affairs and should be considered 'less as the interferer whose insertion is welcome (when it accords our needs) and more as the immensity whose reality is our prefiguration' (A. A. Cohen 1981, p. 95). The death camps are *sui generis* incomparable to any other event (A. A. Cohen 1981, p. 12), and, as a result, while it is understandable that people feel a need to engage in rational discourse, to do so 'is simply inappropriate and unavailing' (A. A. Cohen 1981, p. 8). This is a detached divine gaze that can be deemed neither to fail or to succeed. Whereas others seek to justify God's hiddenness, David Blumenthal contends that God has an abusive 'mode' and, in this sense, 'God "caused" the holocaust, or allowed it to happen' (Blumenthal 1993, p. 247). In a tradition of protest against God, Blumenthal concludes that Jews must learn to 'cope with God and God's actions' (Blumenthal 1993, p. 262); a God who may well feel 'shame at His own hateful actions' (Blumenthal 1993, p. 285). This is a failed gaze, not in the sense of a failure to do as promised but in keeping with a character that is flawed.

The challenge becomes one of recovering a way of speaking about, and living within, a form of a compassionate divine gaze that keeps the fate of the victims of Nazi surveillance identification in view.

A compassionate gaze

Melissa Raphael identifies post-Holocaust theology as a 'thoroughly gendered enterprise' (Raphael 2003, p. 4) because it fails to interrogate patriarchal assumptions around the nature of the divine presence and to engage with women's experience of the degradations of the Nazi project. Raphael's emphasis on the filth and impurity of the camps resonates with our own discussion of purity, and her conclusions on compassion offer a fruitful engagement with the reframed paradigm of holiness.

Raphael does not seek to discount men's experience but makes the astute observation that 'to be a Jewish man in the ghettos and camps was in almost all cases to be stateless, unarmed, and left in a state of alterity and uncleanness more customarily ascribed by gynophobic religious ideologies to women' (Raphael 2003, p. 2). Alterity is not here an analytical category but an experience within the broader attack by the Nazis from 1933 to 1945; to be treated as an attack upon the image of God.

Raphael finds the theological responses to be generally patriarchal. In Maybaum, 'masculine power is made the strong arm of God' that thereby destroys relationality in order to achieve good (as Maybaum defines it; Raphael 2003, p. 34). Berkovits's argument is predicated on autonomy but without appreciating that this is 'an elitist masculine project' as if autonomy were 'the first or only prerequisite of human dignity and becoming' (Raphael 2003, p. 43). The commanding voice of Fackenheim's call to collective survival preserves, insufficiently critically, God's 'monarchical prerogative' (Raphael 2003, p. 30). The wholly inaccessible God of Cohen's position, Raphael concludes, ignores the conditions of God's presence that were not destroyed, namely 'women's relational labours' (Raphael 2003, p. 52). Blumenthal's partly abusive God 'ontologizes patriarchal alienations of power', ending up with 'an eternalized cycle of violence' (Raphael 2003, p. 48). Standing back somewhat from the various post-Holocaust theologies, it is Raphael's reminder from feminist theology that is particularly apposite: 'God's omnipotence is as much a political value as it is a religious hope' (Raphael 2003, p. 38).

What is key for Raphael is the observation that in the camps, and I think we can rightly say well beyond their perimeters in time and space, 'freedom was not necessarily the guarantor of human dignity; human dignity could consist in the capacity, however vestigial, to honour communal or familial obligations' (Raphael 2003, pp. 43–4). When freedom is taken away, the loss is immense and is an attempt at dehumanizing people. However, when freedom is not possible, 'responsiveness to the other was not, and could not be, a bid for freedom but for the conservation of love against the gross profligacies of hate' (Raphael 2003, p. 44). It is, in Raphael's view, in those moments of compassion from one prisoner to an inmate that resistance to being dehumanized is performed, when, whether claimed as such or not, the image of God is enacted, likely in desperation but in a refusal to succumb: 'Human dignity lay in the preservation of the capacity to love, not in the freedom to love' (Raphael 2003, p. 44).

Raphael turns to the tradition of Shekhinah to thereby frame this refusal to be dehumanized as the presence of God-She. Shekhinah denotes 'God's accompanying presence in Israel's exile' (Raphael 2003, p. 81). It is the conditions of gross inhumanity and brutality that hide the divine:

> The Shekhinah is a manifestation of God defined by her presentness. While the conditions in Auschwitz were wholly non-ordinary, God-She may have been so 'ordinarily' present among women whose personhood was getting ever less perceptible that she was herself imperceptible. But that is not to say that she had deliberately hidden herself. If she seemed hidden it was by virtue of the non-luminousness of the medium of her presence, the depth of evil into which she was plunged, and her very soft tread ... She remained among us, perhaps unknown and unknowable, but not hidden. (Raphael 2003, p. 54)

This is not an omnipotent God, absent, hiding Godself, in exile or providentially complicit in evil for some wider purpose. There is no need to turn camp prisoners into unwitting heroes if they were able to wrest their humanity back from the Nazis or as failures when the horrors were too much to watch or they were too exhausted and powerless to resist succumbing. The degree of atrocity was so severe that Shekhinah was all but thoroughly hidden and so we ought to avoid any hint of imputing criticism upon those who died brutalized, especially as reports on individual actions are so scarce among the millions who died with no testimony of their final days being passed on. The filth in the overcrowded train carriages used to transport prisoners to the camps, and the squalid conditions of the barracks, meant ritual purity was impossible but, argues Raphael, the Levitical command to distinguish between clean and unclean was fulfilled in women's relationships with one another:

> they could 'wash' Auschwitz from themselves in ways that were presentative of divine presence and that are generally overlooked by

androcentric religious and historical studies of the Holocaust. Women's acts of care for bodies – washing, holding and covering them – were acts of separative purification that not only fulfilled Israel's covenantal obligation to make the world fit for divine presence, but also, and more immediately, separated women from the engulfing profanation that was Auschwitz itself. (Raphael 2003, p. 60)

The particular acts of intimate bodily care are not incidental but integral to defiantly clinging to their humanity by women for whom purity of bodies was deeply spiritually significant. Defiled by camp conditions in one sense, purity as compassion is asserted, and thus, 'As Shekhinah, God's presence in Auschwitz was that of a God whose power was such that she could consent to be defiled by virtue of her immanence and still be God, then, now, and in the times to come' (Raphael 2003, p. 85). This is God-She, 'smuggled into Auschwitz' (Raphael 2003, p. 156).

Drawing as she does upon Emmanuel Levinas's ethical imperative of the face of the other (Levinas 1969; Stoddart 2011, pp. 33–4), Raphael grounds the presence of God in the defiant compassion that is perhaps not best conveyed in gardening metaphors of stems forcing their way through concrete slabs to reach the light. The tenacity, wiliness and indefatigability of the smuggler is much more apt. The divine gaze here is compassionate – but perhaps having to be furtive and so alert to discovery by guards or informants that eyes can scarcely risk looking at the face of the one whose wounds she is bathing. The divine gaze in the one holding to her humanity is that of the trafficker; conveying an illicit material past the boundaries and borders of control.

A Christian theodic gaze

Christian theological perspectives on suffering, not here always with direct reference to the Holocaust, have many similarities with those Jewish approaches that Raphael has found wanting from a feminist standpoint. A brief overview of the main Christian approaches leads us to the anti-theodicy advocates for whom creating communities able to lament is a better response than philosophical or theological discourse. Rivera's relational transcendence will then enable us to bring together surveillance from the cross with a compassionate gaze that avoids retreat into traditional theologies of watching from above and of divine rescue. This move prepares the way for considering the common gaze as a hopeless and wounded, but still active, gaze.

Theodic community

Alvin Plantinga's classic argument is the free-will defence: God's omni-potence, omniscience and perfect goodness is not inconsistent with the existence of evil, because evil exists due to the free, rational and fallible actions of creatures (Plantinga 1973). A variation on this theme is offered by Richard Swinburne, who eschews a place for a devil's agency. For Swinburne, in a natural law argument, the possibility of suffering is a logical necessity if people are to develop virtues (for avoiding natural harm and disasters) and if people are to have freedom and demonstrate respon-sibility. Such good states would not otherwise be possible (Swinburne 1998).

A process theology argument contends with the classic attribution of omnipotence to God, proposing instead God as Persuader. The nature of existence is becoming, rather than being. It is towards actualization that God lures the cosmos. With respect to God's concrete (but not God's abstract) aspect, God's experience of Godself is created by such choices that creatures make. The process God is not in complete control, there-fore the occurrence of suffering is not incompatible with God's goodness (Cobb and Griffin 1977). In the frame alongside free will, natural law and process theism we find John Hick's 'soul-making' theodicy. We require, he argues, a 'person-making environment' in which to develop towards the ultimate completion within the life of God; a process that is not restricted to this life but continues in other, post-mortem ways (Hick 1977).

While debates continue among philosophical theodicists, these are generally not those that concern anti-theodicists. Theirs fall broadly into two aspects: the moral and the practical critiques. (Although it is important to note that separating the moral and the practical is itself a criticism raised by some.) The moral critique has two aspects: the philo-sophical theodicies (i) mis-declare evil and (ii) have harmful consequences when brought into actual circumstances rather than reserved to abstract discussion. A principal contention of anti-theodicy is that theodicy is a temptation that entices people 'to make evil comprehensible and God innocent, it tempts us to justify useless suffering' (Roth 2004, p. 284). The accusation is that, either directly or indirectly, philosophical theodi-cies contain a proxy endorsement of horrendous suffering. Actions that are life-diminishing and devoid of what is generally recognized as 'good' are re-designated as meaningful, necessary and even valuable. While this seems harmless at the abstract level, when brought into concrete experiences such a theory denies the horror of particular suffering by spiritualizing away its pain (Swinton 2007, p. 19). Terrence Tilley makes the important point that theodicies are, in effect, speech-acts – they 'do not describe, but declare, what is evil' (Tilley 2000, p. 235).

Grace Jantzen, similar to Raphael, challenges what she perceives to be the evasion of concrete issues of power when abstract, Western formulations of the divine are preferred. Attention is diverted away, argues Jantzen, from what humans are doing when priority is given (if not even sole attention is paid) to defending God. Such necrophilia neglects the face of the Other as it presents itself in those who sleep rough or in battered women or people displaced by war (Jantzen 1998, p. 262). Too readily, 'them' and 'us' is a paradigm of privilege, which, in a particularly insidious form, results in 'their' suffering enabling 'our' moral development (Jantzen 1998, p. 260). Dewi Phillips captures this effectively in his contention that suffering in traditional theodicies encourages concentration on the self (Phillips 2004, p. 58). The suffering of others ought not to be 'instrumental to the [that is, my] self' (Phillips 2004, p. 59). For Jantzen, the key questions are those around the ways that the resources of religion are deployed by some to inflict suffering on others, and following Levinas, 'what does the face of the Other require of me, and how can I best respond for love of the world?' (Jantzen 1998, p. 264).

Nel Noddings argues that theodicies are gendered and patriarchal, or at least paternalistic. Those built on the theological framework of Augustine of Hippo rely, contends Noddings, on some explanation of the first sin. Because this rests on the myth of Adam and Eve, 'the burden on woman becomes enormous' (Noddings 1989, p. 20). Where such approaches also include the notion of retribution as an explanation for suffering, they are built on 'the fear of incurring the father-God's wrath' (Noddings 1989, p. 20). Such patriarchal perspectives converge with paternalism that demands that, in the face of 'impenetrable mystery', those who are powerless are taught that they must trust authority – of God and of his representatives (Noddings 1989, p. 20). The task, according to Noddings, is not to explain but to alleviate evil. This is acutely so when theodicies are deployed to rationalize the ways in which more powerful groups oppress those who are subordinate. The construction of the sufferer takes a distinctive hue within such critiques. Rather than one who, as Wendy Farley eloquently captures, is 'resigned or stoic or glib', sufferers are defiant (Farley 1990, p. 27). We live in a world of 'tragic fragility' and 'radical brokenness' (Farley 1990, p. 69). The hope is twofold for Farley: first, that the presence of divine compassion energizes resistance; and, second, that where change cannot be effected, divine love enables people to 'break the dominion of suffering over the spirit' (Farley 1990, p. 117). Integral to both aspects are the twin activities of identifying the conditions that are to be defied and holding on to one's humanity lest suffering rob one of one's sense of self (Farley 1990, pp. 56–7).

In general, anti-theodicists call for the focus to be upon particular experiences of suffering rather than it being an abstract concept for philosophical debate. Where the suffering cannot be halted, efforts to alleviate its dehumanizing effects are vital. Resisting suffering incorporates political protest and other activism. Redeeming the human spirit when it is being crushed by the physical and emotional weight of suffering is a communal effort; both pastorally (in the traditional sense of caring for individuals and families) and politically.

John Swinton offers a multifaceted agenda, developing Stanley Hauerwas's proposals, in just such a direction. Hauerwas argues that the early Church did not attempt to 'explain' suffering but to live lives of faithful response (Hauerwas 1990, p. 53). Swinton presents a multilayered vision of what such theodic communities might look like. For Swinton, there are four key theodical practices: lament, forgiveness, thoughtfulness and hospitality (Swinton 2007). At the heart of Swinton's model there lies a theodical question, but not one framed by philosophical theodicies. Swinton's approach is not to ask why God allows evil but rather: 'What does God do in response to evil?' (Swinton 2007, p. 42). The self-giving solidarity of Christ on the cross is the paradigm of divine grace that thereby shapes the response of theodic communities to the suffering of their own members and the wider world. However, theodic communities in the tradition of Hauerwas and Swinton still tend to rely on God watching *over*, even when not seeking to explain suffering but helping people to lament and support one another. There is a need, I propose, for the common gaze to more clearly represent that turn through 90 degrees envisaged in surveillance under the cross. To that end we use points of similarity to Raphael that lead us to understand the common gaze as a wounded gaze, *with* rather than over others.

Relational transcendence

Raphael's Shekhinah presence, bridging the duality of transcendence–immanence, has considerable similarity with Mayra Rivera's Christian proposal of relational transcendence. Rivera asks how transcendence might be deployed as a way of talking about our neighbour who is not knowable to us, or anyone, in her totality: 'Transcendence is always in relation to something that the self can never fully contain within itself, something that is always beyond its full grasp' (Rivera 2007, loc. 365). This 'excess' is 'grounded in God', for 'God, other creatures, and we exceed all our representations' (Rivera 2007, loc. 547). There is 'a contextual structural difference without implying a duality' (Rivera 2007, loc. 621).

Like Raphael, Rivera draws on Levinas's notion of transcendence gleaming in the face of the Other (Rivera 2007, loc. 827) and, although acknowledging Levinas's hint at the Shekhinah, she does not use this term. Rivera helps us move beyond the particular horrors of Nazi concentration camps to consider encounters within any system of dominance; for her the context is Hispanic post-colonialism. Rivera wants to acknowledge the often violent othering that takes place but theorizes this as 'an understanding of the other as Other, not absolutely Other' (Rivera 2007, loc. 1109). Her key axiom helps in the reframing of both the transcendent divine gaze (through the 90-degree turn to surveillance from the cross) and the gaze of compassion as holiness: 'Transcendence designates a relation with a reality irreducibly different from my own reality, without this difference destroying this relation and without the relation destroying this difference' (Rivera 2007, loc. 1151).

It is in totalitarianism that the destruction of difference and the priority given to sameness becomes acute and against which relational transcendence can offer a bulwark:

> In such systems there is no place for real otherness. Totalities reduce persons to categories within a self-enclosed system, defining them as instances of the same, to functions within a state, a philosophical model, or an ontological logical and/or theological structure. Persons are thus stripped of their irreducible otherness. (Rivera 2007, loc. 790)

Refusing to be dehumanized expands to resistance with any culture of categorization. This is, most certainly, resistance on one's own behalf but in the life of Shekhinah it is resistance on behalf of others, and acts of compassionate re-humanizing in defiance. Rivera names 'the intimate and yet insurmountable space between our differences' as divine, and 'what flows in and between us and nurtures us all is God among us, a living and dynamic, fluid envelope that both links – within and throughout – and subtends the space of difference and thus opens creatures to a relational infinity' (Rivera 2007, loc. 1907). Here, in the language of gaze, is the compassion of relational transcendence. However, lest we get carried away into romanticism and lose touch with the brutish constraints, opposition and moments of interrupted (or hidden) compassionate watching, Miguel De La Torre argues for hopelessness.

A hopeless gaze

Miguel De La Torre asks of the plight of those on the margins the same question posed over the notion of a transcendent, omnipotent God in light of Auschwitz:

> The horrors of concentration camps bear terrible witness concerning the failure of promises to materialized (*sic*). Because too many bodies of the innocent have piled up to the Heavens, hope of future promises is obscured by the tang of rotting flesh ensnared in the nostrils of God and all who are repulsed by Eurocentric futuristic fantasies based on a religious ideology constructed to provide the answer to the unanswerable. (De La Torre 2017, p. 74)

Theologies that point towards hope as the foundation of our approach to salvation history are, according to De La Torre, posited upon the arc of history bending towards justice, 'But if the past and present are any guides, the existence of such an arc is an article of faith presumed without proof or evidence' (De La Torre 2017, p. 49). In the terms we have used in this chapter, there would appear to be rather too much collateral damage for hope of this sort to be acceptable. De La Torre touches a core problem of hopefulness, that it can, whether intentionally or otherwise, normalize and legitimize systems of oppression.

Reminding those in privileged positions of stark everyday experiences of people on the margins, De La Torre invokes the prison (an instrument of discriminatory suppression for many ethnic categories of people) and the iconography of the political cults of authoritarian leaders:

> For all too many, God is the guard in the panopticon tower. Or maybe God is the Great Leader of political posters who always gazes with an unblinking eye at creation. Because we are always being watched by the Divine, unable to hide from the relentless gaze, we have learned to impose upon ourselves our own discipline, becoming our own dominatrix. (De La Torre 2017, p. 37)

In buildings and on billboards are symbols of omnipotence that, to a greater to lesser extent, draw legitimation from theologies of power and that, in a destructive feedback loop, shape people's understanding of the divine. Christian theologies of hope are perceived differently on the underside of marginalization, particularly by those who suffered massacres in their history of encounter with this faith. The compulsion to hope seems, in De La Torre's assessment, to be a final word explaining reality as a construct that sweeps all Christian atrocities under the rug of salvation history (De La Torre 2017, p. 51). Here we see Jantzen's concern that philosophical abstractions occlude individuals' actual experiences writ large upon whole communities. The providential use of horror by God for some greater good is seen for the commitment to an article of faith in progress that it turns out to be. Such a faith has a soporific acquiescence of oppression built into it because it allies itself with history as written by oppressors, which constructs the chaos of the Holocaust, or Indian genocide, as a necessary conflict pushing humanity towards the next elevated historical stage (De La Torre 2017, p. 63). The result is 'a demobilizing conformity' of optimism, which is not the solidarity with the perishing that the gospel requires (De La Torre 2017, p. 64). Hope becomes little more than 'an antidote for the guilt of the privileged' (De La Torre 2017, p. 155).

In language echoing our proposal of surveillance from the cross, De La Torre gives compassion an extensive arena: 'Christ becomes one with the crucified people of this time, as well as with all who are crucified today on the crosses of classism, colonialism, racism, sexism, heterosexism, and religious discrimination' (De La Torre 2017, p. 66). As God chose self-negation on the cross, so the person who pursues liberation needs to be converted to 'the self-negation of the existential self before that same cross' (De La Torre 2017, p. 93). As well as being a commitment to compassion it is an invitation to 'de-intellectualize reality', what we might call an equivalent 90-degree rotation of a Christian's gaze (De La Torre 2017, p. 94). Instead of looking from above (from a position of optimism, what is actually a hope in the arc of (salvation) history) a Christian looks horizontally, at the particular; the one requiring feeding, visiting or clothing. For De La Torre, in terms highly reminiscent of Raphael's Shekhinah, 'the face of God is found on the faces of Dachau's condemned and all who are marginalized and disenfranchised today' (De La Torre 2017, p. 94).

In place of hope, De La Torre calls for 'a theology of desperation that leads to hopelessness' (De La Torre 2017, p. 139). A hopeless gaze is therefore a watching in solidarity with those who share the 'contradictions and ambiguities of being human' (De La Torre 2017, p. 95). This is first and foremost a gaze of compassion shared between people who are being marginalized – and this may well be due in part to algorithmic categorization, but it will not be limited to these systems. The gaze of allies from among the privileged is complicated not least in the dangers of paternalism and speaking on behalf of others without the endorsement of those who are oppressed. De La Torre's liberative ethics are driven from below, from communities that suffered, and suffer, at the hands or, we should say here, under the gaze, of colonizing powers. The hopeless gaze is theirs, and it is by invitation that the privileged might share in it.

A wounded gaze

The readiness by which the privileged rush to speech is often predicated on that recourse to philosophical abstractions that glosses over the experience of particular suffering people. The proposals we have considered in this section to prevailing theodicies have each, in their own way, refused to accept the notion of collateral damage as the price to be paid for reassurance that all will, eventually or ultimately, be well. The need to offer consolation is in many respects commendable. However, if an onlooker finds it too uncomfortable to sit with others in pain, that onlooker may unconsciously silence the other's emotions. Such 'rescuing' is more for the sake of the onlooker (assuaging his or her discomfort) than for the person in pain. Frightened at the contingencies of life, let alone the horrors meted out by cruel oppressors, those called or self-appointed to speak on occasions of terror and hardship can rush to one or other of the theodicies we have seen in this section. Christopher Brittain interprets Rowan Williams's approach to speaking of God in times of terror as 'wounded speech' and this can be usefully extended to talk here of 'a wounded gaze' (Brittain 2011).

Brittain points to Williams's sermon while Archbishop of Canterbury at a memorial service in November 2005, delivered in the aftermath of the terrorist bombings in London on 7 July that year, and in the shadow of the still recent 9/11 terrorism crimes in the USA. Williams makes the crucial point that terrorism regards human lives as of no individual significance; any deaths will do. This philosophy is the antithesis of a humanist and Christian standpoint that 'we are each of us unique and responsible and non-replaceable' (Williams 2005). Grief is for the loss of a particular loved one and mourning is an act of defiance against ideologies that claim otherwise: 'There are no generalities for us, no anonymous and interchangeable people. We live by loving what's special, unique in each person. Everyone matters.' This, for Williams, is the import of the divine gaze upon sparrows falling to the ground but not forgotten by God: 'Every life is a special sort of gift.'

In words that resonate with Raphael's notion of Shekhinah in the clinging to humanity by acts of compassion in the camps, Williams seeks to help this congregation fear rightly:

No, it is not death itself that should be the focus of fear. Rather, we should be afraid of losing just that passionate conviction about the beauty and dignity of each unique person that brings us here today. We should be afraid of losing the thing that, above all else, sets faith, humanity, civilisation apart from the mind and the world of the terrorist. (Williams 2005)

Brittain recognizes that Williams is grounding his theology in the perspective of the sufferer and not attempting to answer 'why'. Rather, Williams shows what needs to be challenged in the horror of terrorism. This, argues Brittain, is an example of theology 'broken by the wounds it witnesses to' (Brittain 2011, loc. 4090). We have here an avoidance of the rush to hope; it is wounded speech that holds lacerations open, not ignored or plastered over to avoid distress:

> Hoping against hope emerges from a perspective that acknowledges the particularities of the sufferings of the world as they present themselves, so as to avoid the temptation to cover over the wounds of history or to sublate them into a consoling narrative. (Brittain 2011, loc. 4196)

This paradigm is transportable from speech to sight. A wounded gaze is a way of seeing what is marred by encounters with particular people's suffering. It is imperfect vision, damaged by gazing upon the horrors experienced by unique, non-replaceable people. A wounded gaze is not panoptic and knows its limits. It is injured by compassion and offers compassion that does not insult with solutions, but sees enough to respond with humanity when objectification and desecration by brutal regimes and individuals almost succeed in dehumanizing victims (and sometimes succeed in so doing). It is a hopeless gaze that, on the part of those privileged to be spared oppression, is a learned quality.

Terms like 'surveillance' have such a weighty tradition and ubiquity in usage that appealing for a substitute is an almost futile task. But if the prefix 'sur' and its associations with looking *upon* others might be replaced with one that points more readily to solidarity as envisaged in the wounded gaze, perhaps *comveillance* holds possibilities. Whether or not such a neologism has a chance of being adopted, watching with and watching for one another points to identification and indeed classification tempered at least, and reshaped at best, for liberative and less oppressive purposes.

In Part 3 we return to the idea of the common good to ask what our enquiry into influence, identity and identification suggests for the practice of the common gaze in the situations we have considered.

Part 3

6

Common Gazing as Public Practice

The common gaze takes discussion of surveillance into fundamental challenges around the nature of the democracy and society we might want to foster. When so much focus in the public square is on individual privacy, the common gaze turns attention to ways our personal flourishing is not only integrally bound up with the flourishing of others but also to the notion that part of flourishing as an individual is being attentive to and contributing to others' authentic development. In this chapter we anticipate a number of criticisms of the common gaze perspective before articulating its most significant contributions to public practice.

Concerns

The common gaze imposes a vision of the good

This is a core challenge to articulations of the common good that conceive of it as a destination rather than a journey. It is the criticism with which any attempt to articulate a notion of justice has to contend. There is, however, a significant difference between *having* and *imposing* a vision of the good. Many will not share the particular theological standpoint proposed here that the vision of the common gaze contains a preferential optic for people who are poor (understood not only materially but in terms of broader disadvantage). Michael Walzer's reiterative process of social criticism argues that we find confirmation of our community's truths when we see others reiterating them in their own social criticisms and articulation of what they hold to be true (Walzer 1990, p. 533). Contributing our particular vision is not to close down but to open up discussion. Such a reiterative process holds true for the common gaze as it discloses our respective social imaginaries. The common gaze is not a political philosophy and is not offered as a step towards a resolution of the question of justice. The common gaze is, however, a provocation to question how we navigate the choices made to implement surveillance in its particular forms.

There is a further component to this concern: that the common gaze assumes a Western model of flourishing. By avoiding ranking the components of flourishing, the common gaze leaves space for cultural and religious diversity. It may be that some Christians determine that flourishing has to be shaped such that the capability of practical reason takes priority over life; martyrdom is preferred to apostasy. Where this is not going to be a choice that ever needs to be made, other Christians may rank life considerably ahead of being able to flourish, for example through play. It will be the habits and traditions of faith communities that shape their respective formulations of flourishing, as will be the weight of philosophical reasoning for non-religious perspectives.

In this way, the common gaze holds the door open for discussions of surveillance technologies that encompass more than scientific rationalism. It is easy to assume that because someone uses digital technology their world view is wholly and unequivocally technological. The person who uses a mobile phone to arrange an appointment with a practitioner of traditional medicine holds a hybrid world view. Newer spiritual healing traditions, for example crystals, can also be procured by means of digital technologies – and contribute to a person's digital footprint that is valuable to marketing companies. This hybridity cannot be presented as merely people compartmentalizing in the sense that they use a technological approach to communicate but a spiritual means for healing. The situation is much more complex, given that someone might both trust in security systems at an airport *and* pray for God's protection on their journey. Those for whom the world remains in one way or another enchanted may hold this in tension with their own commitment to science and technology. The common gaze invites much deeper probing of hybrid world views of watching – without rushing to a scientific positivist conclusion.

The common gaze is a collective, but not a common, good

Surveillance certainly requires collective action; we are not able to each set up our own data-collection and analysis system beyond, perhaps, the rudimentary observation of our own home. Even in such a case, once we start remote monitoring we are reliant on collective action involving internet connectivity. So surveillance in its multiple forms is a collective good in which people are better off than if they acted individually. Crucially, this needs to be qualified because, as we have seen, it is not *all* people who are always better off as a result of surveillance. There are differences in benefits and, of greater concern still, disbenefits to some categories of people.

To think of the gaze as only a collective good is to fail to appreciate its *intrinsic* good. It is more than a matter of benefiting from surveillance in terms of security or consumer choice. The practice of watching out for and watching with one another in solidarity is an intrinsic good. We benefit from the good by participating in its action, as we do as musicians and audience at a concert (Deneulin and Townsend 2007, p. 26). In this sense, understanding the gaze in terms of the common good is to deepen our appreciation of being involved in surveillance culture. Surveillance can easily be rendered as a threat but to do so fails to appreciate the benefits it brings and the valuable contribution of those who work in surveillance industries. Sharing in the common gaze means having to re-examine our social imaginaries because these influence how we perceive those upon whom we gaze together – and for their good.

It might be further argued that the common gaze fails to recognize that surveillance is a commodity, purchased by states, corporations and individual consumers. The claim is that faced with contingency and danger, quantified in terms of risk, people are motivated by utility maximization to obtain the greatest possible benefit for the least necessary expenditure. A call for a common gaze is one that goes against the grain of economic decision-making. The common gaze is indeed a challenge to prevailing models because it confronts the social imaginaries that shape and are shaped by quantifications of risk. Common-gaze thinking encourages reflection on the preferences held by states, corporations or individuals. Purchasing (or financing the design of) particular surveillance devices is certainly an economic decision, but the common gaze claims the decision to be also political, social and spiritual. What one conceives as a threat, and the level of that threat, are bound up with how one understands one's own place in the universe, one's core values, one's experience of society and one's political perspectives. Racism, classism and gender are the most visible (although still rather occluded) practices of categorization that are reproduced, even amplified, by surveillance technologies. Even where a surveillance system is a commodity it is not *only* a commodity. A common gaze offers a broader depth of field.

The common gaze relies on trust

The rationale underlying such a criticism is that the primary disposition of social and political relations ought to be suspicion, if not outright distrust. Contracts are required because promises are inadequate. Surveillance systems are required because ill intent, fraud and other deceits are presumed. Similar to the problem of opportunism in discussions of gifts, deceit haunts justifications for surveillance. Appeals to the common gaze can seem naive, even dangerously negligent, because rights of privacy or justice, for example, hinder the deployment of surveillance towards 'obviously dangerous' groups.

This is a form of pitting freedom against security, failing to appreciate that security is *for* freedom, and freedom *requires* security – but neither can be guaranteed as absolute conditions. The common gaze does raise important dimensions of trust, not least in presumptions of guilt laid upon categories of people designated, for a complex set of reasons, as 'dangerous'. But the common gaze is not an appeal to rely *only* on trust and thereby dispense with systems of accountability, monitoring and control in particular domains. Yet there is an important element that might be described as cultivation of a disposition, arguably even a virtue, of trust. As Robert Reich observes, 'the common good depends on people trusting that most others in society will also adhere to the common good, rather than lie or otherwise take advantage of them' (Reich 2018, p. 27). This comes to the fore in the challenge to incorporate human intervention in AI systems that control entitlement to welfare provision. Some professionals demonstrate bias. The solution is not to remove all expert human decision-making but to have systems of transparent accountability and redress at the same time as cultivating trust by placing it in properly trained people.

The common gaze assumes citizenship and duty to country

Who it is that constitutes the 'common' of common good is not straightforward. Historically it would have been citizens or subjects of the city state or later nation state. Appeals to the common good by politicians, when these are made, are by and large directed at electors. Campaigners for the common good as it relates to transnational environmental concerns have in mind the global community of humankind. If we restrict ourselves for the moment simply to the nation state, the common gaze enfolds citizens and non-citizens alike. The latter comprise undocumented persons because of illegal migration or state action, those claiming asylum and others seeking refugee status. As expected, while sometimes rendered less visible by a state so it can avoid taking responsibility, people on these margins can simultaneously be made hyper-visible as objects of abuse and threat. Surveillance is thereby an action of the state against them, although campaigning organizations may encourage legible identification in order that people's status has the possibility of being acknowledged and positively addressed.

The common gaze – in its preferential optic for those who are poor – does not make citizenship a criterion for sharing in the good that is watching over and watching with. Non-citizens, and particularly those with no or incomplete documentation, are prime candidates for the compassion to which the common gaze, in its Christian version, pays special attention.

Critics may be concerned that relying on the common good appeals to duty to country, concealing disadvantage. The criticism here is directed at what are actually appeals to the collective, rather than the common, good. Rhetoric of the type, 'we are all in this together' or 'for the sake of the nation', or more insidiously, 'for the fatherland', are indeed claims for the good of the whole superseding those of individuals or minority groups. Such a notion of the collective good very easily glosses over current or newly generated disadvantages for some; a price considered worth paying. In war, it may well be that conscription and death toll hit poorer people disproportionately when troops with lower educational attainment are cannon fodder, while wealthier people can secure roles with less exposure to the front line.

There are forms of nationalism that appeal to disadvantaged groups by promising to inhibit the others who are 'taking your jobs' and thereby displacing blame on the other while ignoring structural barriers of injustice. This can become acute in broad appeals to 'national security' as legitimations for intrusive surveillance of those framed as dangerous communities. The common gaze is not the nationalist gaze. Rather, the common gaze aims to disclose the prejudices of rhetoricians and probes the reasons underlying discrimination. If it were to be taken to an even more extensive *global* common gaze, then its interrogation of national identity in relation to less powerful countries could be ever more acute.

The common gaze fails to rank within its preferential optic

If the common gaze is concerned about everyone's flourishing, then because flourishing is a conglomeration of different components, the challenge here is that the concept only highlights lack but gives no guidance on priorities for remedial action. If surveillance contributes to health outcomes by identifying national or global trends of a disease, is that more important than chilling of freedom of expression that other forms of surveillance might impose? Is bodily integrity, perhaps at borders, of higher priority in protection than surveillance that develops the capability of play by means of self-quantification in sports training?

Without recourse to a hierarchy of needs it is not clear how trade-offs between flourishing in one capability might be secured by accepting diminishment in another. Where does the common gaze help in tackling restrictions on religious liberties when a state considers these constraints necessary for preserving life (the case of the Uyghurs is a current example)? To put this in the terms of the compassion code, to whom in need does one go first when faced with a sick person, one who is unclothed, another who is in prison and one who is hungry? More broadly, with limited resources, the common gaze might disclose need but overwhelm responders. It has no obvious mechanism for directing remedial action first to injustices of surveillance against bodily integrity and only then to, say, diminishing of liberty of conscience. The response to this criticism returns to the reiterative process of social critique and, importantly, including the voices of people who are poor. This is not deciding on their behalf but *with* them – another reason for talking about *com*veillance rather than *sur*veillance, even solidaristic surveillance.

Contributions

Resistant democracy

The common gaze has the potential to energize democracy and make it more resistant by asking what sort of democracy it is that people actually want at the same time as disclosing how, through propaganda and advertising, those desires are being shaped. It may be that with greater awareness of how propaganda and micro-targeting overlap, many people come to find the strategies of the likes of Cambridge Analytica increasingly distasteful. Arguments over limits on campaign spending and the role of lobbying firms with money influencing policy are legion, taking their own shape in different countries (IDEA 2020). The role of exceedingly wealthy funders in political processes is problematic for the common gaze, let alone the common good. (On disproportionate influence of business elites on US government policy, see Gilens and Page 2014.) It may be almost impossible to think of a polity in which money does not talk, especially given the expense of running technologized campaigns. The practical impossibility of automated censorship with human intervention when social media platforms are all but monopolies on a global scale is a point well made by Cory Doctorow, who recognizes that overblocking (too stringent automated filtering algorithms on social media sites) can, albeit inadvertently, silence the voices of victims and legitimate protest. His call is for a break-up of corporations so that there can be communities deciding on and enforcing rules (Doctorow 2020b). To what extent is it desirable that one man can decide for 2.6 billion people what can and cannot be said in a public forum (Doctorow 2020a)? Alfred Kahn's theory of the tyranny of small decisions is highly relevant (Kahn 1966). If the small decisions taken along the way had been taken with knowledge of where we have ended up, the question is whether those small decisions would have been made. So rather than some great conspiracy, the cumulative effect of quite minor decisions has brought us to an undesirable situation that we would never have accepted if presented as one, single step.

In forcing the question of how vulnerable people are affected by data analytics, the common gaze lifts the public's vision to the likely future of its acquiescing to political decisions around surveillance in the present. Although not the most noble of appeals, the common gaze reminds people that they could become some of the collateral damage of surveillance at some point in the future. The economic consequences of the coronavirus pandemic have certainly hammered home the reality for many that job security, health stability and social interaction cannot be taken for granted and can collapse with frightening rapidity. With history in view, the common gaze reminds the public how data gathering and analysis can be a powerful tool in the armoury of those who turn against minorities. Populist politicians are well aware how successful it can be to dehumanize, indeed to demonize, minorities. Purity language, if not necessarily within religious rituals, can be deployed to construct and maintain a perception of the threat of contamination – possibly in cultural terms but also in health terms. The vilification of LGBTQI+ communities during the HIV/AIDS crisis serves as a reminder of the conjunction of moral and health pollution fears that remain significant in otherwise highly secularized countries. It is too soon, in the early summer of 2020, to know what stigma will be attached to having been a person who has spread Covid-19.

The common gaze is *resisting* prevailing assumptions that collateral damage from surveillance is acceptable. In military attacks collateral damage includes not only infrastructure but non-combatants or the civilian population. The point is that, although not directly targeted, certain categories of people are viewed as dispensable, albeit regretfully. As problematic as it is to adopt military terminology within contexts of everyday surveillance outside war zones, to refer to collateral damage is important as a means of exposing the value-laden terminology. Where algorithms are deployed that result in oppressive discrimination, the people so affected very much matter. They are not data points in a risk-analysis exercise but equally members of the community, despite whatever social stigma or opprobrium is attached to them. Often already living in the borderlands of poverty and social exclusion, the common gaze places them centre stage in evaluating surveillance systems of entitlement. The common gaze resists neoliberal economic modelling that privileges the market and in some cases makes market reasoning paramount. So if welfare provision is to be cut then the common gaze contests ideologies of austerity, asking instead who gains at whose expense and, in placing those who are poor centre stage, counters argument that it is they, and not the privileged, who are to bear the burden. Indeed, the common gaze is deeply political and also civic, in the sense that it engages the energy and experience of civil society as a means of constraining politics as the sole rationalizing discourse. Civil society practising a common gaze will require access to surveillance data in order to stand with, and sometimes on behalf of, those who are in the borderlands. Charities and advocacy groups need to be assured that proper authorities know who is denied services, discriminated against or otherwise marginalized. For example, Age UK, advocating for those in advanced old age, have a crucial role in the common gaze (Age UK 2020). They shine a light on the needs of this category of people as well as supporting individual elderly clients. In this sense, algorithms allocating services can liberate and oppress at the very same time. They can be liberative in unveiling need and oppressive when used to avoid government taking appropriate responsibility – or in some cases actively marginalizing.

Resilient society

The common gaze turns attention not just to the communal implications of surveillance but to the effects upon those who are particularly vulnerable. In so doing, the common gaze breaks the mesmerizing of which Floridi warns within the context of self-quantification. The allure of technological solutions combines with the ubiquity of the digital gaze to leave us inured to other options. A few parallels are salutary: for a time, doctors prescribed antibiotics as the go-to response for many patients until it became clear that, in the long run and across the population as a whole, overprescription increases resistance to this treatment (WHO 2015). Until only very recently, plastics were the solution to cheap and convenient packaging and to the need for products to be long-lasting and washable. Marine ecologists now warn of the destructive effects on the environment (United Nations n.d.). In a very different domain, the possibilities for alternative methods of policing advocated by groups in the USA, under the rather misleading banner of 'defunding the police', are resisted as being too far removed from known models. A turn to restorative approaches in criminal justice involves victims in processes to a far greater extent than retributive methods that are more traditional.

If we step some years into the future and imagine looking back at the early twenty-first century, this period might well be known as one in which surveillance was the go-to prescription and ready solution upon which our generation were unwilling to loosen their grip. When we ask what surveillance is *for* and conclude that the answer is best framed in terms of the common gaze, we begin to open up not only its effects against *social* justice (not just individual justice as in privacy concerns) but the deeper community dimensions surveillance is relied upon to address.

The notion of each person as not so much a living human document as a living human database is helpful – as long as we do not make the mistake of thinking of ourselves as *merely* biological algorithms. We are affected by a multitude of correlations among our interactions with other people. Our responses are to stimuli from those very much like us, a little like us and those who are very different from us. At our best, we do not live at the superficial level of emotional reaction but are sufficiently self-conscious to modify our responses; sometimes energizing by religious commitments but often by other values we have acquired or absorbed. The value of thinking of ourselves as living human databases lies in appreciating our being nodes in complex networks of relationships. To address conflict and uncertainty only with technological means, such as surveillance devices, is quite a superficial response. If democracy and citizens are hacked, then certainly it is important to regulate micro-targeting and associated data analysis, but the common gaze pushes us towards seeking ways of cultivating a social culture that encourages a best practice that arises from deep appreciation of the dignity of all people. The common gaze ushers us into the realm of virtue and not mere procedural solutions. We reiterate: the common gaze needs to be understood not as promoting one community's vision of the good but as that commitment to navigating multiple visions of the good.

There are *subversive* and *reparative* components to the common gaze. To conceive of our data as a gift, and to receive others' data similarly, undercuts strictly monetizing agendas. It subverts our being treated as data-generating agents for whom individual benefit is appealing. The common of this gaze undermines the atomism of economic and political models that aim to motivate and govern us on that basis. The reparative dimension is partly connected to the subversive trafficking of love into situations that otherwise show little evidence of being shaped by compassion. The conservation of love to which the wounded gaze aims is a radically different way of approaching the challenge of chaos, contingency and danger than digital categorization. Whereas self-quantifying apps turn attention to the self and to those doing the same activity, the common gaze is more outward looking. That same turn inwards is apparent in simplistic appeals to national security or national prosperity, as if those are not integrally connected to the flourishing of others in the world. The common gaze aims to repair the social fabric where it has been torn by aggressive atomism and individualism. The common gaze attends to the importance of our own dignity being inextricably linked to how we dignify others' lives. It is a gaze not only of connection but of solidarity. The common gaze is a counterforce to that which makes self-optimization a means of averting one's attention from systemic injustices within the surveillance industry. It is convenient to turn a blind eye towards those who work in the manufacturing plants that make affordable, wearable technologies. A self-tracking device may come at the cost of low wages for those much earlier in the production chain. This could be equally true of other surveillance and digital devices in everyday use.

To practise the common gaze is to subvert the prevailing technological and economic paradigms and to foment resistance that is political and radical against assumptions that more surveillance is the best response to each social challenge. The common gaze foments dissatisfaction at the prevalence of marketization of everyday life by injecting notions of gift and of love as bulwarks against the dehumanizing of people.

7

Common Gazing as Church Practice

The common gaze is not limited to addressing the public sphere but has implications for the practices of Christian communities. In this chapter we consider how the Church might welcome surveillance upon its activities, and what challenges arise as to how a church uses surveillance systems in its pastoral care and political campaigning. First, however, we ponder what rereading of the Bible is required in the light of our discussion of the common gaze and its preferential optic.

Rereading the Bible

Texts in denial

Feminist readers have identified 'texts of terror' to be reframed or expunged because of their propensity to legitimate violence, particularly against women (Trible 1984). Our rendering the common gaze in the presence of the burning children of Auschwitz requires us to reread *texts in denial*, where the unpleasant realties of a failed divine gaze are kept out of conscious awareness. 'The LORD will keep you from all evil' (Ps. 121.7) has to be absorbed in the knowledge that, not only in the Holocaust but in the experience of many who have been immersed in brutality and oppression, liberation can come too late. Most of the weight of Christian imagery, particularly in its hymns, pushes against the wounded and hopeless gaze to which Williams and De La Torre point. Countless Christians have found solace in songs like 'His Eye is on the Sparrow', by the lyricist Civilla D. Martin and composer Charles Gabriel, published in 1905. The chorus expresses what many might like the divine gaze to be:

> I sing because I'm happy,
> I sing because I'm free,
> For His eye is on the sparrow,
> And I know He watches me.

The common gaze cuts across this theodicy, destabilizing expectations of God in a way that is admittedly discomfiting. Timothy Rees's 1922 hymn, 'God is Love, let Heaven adore Him' can serve as a further example of the need for rereading against the grain of a hermeneutics of denial:

> God is Love: and he enfoldeth
> all the world in one embrace;
> with unfailing grasp he holdeth
> every child of every race.
> And when human hearts are breaking
> under sorrow's iron rod,
> then they find that selfsame aching
> deep within the heart of God.
> (verse 2)

Rees's theodicy is of a final resolution, beyond time, of the pains of this life: 'God is Love, so Love for ever o'er the universe must reign' (verse 3). Again, this belief satisfies and reassures many Christians, but the common gaze stimulates careful critical attention to the underlying assumptions of God's watching. This is also the case for texts that extol the shepherding of God, such as we have seen in Luke 15.4. Not every lost sheep is found. We do not expect this or any parable to provide a comprehensive reflection across the breadth of theological issues. The pressing challenge is detecting when a passage is deployed as a text in denial. Rereading this parable would mean pondering how the flock (the 99 'un-lost') are watching with and over one another. Naturally, the metaphor of sheep and shepherd rapidly breaks down, but the responsibility remains for creating an environment where sheep may safely gaze.

Sorting texts

Having a preferential optic for those who are poor means that the common gaze does not disregard categorization but seeks to put this process to good use as a way of identifying needs. A critical reading of biblical texts that feature social sorting is another of the contributions of the common gaze, when purity thinking proves so difficult to dislodge from its primacy with many Christian social imaginaries despite Jesus' reframing of the holiness paradigm. There is no way to avoid the associations with purity that arise in arguing that the Christian's body is a temple of the Holy Spirit (1 Cor. 6.19; 2 Cor. 6.16). However, the metaphor needs to be brought under control lest the defensiveness of protecting purity (as we observed in the ideational mapping in Ezekiel) inhibits compassion.

Radical hermeneutics is a reading from the outer side of boundaries, not, as we have seen, merely asking for admission but challenging the need to name and control those borders. Lists of categories such as those found in 1 Corinthians 6.9–10 come under the scrutiny of the common gaze. Who claims authority to define 'fornicators'? Remembering the challenge taken on by post-colonial readers against those who rushed to denigrate indigenous culture, we ask how the category of 'idolater' is legitimated, and to whose benefit and whose detriment? Knowing full well that Christians have selectively redrawn the boundaries of 'adulterer' to acknowledge complexities for people who have divorced and remarried, the notion of dismantling once-sacrosanct categories is widely, although not universally, established among churches. The common gaze interrogates the ways 'thieves' is constructed as another category that, at least for the apostle Paul, is not included in inheriting the kingdom of God. Where discrimination in algorithmic sorting generates automated inequality, readers of the Bible have to confront not only distinctions between blue-collar and white-collar financial crimes, but what thieving means in relation to a preferential optic for those who are poor across the globe. How complicit are Christians in a surveillance culture that advantages those in already privileged contexts?

In 1 Corinthians 6.9–11, Paul is making a point about repentance and the new way of living to which Corinthian Christians have turned. However, it is one of the 'sorting texts' that lend support to appreciating that categorization is an innately human activity. Because it is part of human life, categorization requires continual reappraisal to limit its use by people with more power to exert control over less powerful others.

Reversing texts

It takes little effort for a reader to distance him- or herself from the 'bad guys' of the Bible. No one wants to cast themselves as one of the false prophets, fickle crowd or traders colluding with the brutalities of imperial Roman commerce. Without going too far down a road of self-condemnation, the common gaze prompts a hermeneutics of suspicion not only towards readings that instantiate the ideologies of others but as to our own positions of power. In this sense we can talk of reversing roles within texts where we are the ones under notice from Mary of being cast down from our thrones and scattered in our imaginations (and imaginaries).

So a reversed reading of Jeremiah 23 on false prophets invites us to consider in what we put our trust for the future. It is unlikely to be in Baal, but do the CEOs of global data-analysis companies serve a similar function in our hopes when we accept their mantra of 'sharing to connect' or their redefinition of 'smart' as enabling the rendition of our data? Our faith might not be placed quite so personally in those executives, but the lure towards feeling secure might be recognizable by our forebears. The false prophets 'walk[ed] in lies', and at the moment of posting to social media it may be that Christians follow in their footsteps with fake news and disinformation. Are we the evildoers whose hands are strengthened?

We can self-affirm by picking the better moments of the behaviour of the crowd in the Gospels against which to compare ourselves. There is a hackneyed evangelistic rhetoric that asks unconverted audience members if they would be among those who would have condemned Jesus and called for the freeing of Barabbas. A hermeneutics of reversal would instead read ourselves into the text as those who might be the ones under adverse influence and unable to see what is happening to us. We could be the traders grieving at the loss of Babylon's power by which we have been able to accrue prosperity. As much as we might be prosumers within surveillance capitalism, our advantageous economic status could be under threat if a turn to the common gaze were to give priority to those in need.

Complicity in informational capitalism and the discriminatory inequities of twenty-first-century surveillance systems pose challenges for how Christians read these biblical texts. It is more pleasant to sit on the side of the fence that rejoices at Jesus' manifesto in Nazareth, anticipating the benefit of God's salvation. But we can reverse read the text to disclose where we, as users, developers, marketers or purchasers of surveillance technologies are the ones causing the captivity, the blindness and the oppression from which Jesus declares God's intention to deliver. A reversed reading is a necessary, but not the only, step. It may be that the manifesto is partly fulfilled when those unable to exercise a common gaze are given the resources to deploy surveillance with, and for, their particular communities; blindness is lifted. Similarly, those held captive by algorithms of oppression might be released by the application of surveillance that has exposed their plight and keeps holding policy-makers accountable for better practice.

It is unsettling to step from denial into acceptance of reality, and reading the Bible in theodic communities means being conscious of the wounded gaze that declines trite answers in the face of oppression. To fix the texts about sorting demands a less defensive posture towards the categories that we can find so reassuring. Reverse reading is a practice that guards from self-deception so that we can keep our distance from the ideologies of surveillance capitalism. Reading is itself a practice, but we can turn to specific challenges to how the Church engages with surveillance in the light of the common gaze.

Challenges to Christian practice

Church under surveillance

The Church certainly ought not to be reticent to be under surveillance in a number of particular situations. It needs to be under surveillance to ensure safety compliance for its property. While maintenance of church buildings might well be viewed from the theological perspective of Christian stewardship, the state does not leave this to spiritual discretion. As public buildings, churches are, at least in the UK, subject to quite stringent fire, health and safety regulations. A Christian of sound mind is never going to plan to make a church building a fire risk or a death trap to the unwary visitor. Nevertheless, I am confident that most, if not all, people who have had some management responsibility for church premises could tell stories of neglected kitchen equipment, flagstones causing a trip hazard, flammable materials forgotten about in the basement, or other frightening accounts. Lack of personnel, limitations on funds or sheer carelessness might be explanatory factors, but these are culturally – and legally – unacceptable in affluent countries.

The Church also needs to be under, and to welcome, surveillance to respect its charitable status (however that is determined within different legal jurisdictions). It is not enough to take the approach of 'Render unto Caesar that which is Caesar's – and remember it might be tax deductible'. Regulations also exist for the conduct of the wider financial affairs of charities, and thereby churches, most significantly in terms of what financial benefits arise for the trustees. A supporter of the Church should find no problem at all in welcoming the bureaucratic surveillance of the state in this regard. The opportunity is presented to demonstrate Christian probity and thus display good deeds before unbelievers.

The Church needs to be under surveillance for the protection of its vulnerable members. Detailed systems of surveillance and accountability are required of churches by the state to make Christian activities safer places for children and vulnerable adults. Child-protection requirements vary from country to country but in the UK there are stringent rules about vetting (through state-administered systems) not only full- or part-time professionals but also volunteers. These regulations apply to public bodies and charitable institutions alike. Churches are not discriminated against in this regard; the regulatory framework is applied across the sectors. Historic (and likely current) complicity of some churches in the abuse of vulnerable people demands rigorous accountability and transparency that relies on data gathering and cross-checking of the criminal records of volunteers who have direct engagement with particular categories of people.

The paradox of surveillance can be made to work to people's advantage. The Church under surveillance might be a better Church because her unjust actions are brought to light. Similarly, the internalized disciplinary process of being under surveillance might serve as a deterrent against bad practice (and bad theology).

The prospects for the Church can be bleak as it is perceived as an institution that has breached trust – whether over child abuse, financial corruption or more minor infractions. Reputational damage has been serious, and quite rightly the Church cannot be trusted to do good. I suggest that surveillance can contribute as acts of verification of truthful practice. The parallel I have in mind is that used in processes such as the Strategic Arms Limitation Talks that began in the 1970s to reduce the level of nuclear weapons held by the United States and the Soviet Union. Whether steps are unilateral or bilateral, these depend upon verification. Neither side trusts the other but incremental, verified, moves enable an agreement to be implemented. Other forms of peacemaking and conflict resolution use a similar process. The tortuous decommissioning of IRA arms in 2005 relied on the verification/oversight of the retired Canadian general John de Chastelain.

It is not enough that a Church says to the wider world, 'Sorry, we've failed in the past, but look, we follow Jesus and we have high ideals – we'll do better in the future.' Such assertions might help the faithful feel better when a preacher can point to corrupt figures and put them at a distance, claiming 'We're not like them'. Thankfully, the proverbial penny dropped and no serious Christian leader resists child-protection regulations. In fact, the horror of learning about abuse within and by the Church has prompted Christians to take these responsibilities with great seriousness. Here, at least, there is a welcome of what rightly needs to be named as surveillance. It is an example of surveillance as acts of care.

To embrace and welcome forms of surveillance is not to deny the social shaping that these technologies foster. It is too early to know how a culture of child protection will alter relationships within the Christian community, both for good and for ill. Relations of trust, aversion to risk and assuming a suspicious posture could become significant factors that tear the delicate fabric of Christian discipleship and basic human interaction. Perhaps this will be the price that all pay for the past sins of others.

Church using surveillance for pastoral care/growth

If these are aspects of the Church *under* surveillance, for the common good and as a dimension of the common gaze, there is also the matter of using big data as an administrative tool within congregations.

Gloo proposes using big data to 'engage your people and grow your church' (Engel 2019). The company contends that 'Using data is an accurate and efficient way to gain insights about your people and make confident decisions.' The methods include social media analytics, surveys and assessments, demographic reports and third-party vendors. The context is the USA, where data protection regulation is patchy and often very weak, so the company can extol the possibilities: 'This information creates predictive models of behavior. In other words, you'll be able to know things like a specific person's likelihood to get divorced or your congregation's need of financial support.' Gloo's products resonate with Michael Gutzler's enthusiastic embrace of big data in congregational development and pastoral care in a 2014 article in which he presents big data as the key to deepening the faith life of a congregation because it discloses the 'faith needs' of members (Gutzler 2014, p. 24). Gutzler recognizes that people raised in, or now seeped in a digital environment require relevant communication from the Church. Members are now dipping into, rather than being embedded in, church so have different 'circles of commitment', which can only be addressed if the pastor knows someone's 'personal data profile' (Gutzler 2014, p. 24). Circles of commitment (from Rick Warren's *The Purpose Driven Church*) are, in surveillance terms, social-sorted-categories. These include key data points: frequency and regularity of attendance; relative hours of volunteering activity in church life; offered demographic information supplemented by online data for their locality, for example, typical salary, monthly mortgage payments; personal financial giving to the church; participation in spiritual development initiatives run by the church. This allows the construction of a 'total level of commitment' index plotted against categories of core lay ministers, committed maturing members, congregation members, crowd/regular attenders and the community of the unchurched (Gutzler 2014, p. 26). In Gutzler's view, a church leader can then use data to target events that will move someone from an outer to an inner category of these concentric circles. The data can also demonstrate which church events are helpful and which harmful to such objectives. Taken together, the process involves mapping spiritual growth, which Gutzler reassures is 'easier than one thinks!', with variables such as participating in a retreat, an illness, a bereavement or attending a preaching series (Gutzler 2014, p. 28).

Unfortunately, Gutzler's proposal is ignorant of the shaping of attitudes that occurs by categorization. As we have seen, categories are performative, in the sense that our encounter with a category into which we have been placed shapes our behaviour. Furthermore, practice such as is envisaged by Gutzler offers no acknowledgement that categories are constructed based on what is measurable, not necessarily what is valuable. Gutzler ignores ethical questions of whether particular data should be collected or not. He sidesteps important technical questions about capturing accurate data (for example, of attendance). If the data is inaccurate then people could be wrongly categorized and potentially targeted with an inappropriate invitation or pastoral intervention. Overall, Gutzler seems unaware of the paradox of surveillance: it is helpful and harmful at the same time.

The use of data analytics would constrain the space to develop (through sometimes making mistakes) when a congregation is so closely monitored by its pastor. The power of the monitoring pastor is potentially abusive, not least because he is dealing with information rather than knowledge that is integrally bound into embodied relationships with people. This is perhaps less a problem in smaller congregations, but there the incentive to use data analytics will be weak, if present at all. In large, particularly megachurch settings, there is already significant distance between executive officers and members of the congregation(s). It is worth pondering what new metaphor of pastoral care arises in the vision that Gutzler extols: the pastor as security agent? The pastor's monitorial gaze is, yes, to encourage spiritual development, but where does this elide into protecting the rest of the congregation from those who cannot or will not grow or give? A whole new category is thus constructed: the risky congregant.

Church using surveillance for political engagement

Brian Burch of CatholicVote acknowledges the value of data gathering for engaging, in this case, with worshippers in Catholic churches in the USA, with a view to encouraging their participation in elections in favour of particular candidates:

> I suspect you already know that the vast majority of cell phone users have agreed to share their location data in order to unlock extra features on popular apps. Big corporations like Macy's, Home Depot, big sports franchises and many others purchase this data to reach potential customers.
>
> So we decided to do the same thing ... but with Catholic voters.

Starting last year, we created ad campaigns targeted to mobile devices that have been inside of Catholic churches. (Burch 2019)

Burch's aim for using this geofencing (in which mobile phone data can identify when a user is within a specified area) is with a very specific political agenda:

But consider this: pro-abortion politicians like Claire McCaskill, Nancy Pelosi and Joe Biden have masqueraded as faithful Catholics for decades. And NOTHING ever happens. Our churches forbid the distribution of outside voter guides and flyers in parking lots, and often say little to nothing from the pulpit, while warning of losing their tax-exempt status …

We're done tiptoeing around the Church hoping something will change.

The laity need to step up. And it's our job to deliver the truth. And we are not going to apologize.

We're going directly to our fellow Catholics with the truth about these lying politicians! And we're going to triple our efforts in 2020.

We don't need permission to reach millions of voters. You and I can now reach our fellow Catholics – especially Catholics who regularly attend church and proudly vote for pro-life candidates – with the bold, inspiring truth. (Burch 2019)

In her 2019 book, *Power Worshippers*, Katherine Stewart traces the development of Christian organizations she identifies to be particularly right wing, who are using data analytics, particularly United in Purpose (UiP), which focuses on Christian voter registration and turnout (Stewart 2019, pp. 172–84). Groups committed to the election of Democrat candidates are, as we would expect, also active in data analytics.

We have seen that in the febrile ecosystem of political micro-targeting there exist deeply partisan and rage-inducing strategies to advance the campaign of one party over another. In this same ecosystem sits data gathering to encourage voter registration and tactics to get people to vote in specific elections. Disinformation and attempts to dull people's critical capacities with affect heuristics is not the same as encouraging civic participation. However, in keeping with the liquidity of surveillance, it is of great concern that strategies and ethical assumptions (or the lack thereof) might leak from motivation by fake news and hatred into more worthy projects of registration and mobilization.

If we simply use the self-attested approach of CatholicVote as an example, there are significant issues of *informed* consent, rather than inadvertent consent. It is far from clear that agreeing to location services on a few mobile apps is recognized by Christian users as consent for their attendance at church to become another data point by which they are targeted with spiritual-political advertising. On a broader canvas, if a political agenda favoured by a large proportion of Christians, in for example the USA, can be achieved by the use of data analytics in conjunction with affect heuristics of enmity, does this end justify the means? In the arms race of data analytics and the hefty donations required to fund the most accurate and efficient systems, it is not difficult to envisage challenges for Christians to collude.

Such ventures may well be out of the hands of denominational leaders, if CatholicVote's intentions to reach over their (passive) heads to engage directly with parishioners is anything to go by. Nevertheless, education of people in the pews (or viewing online services at home) in the preferential optic for those who are poor is urgently required given the somewhat Wild West approach of political micro-targeting. Taking a common gaze approach here means confronting Christian complicity in systems of data analytics that either fail to address injustice or directly favour the already privileged at the expense of those who are poor. It really matters what Christians share on social media; the news items they re-post from highly partisan sites and their role in 'the crowd', who may be as fickle and disingenuous as those in the biblical narratives.

When the boundaries between the gospel and forms of exclusive, even racist, nationalism become blurred, the sensationalism and enmity fuelling political campaigning grates with the solidaristic emphasis of the common gaze. It is disturbing that Christians might be engaged in an arms race of weaponizing information targeted at other members of the body of Christ. It is, most certainly, a huge step for Christian campaigners to eschew data tools that might offer a tactical advantage over the opposition – especially when it is gospel values that are believed to be under threat. If a group of progressive Christians declines to deploy some forms of data analytics because these are oppressive and dehumanizing of categories of people, it is possible that those campaigners lose elections to conservative forces that are committed to economic policies that further hurt those at the bottom of the economic ladder. Coming from a conservative position, other groups faced with the possibilities of political micro-targeting might be unable to secure their anti-abortion agenda should they avoid the more disreputable forms of data gathering and influence of voters.

It may well be that Christians would want to uphold more than mere regulatory requirements for a minimum standard of data analytics. Here is one place where the preferential optic for those who are poor becomes particularly disturbing and therefore crucial in the common gaze. Just as many Christians recoil from using violence to achieve their desired political outcomes and opt for civil disobedience in tandem with consciousness-raising, the common gaze is a framework within which to make decisions to stand back from the verbal violence of affect heuristics in political micro-targeting – even if those might prove advantageous for the cause of social justice. Living in a world beyond victory on a particular issue requires repudiating a cycle of violence; here verbal violence (distinguished from robust and passionate declaration and argument). The common gaze challenges progressives not to use dehumanizing strategies even for humanizing goals.

Conclusion

Surveillance is common because we often encounter it and our engagement with these technologies takes place largely in the normal course of everyday life. Those of us in advanced capitalist societies share our data in ways that are so routine that they are unexceptional. Digital technologies of watching and sorting are often unremarkable to those who do not find themselves at the sharp end of the discrimination these systems reproduce. Life under habitual negative categorization, often inferred from proxy elements of our digital footprint, is another matter.

Surveillance is a condition of access to multiple benefits of technological and economic development. People living in countries that crave the improvements that digital systems offer may well see in the forerunners a future that gives them pause to reflect. The opportunity to design-in the common gaze might still be feasible. The window for resisting neocolonialism in the form of Silicon Valley globalization may not yet have closed.

Humans gaze aware of a horizon of mortality that deepens our appreciation of the here and now. Regardless of our social or economic status we die. Religions take different stances on whether this is the end or not, but sharing life that is limited nudges us all in the direction of solidarity. To watch over one another is not necessarily to scrutinize with a piercing gaze but can be wistful in anticipating what others might be able to achieve. We can watch with one another in wonderment at technological skills, the human capacity for inventiveness, and the good that surveillance serves. Machines can monitor, but humans can gaze.

It is important to understand what surveillance is for; the answer we offer here is human flourishing. The more penetrating question lies in asking: *Who* is surveillance for? It can be for those who are digitally poor, those who are digitally comfortable, those who are digitally affluent and those who are digitally mega-rich. The opportunity to step over discrimination or to withdraw from others' gaze is much less for those with few resources than for those with many. The common gaze puts those with least at the front of the queue for surveillance that benefits their flourishing. People who are better off have a place in the queue, but not at its head.

What it means to flourish is inflected differently across, and within, diverse religious and philosophical traditions. This book attempts to reframe the divine gaze from a Christian standpoint as a way of doing theology in public. With different perspectives, symbols, myths and communities of practice, people of other traditions will bring other dimensions to a common gaze. A Muslim, Hindu or Shinto exploration of surveillance through the lens of the common gaze will not be identical to the one offered here. The possibilities of rich encounters in inter-religious and intra-religious dialogue around the common gaze lie in future projects.

Afterword

Although much of this book was written during lockdown in the late spring of 2020, it has not been focused on the global pandemic. Given the rapidly developing situation, and despite its continuing to be in flux in mid-September 2020, it seems appropriate to add some brief reflections on how my proposals relate to the current emergency.

The common gaze in a pandemic

Particular forms of watching have become a way of life during the global pandemic of 2020 (and beyond). Health scientists are gathering data on the transmission and outcomes of the virus. Officials and politicians provide sometimes daily broadcasts explaining the progress of the pandemic and public health actions that are in some instances mandatory and in others advisory. On public transport and in shops people look around in order to be aware of who is and who is not maintaining social distancing regulations and/or mask-wearing. The authorities, perhaps as the result of a neighbour's tip-off, keep an eye on house parties that breach local restrictions. While some leaders are applauded for their government's response to Covid-19, others face severe criticism for carelessness and corruption. At the heart of many public debates has been the value of the most vulnerable members of society relative to the inconveniences imposed upon the majority. In the language of the parable of the lost sheep, some of the 99 have taken umbrage at the measures taken to care for the missing member of the flock.

Often, appeals are being made to act for the common good; in effect for a common gaze that this book is proposing. National slogans encouraging community-minded responses appear on websites, flyers and behind politicians during broadcast briefings. In Indonesia, it is, '*Maskerku melindungi kamu, maskermu melindungi aku*' – 'My mask protects you, your mask protects me'. The Saudi campaign in English is 'We're all responsible'. New Zealand is going with, 'United against Covid-19'. Italy emphasizes the experience shared by many: '*Insieme senza paura*' –

'Together without fear'. Spaniards have been presented with '*Este virus lo paramos unidos*' – 'This virus, we stop it together'. The early slogan of the United Kingdom government was 'Stay home, protect the NHS, save lives'. The state of Victoria, Australia, focuses on the justification for restricting social contact: 'Staying apart keeps us together'. As the first wave hit in the northern hemisphere's spring of 2020, public health officials and politicians appealed not only to individuals' sense of self-preservation but also to the close interdependence of each person's health with that of others. At their best, communities could respond to the virus in an expression of the common good; embracing restrictions on liberty as a communal effort in an emergency for the sake of everyone. Staying home, missing funerals, weddings and family milestones, maintaining social distancing and wearing a mask could be not simply *for* the common good but a moral engagement *of* the common good.

The preferential optic for those who are poor includes not only those in material poverty but people with poor health, perhaps through underlying medical conditions. The relationships between health and poverty, and between poverty and possibilities for social distancing and self-isolation, have come to the fore. Once the almost total closure of businesses has been eased, it matters greatly if a person works for a company that respects (and absorbs) the costs of an employee self-isolating should a family member show symptoms of infection. A preferential optic for those who are poor does indeed mean, as this book advocates, putting the needs of those who are most in need first. As the pandemic has unfolded it is possible that in some contexts we are seeing not so much a *preferential* but a *neglectful* optic for those who are poor. People who are already in poor health may well be left unseen by those whose responsibility it is to make evidence-based policy decisions. This need not be a disproportionate oversurveillance of people but an *absence* of attention to remedy the ways existing disadvantage is exacerbated by Covid-19.

The extent to which authoritarian states are able to respond to a pandemic better or worse than those that are democratic will be debated for years to come. All we can do here, at this stage, is to acknowledge that global public health is an issue around which political careers are made or broken – in either case justly or unjustly. Without forgetting those who are stateless or without citizenship, it is the case that the virus is transmitted between citizens; those who are in some way or another invested with decision-making power in elections. Datafied citizenship comes to the fore during this pandemic most obviously in people's health information being collected, analysed and sometimes shared. The common gaze challenges those who weaponize information and therefore confronts attempts by political actors to manipulate health data for their own ends. How independent are public health agencies from political pressure? Such a question has to be posed in an open, not closed, form as the *degree* of independence is of much more concern than assurances based on crude dichotomies such as 'independent' and 'politically controlled'. Our discussion here of gazing on democracy draws attention to attempts to hack democracy by social sorting of citizens into diverse categories that, arguably, are thus more open to being the focus of undue manipulation. 'False prophets' during a pandemic are not merely those who promulgate a religious message of divine protection for particularly faithful believers. Attempts to use data to shape citizens' self-perception and especially their view of others in their communities may be a careful tightrope walk between reassurance and alarm. On the other hand, less scrupulous politicians actively undermine a common gaze in favour of virulent individualism that panders to ethnic, religious or social prejudices. Today's successors of 'the crowd' in the biblical narrative are vulnerable not only to Covid-19 but to propaganda attempting to hide under the skirts of scientific data or overtly rejecting scientific method. The mantra in the UK's Brexit campaign – 'We've all had enough of experts' – has been blown away by the winds of Covid-19. However, rejection of scientific advice in public pronouncements by some politicians in the USA attempts to take the public in the opposite direction.

A major justification for lockdowns during the first wave was the need to avoid, if at all possible, overwhelming the health services, particularly hospitals, where the availability of critical-care equipment such as ventilators can outstrip demand. Rationing of life-sustaining interventions poses ethical and political challenges not normally confronted by healthcare officials in affluent countries, although it is a much more common everyday experience for their colleagues in many parts of the world. The choice to place Mrs X rather than Mr Y on the one remaining available ventilator might have to be made on the basis of a number of metrics, but the final decision lies with a medical practitioner rather than a machine-learning algorithm. Similarly, we might hope any decision to withdraw Ms W from a vital ventilator in order to accommodate the need of Ms Z is made by expert humans, not solely by an artificial intelligence processing health data. The common gaze calls for compassionate solidarity to prevail, which is not possible within the decision-making systems of AI, and thus places obstacles in the path of those eagerly advocating that humans stand aside in deference to supposed superior intelligence.

The good citizen, so it would seem, is one who tracks his or her own symptoms and movements. This does not necessarily mean downloading and using a specialist symptom-reporting or contact-tracing phone app. A non-digital memory or written note might well suffice as a log of social encounters over the previous 14 days. There is the possibility that familiarity with self-quantification apps predisposes people to use state-sponsored apps. However, there were early concerns in a number of jurisdictions over systems that might hold contact data centrally rather than this being dispersed and thus held on a user's own device. The good citizen is likewise one who fully cooperates with data gathering at restaurants, for example, who need a way of contacting patrons in the event of another customer or a staff member later testing positive for the virus. We might say that identity construction during the pandemic includes a dimension (perhaps a major dimension) of the assertion that 'I count therefore I am.' A contentious battle may yet ensue over the data that has been gathered and could be accessed for commercial or state advantage. Surveillance capitalism can be expected to push as far as regulators will permit in monetizing health data. As vaccines become available, any requirement to prove that one has received it will surely turn out to be a major tension between privacy and the common good. The concerns raised in this book offer some paths through this dense undergrowth of competing claims by keeping in the foreground a fundamental question: Who is surveillance *for*?

It has been health surveillance that has enabled correlations to be identified between the impact of the virus and some ethnic and socio-economic factors. One of the challenges ahead lies in how not only government but civil society responds in the long term to systemic disadvantage and Covid-19. The common gaze draws attention to discrimination, not least when climbing out of an economic recession might be given priority over caring for those most affected, but who have the least voice. Without considerable effort it is likely that those found to be 'out of place' in a post-Covid-19 society will be shunned. A human predilection to identify scapegoats could too easily blame communities in those parts of a country that have experienced spikes in transmission rates when responsibility lies elsewhere. As many of the public become weary of the pandemic and more resistant to public health restrictions, the urge to lay blame could intensify. Politicians will bear a heavy ethical burden to take responsibility for their actions or inactions.

With its theological roots in a wounded gaze, the common gaze is positioned to restrain Christians from rushing to simplistic or universalized responses to the pandemic. When it is health liberation, in the form of vaccines and treatments, that comes too late, the human casualties and bereaved people's pain cannot be brushed under any doctrinal carpet in a rush to defend a traditional, transcendental, omnipotent God. It will be important to address theologically the form of God's watching during the pandemic and how watching over one another can be the divine gaze. When high-profile Christian leaders have ridiculed mask-wearing and resisted restrictions on public worship there are trashed reputations to be rebuilt; not just their own but those of Christians who are found guilty by association in the minds of the wider public.

The common gaze offers a way of thinking critically towards reconstructing democracies that have been found wanting, ill prepared for resilience in the face of a global pandemic. Provision of medical equipment and health-care services is of course vital but, as the crisis rolls on, the social fabric is torn in many places but holding fast in others. To watch for, with and over one another is not to be reduced to technological apparatuses but, as this book argues, is fundamentally about human relationships committed to flourishing by enabling others to flourish.

Bibliography

Acxiom, 'When Experience Matters', available at www.acxiom.com/, accessed 19.03.20.

Age UK, 'Love Later Life', available at www.ageuk.org.uk/, accessed 19.06.20.

Airbnb, 'Hosting in 3 Steps', available at www.airbnb.co.uk/host/homes, accessed 16.06.20.

Ajana, B., 2018, 'Introduction: Metric Culture and the Over-Examined Life', in Btihaj Ajana (ed.), *Metric Culture: Ontologies of Self-Tracking Practices*, e-book edn, Bingley: Emerald Publishing Ltd.

Albrecht, K. and L. McIntyre, 2006, *The Spychips Threat: Why Christians should Resist RFID and Electronic Surveillance*, Nashville, TN: Nelson Current.

Alencar, A., K. Kondova and W. Ribbens, 2018, 'The Smartphone as a Lifeline: An Exploration of Refugees' Use of Mobile Communication Technologies during their Flight', *Media, Culture & Society*, 41:6, pp. 828–44.

Ananny, M., 2016, 'Toward an Ethics of Algorithms: Convening, Observation, Probability, and Timeliness', *Science, Technology, & Human Values*, 41:1, pp. 93–117.

Andersen, J., 2018, 'Archiving, Ordering, and Searching: Search Engines, Algorithms, Databases, and Deep Mediatization', *Media, Culture & Society*, 40:8, pp. 1135–50.

Anzaldúa, G., 2012, *Borderlands – La Frontera: The New Mestiza*, San Francisco, CA: Aunt Lunt Books.

Aquinas, T., 1945, *Basic Writings of Saint Thomas Aquinas*, Anton C. Pegis (ed.), Man and the Conduct of Life, volume 2, Indianapolis, IN: Hackett Publishing Company.

Arendt, H., 1958, *The Origins of Totalitarianism*, Cleveland, OH and New York: Median Books – The World Publishing Company.

Aristotle, 2017, *Politics*, Brooklyn, NY: Sheba Blake.

Arvidsson, A. and E. Colleoni, 2012, 'Value in Informational Capitalism and on the Internet', *The Information Society*, 28:3, pp. 135–50.

Bach, R. L. et al., 2019, 'Predicting Voting Behavior Using Digital Trace Data', *Social Science Computer Review*, October, available from https://journals.sage pub.com/doi/full/10.1177/0894439319882896, pp. 1–22, accessed 08.09.20.

Bailey, J., 2015, 'A Perfect Storm: How the Online Environment, Social Norms, and Law Shape Girls' Lives', in Jane Bailey and Valerie Steeves (eds), *eGirls, eCitizens*, Ottawa: University of Ottawa Press, pp. 21–53.

Bailey, K. E., 1983, *Poet & Peasant and through Peasant Eyes: A Literary-Cultural Approach to the Parables of Luke*, Grand Rapids, MI: Eerdmans.

Bakir, V. et al., 2018, 'Organized Persuasive Communication: A New Conceptual Framework for Research on Public Relations, Propaganda and Promotional Culture', *Critical Sociology*, 45:3, pp. 311–28.

Barbour, I. G., 1999, 'Neuroscience, Artificial Intelligence, and Human Nature: Theological and Philosophical Reflections', *Zygon*, 34:3, pp. 361–98.

Barstad, H. M., 2009, 'What Prophets Do: Reflections on Past Reality in the Book of Jeremiah', in Hans M. Barstad and Reinhard G. Kratz (eds), *Prophecy in the Book of Jeremiah*, Berlin: Walter de Gruyter, pp. 10–32.

Bauckham, R., 1993a, *The Theology of the Book of Revelation*, Cambridge: Cambridge University Press.

_____, 1993b, *The Climax of Prophecy: Studies on the Book of Revelation*, Edinburgh: T&T Clark.

Bauman, Z., 1990, *Work, Consumerism and the New Poor*, Buckingham: Open University Press.

Bauman, Z. and D. Lyon, 2013, *Liquid Surveillance: A Conversation*, Cambridge: Polity Press.

Bellar, W., 2017, 'Private Practice: Using Digital Diaries and Interviews to Understand Evangelical Christians' Choice and Use of Religious Mobile Applications', *New Media & Society*, 19:1, pp. 111–25.

Benedict XVI, 2005, *Deus Caritas Est*, available at http://w2.vatican.va/content/benedict-xvi/en/encyclicals/documents/hf_ben-xvi_enc_20051225_deus-caritas-est.html, accessed 31.12.15.

_____, 2009, *Caritas in Veritate*, available at www.vatican.va/holy_father/benedict_xvi/encyclicals/documents/hf_ben-xvi_enc_20090629_caritas-in-veritate_en.html, accessed 28.05.18.

Benkler, Y., 2006, *The Wealth of Networks: How Social Production Transforms Markets and Freedom*, New Haven, CT: Yale University Press.

Bennett, C., 2013, 'The Politics of Privacy and the Privacy of Politics: Parties, Elections and Voter Surveillance in Western Democracies', *First Monday*, 18:8, online.

Bergier, J.-Y. and C. Faucher, 2016, 'Persuasive Communication from a Military Force to Local Civilians: A Psyops System Based on the Elaboration Likelihood Model', *2016 IEEE 15th International Conference on Cognitive Informatics & Cognitive Computing* (ICCI*CC), pp. 160–6.

Berkovits, E., 1973, *Faith after the Holocaust*, New York: Ktav Publishing House.

Bhabha, H., 1995, 'Unpacking My Library Again', *The Journal of the Midwest Modern Language Association*, 28:1, pp. 5–18.

Black, E., 2009, *IBM and the Holocaust: The Strategic Alliance between Nazi Germany and America's Most Powerful Corporation*, 2nd edn, Washington, DC: Dialog Press.

_____, 2012, 'IBM's Role in Holocaust – What the New Documents Reveal', *HuffPost – The Blog*, 27 February, available at www.huffingtonpost.com/edwin-black/ibm-holocaust_b_1301691.html, accessed 4.12.18.

Blenner, S. R. et al., 2016, 'Privacy Policies of Android Diabetes Apps and Sharing of Health Information', *JAMA*, 315:10, pp. 1051–2.

Blumenthal, D., 1993, *Facing the Abusing God: A Theology of Protest*, Louisville, KY: Westminster John Knox Press.

Boisen, A. T., 1960, *Out of the Depths: An Autobiographical Study of Mental Disorder and Religious Experience*, New York: Harper & Row.

_____, 1971 [1936], *The Exploration of the Inner World: A Study of Mental Disorder and Religious Experience*, Philadelphia, PA: University of Pennsylvania Press.

Bölsche, J., 'Kirche im Nationalsozialismus: Verrat unter Brüdern', updated 17 February 2008, available at www.spiegel.de/einestages/kirche-im-nationalsozialismus-a-946648.html, accessed 29.11.19.

Borg, M. J., 1998, *Conflict, Holiness and Politics in the Teachings of Jesus*, London: Continuum.

Boutang, Y. M., 2011, *Cognitive Capitalism*, Ed Emery (trans.), Cambridge: Polity Press.

Bowden, M., 2012, 'The Measured Man', *The Atlantic*, July/August, available at www.theatlantic.com/magazine/archive/2012/07/the-measured-man/309018/, accessed 10.10.18.

Bowker, G. C. and S. L. Star, 1999, *Sorting Things Out: Classification and its Consequences*, Cambridge, MA: The MIT Press.

boyd, d. and K. Crawford, 2012, 'Critical Questions for Big Data', *Information, Communication & Society*, 15:5, pp. 662–79.

Brenkert, G. G., 1998, 'Ethics in Advertising: The Good, the Bad, and the Church', *Journal of Public Policy & Marketing*, 17:2, pp. 325–31.

Brittain, C. C., 2011, *Religion at Ground Zero: Theological Responses to Times of Crisis*, London: Continuum.

Brock, B., 2010, *Christian Ethics in a Technological Age*, Grand Rapids, MI: Eerdmans.

Brother Lawrence, 1981, *The Practice of the Presence of God*, E. M. Blaiklock (trans.), London: Hodder and Stoughton.

Brown, M. J., 2008, 'Performance Anxiety: The Use of Ὑποκριτής in Matthew 6:1–18', in Patrick Gray and Gail R. O'Day (eds), *Scripture and Traditions: Essays on Early Judaism and Christianity in Honor of Carl R. Holladay*, Leiden: Brill, pp. 115–36.

Brustein, W., 2003, *Roots of Hate: Anti-Semitism in Europe before the Holocaust*, Cambridge: Cambridge University Press.

Bugan, C., 2016, *Releasing the Porcelain Birds*, Bristol: Shearsman Books.

Burch, B., 2019, 'Untitled Blog Post', updated 15 October 2019, available at https://catholicvote.org/front-page-story/, accessed 15.06.20.

Butler, P., 2018, 'MPs Call for Review of "Pointlessly Cruel" Benefit Sanctions', 6 November, *The Guardian*, available at www.theguardian.com/society/2018/nov/06/mps-call-for-review-of-pointlessly-cruel-benefit-sanctions, accessed 11.06.20.

Cadwalladr, C., 2018, 'Our Cambridge Analytica Scoop Shocked the World. But the Whole Truth Remains Elusive', updated 23 December 2018, *The Guardian*, available at www.theguardian.com/uk-news/2018/dec/23/cambridge-analytica-facebook-scoop-carole-cadwalladr-shocked-world-truth-still-elusive, accessed 15.01.20.

Cahill, L. S., 2004, *Bioethics and the Common Good*, Milwaukee, WI: Marquette University Press.

Callahan, A. D., 1999, 'Apocalypse as Critique of Political Economy: Some Notes on Revelation 18', *Horizons in Biblical Theology*, 21:1, pp. 46–65.

Camdessus, M., 2012, 'From a "Culture of Greed" to a Culture of Common Good', in Martin Schlag and Juan Adrés Mercado (eds), *Free Markets and the Culture of Common Good*, Dordrecht: Springer, pp. 111–19.

Cameron, H., 2014, 'The Morality of the Food Parcel', *Practical Theology*, 7:3, pp. 194–204.

Carroll, R. P., 1981, *From Chaos to Covenant: Uses of Prophecy in the Book of Jeremiah*, London: SCM Press.

_____, 1986, *Jeremiah: A Commentary*, London: SCM Press.

Caruso, L., 2017, 'Digital Capitalism and the End of Politics: The Case of the Italian Five Star Movement', *Politics & Society*, 45:4, pp. 585–609.

Castells, M., 2000, *The Rise of the Network Society*, 2nd edn, Oxford: Blackwell.

Castoriadis, C., 1987, *The Imaginary Institution of Society*, Kathleen Blamey (trans.), Cambridge, MA: The MIT Press.

CELAM (Consejo Episcopal Latinoamericano), 1979, 'Documento De Puebla III Conferencia General Del Episcopdao Latinoamericano', *Latin American Episcopal Council*, available from www.celam.org/doc_conferencias/Documento_ Conclusivo_Puebla.pdf, accessed 21.06.20.

CGCM (Common Good Capitalism Movement), *Common Good Capitalist Movement*, available at www.commongoodcapitalism.org/, accessed 06.02.20.

Chang, L., 2015, 'Third-Party Websites are Getting a lot of Your Personal Data from Your Mobile Apps', *digitaltrends*, updated 6 November 2015, available at www.digitaltrends.com/mobile/how-much-data-are-your-favorite-apps-really-sharing-with-third-parties/, accessed 05.02.20.

Cheney-Lippold, J., 2017, *We are Data: Algorithms and the Making of our Digital Selves*, New York: New York University Press.

Citizens Advice, 'Preparing for Your ESA Medical Assessment', available at www. citizensadvice.org.uk/benefits/sick-or-disabled-people-and-carers/employment-and-support-allowance/help-with-your-esa-claim/esa-medical-assessment/, accessed 11.05.20.

Cobb, J. F. and D. R. Griffin, 1977, *Process Theology: An Introductory Exposition*, Louisville, KY: Westminster John Knox Press.

Cohen, A. A., 1981, *Tremendum: A Theological Interpretation of the Holocaust*, New York: Crossroad Publishing.

Cohen, J. E., 2019, *Between Truth and Power: The Legal Constructions of Informational Capitalism*, New York: Oxford University Press.

Collins, A. Y., 1984, '"What the Spirit Says to the Churches": Preaching the Apocalypse', *Quarterly Review*, 4.

Combs, C. D. and S. R. Barham, 2016, 'The Quantifiable Self: Petabyte by Petabyte', in C. Donald Combs, John A. Sokolowski and Catherine M. Banks (eds), *The Digital Patient: Advancing Healthcare, Research, and Education*, Hoboken, NJ: John Wiley & Sons, pp. 63–72.

Cone, J. H., 1969, *Black Theology and Black Power*, New York: Seabury.

_____, 1977, *God of the Oppressed*, London: SPCK.

_____, 1990 [1970], *A Black Theology of Liberation: Twentieth Anniversary Edition*, Maryknoll, NY: Orbis Books.

Congregation for the Doctrine of the Faith, 1984, 'Instruction on Certain Aspects of the "Theology of Liberation"', available at www.vatican.va/roman_curia/con gregations/cfaith/documents/rc_con_cfaith_doc_19840806_theology-liberation_ en.html, accessed 03.06.20.

Corelogic, 'Powering Housing', *CoreLogic*, available at www.corelogic.com/, accessed 19.03.20.

Crites, S., 1989, 'The Narrative Quality of Experience', in Stanley Hauerwas and L. Gregory Jones (eds), *Why Narrative? Readings in Narrative Theology*, Grand Rapids, MI: Eerdmans, pp. 65–88.

Damasio, A., 2018, *The Strange Order of Things*, New York: Pantheon Books.

Davies, H., 2015, 'Ted Cruz using Firm that Harvested Data on Millions of Unwitting Facebook Users', 11 December, *The Guardian*, available at www.theguardian.com/us-news/2015/dec/11/senator-ted-cruz-president-campaign-facebook-user-data, accessed 29.02.20.

Day, K., 2016, *Religious Resistance to Neoliberalism: Womanist and Black Feminist Perspectives*, New York: Palgrave Macmillan.

DCM&S (Digital, Culture, Media and Sport) Committee, 2018a, 'Disinformation and "Fake News": Interim Report', London: House of Commons.

DCM&S (Digital, Culture, Media and Sport) Committee, 2018b, 'Oral Evidence: Disinformation and "Fake News", Hc363', London: House of Commons.

DCM&S (Digital, Culture, Media and Sport) Committee, 2019, 'Disinformation and "Fake News": Final Report', in Digital, Culture, Media and Sport Committee (ed.), London: House of Commons, 18 February 2019.

De La Torre, M. A., 2013, 'Introduction', in Miguel A. De La Torre (ed.), *Ethics: A Liberative Approach*, Minneapolis, MN: Fortress Press, pp. 1–6.

_____, 2015, *The Politics of Jesús: A Hispanic Political Theology*, Lanham, MD: Rowman & Littlefield.

_____, 2017, *Embracing Hopelessness*, Minneapolis, MN: Fortress Press.

Dencik, L. et al., 2019, 'The "Golden View": Data-Driven Governance in the Scoring Society', *Internet Policy Review*, 8:2, pp. 1–24.

Deneulin, S. and N. Townsend, 2007, 'Public Goods, Global Public Goods and the Common Good', *International Journal of Social Economics*, 34:1/2, pp. 19–36.

Desouza, K. C. et al., 2020, 'Weaponizing Information Systems for Political Disruption: The Actor, Lever, Effects, and Response Taxonomy (ALERT)', *Computers & Security*, 88, p. 1–15.

Diphoorn, T., 2016, '"Surveillance of the Surveillers": Regulation of the Private Security Industry in South Africa and Kenya', *African Studies Review*, 59:2, pp. 161–82.

Doctorow, C., 2020a, 'On Zuckerberg and Content-Blocking', 13 June, *Twitter*, available at https://twitter.com/doctorow/status/1271875069770207233, accessed 19.06.20.

_____, 2020b, 'On Cutting Size of Facebook', 13 June, *Twitter*, available at https://twitter.com/doctorow/status/1271875068566532096, accessed 19.06.20.

Dormehl, L., 2016, *Thinking Machines: The Inside Story of Artificial Intelligence and our Race to build the Future*, London: W. H. Allen.

Douglas, K. B., 2015, *Stand Your Ground: Black Bodies and the Justice of God*, Maryknoll, NY: Orbis Books.

Douglas, M., 1966, *Purity and Danger: An Analysis of the Concepts of Pollution and Taboo*, London: ARK Paperbacks.

_____, 2000, *Leviticus as Literature*, Oxford: Oxford University Press.

_____, 2002 [1966], *Purity and Danger: An Analysis of the Concepts of Pollution and Taboo*, London: Routledge.

Dressel, J. and H. Farid, 2018, 'The Accuracy, Fairness, and Limits of Predicting Recidivism', *Science Advances*, 4:1, pp. 1–15.

Dreyfus, H. L., 1979, *What Computers Still Can't Do: A Critique of Artificial Reason*, Cambridge, MA: MIT Press.

Du Bois, W. E. B., 1926, *The Souls of Black Folk: Essays and Sketches*, Chicago, IL: A. C. McClurg & Co.

Dubrofsky, R. E. and S. A. Magnet, 2015, 'Introduction: Feminist Surveillance Studies – Critical Interventions', in Rachel E. Dubrofsky and Shoshana Amielle Magnet (eds), *Feminist Surveillance Studies*, Durham, NC: Duke University Press, pp. 1–17.

Duff, A. S., D. Craig and D. A. McNeill, 1996, 'A Note on the Origins of the "Information Society"', *Journal of Information Science*, 22:2, pp. 117–22.

Duffy, B., 2018, *The Perils of Perception: Why We're Wrong about Nearly Everything*, London: Atlantic Books.

Dunn, J. D. G., 2002, 'Jesus and Purity: An Ongoing Debate', *New Testament Studies*, 48:4, pp. 449–67.

_____, 2010, 'The Thought World of Jesus', *Early Christianity*, 1:3, pp. 321–43.

Dussel, E., 1988, *Ethics and Community*, Tunbridge Wells: Burns & Oates.

Dyson, G., 2012, *Turing's Cathedral: The Origins of the Digital Universe*, New York: Pantheon.

Echo app, 'Echo Exists to Help You Pray', available at https://new.echoprayer.com/, accessed 19.03.20.

Eckhardt, G. M. and F. Bardhi, 2015, 'The Sharing Economy isn't about Sharing at All', 28 January, *Harvard Business Review*, available at https://hbr.org/2015/01/the-sharing-economy-isnt-about-sharing-at-all, accessed 8.10.19.

Edelman, B., M. Luca and D. Svirsky, 2017, 'Racial Discrimination in the Sharing Economy: Evidence from a Field Experiment', *American Economic Journal: Applied Economics*, 9:2, pp. 1–22.

Ellul, J., 1973 [1965], *Propaganda: The Formation of Men's Attitudes*, New York: Vintage Books.

_____, 2003 [1970], *The Meaning of the City*, Eugene, OR: Wipf & Stock.

Engel, M., 2019, 'Use Big Data to Engage Your People and Grow Your Church', 20 February, *Gloo*, available at https://blog.gloo.us/big-data-for-churches-introduction, accessed 15.06.20.

Equifax, 2020a, 'Business', *Equifax*, available at www.equifax.com/business/, accessed 19.03.20.

_____, 2020b, 'Personal', *Equifax*, available at www.equifax.com/personal/, accessed 19.03.20.

Ericksen, R. P., 2012, *Complicity in the Holocaust: Churches and Universities in Nazi Germany*, Cambridge: Cambridge University Press.

Eubanks, V., 2017, *Automating Inequality: How High-Tech Tools Profile, Police, and Punish the Poor*, New York: St Martin's Press.

Experian, 'About Experian', available at www.experian.co.uk/about-us/index.html, accessed 19.03.20.

Facebook, 2020, 'Preparing for Election Day – press statement by Guy Rosen, VY Integrity', https://about.fb.com/news/2020/10/preparing-for-election-day/, accessed 16.10.20.

Fackenheim, E. L., 1967, 'The 614th Commandment', *Judaism*, 16:3, pp. 269–73.

_____, 1970, *God's Presence in History: Jewish Affirmations and Philosophical Reflections*, New York: New York University Press.

_____, 1990, *The Jewish Bible after the Holocaust*, Manchester: Manchester University Press.

Farley, W., 1990, *Tragic Vision and Divine Compassion: A Contemporary Theodicy*, Louisville, KY: Westminster John Knox Press.

Felber, C., 2019, *Change Everything: Creating an Economy for the Common Good*, 2nd edn, London: Zed Books.

Finn, D. K., 2012, 'Reciprocity, Trust, and Social Capital', in Daniel K. Finn (ed.), *The Moral Dynamics of Economic Life: An Extension and Critique of Caritas in Veritate*, Oxford: Oxford University Press, pp. 76–80.

Finnis, J. M., 1999, 'What is the Common Good, and why does it concern the Client's Lawyer?', *South Texas Law Review*, 40:1, pp. 41–53.

_____, 2001, 'Is Natural Law Theory Compatible with Limited Government?', in Robert George (ed.), *Natural Law, Liberalism, and Morality: Contemporary Essays*, Oxford: Oxford University Press, pp. 1–26.

Floridi, L., 2014, *The 4th Revolution: How the Infosphere is Reshaping Human Reality*, New York; Oxford: Oxford University Press.

_____, 2015, 'A Proxy Culture', *Philosophy & Technology*, 28:4, pp. 487–90.

Foerst, A., 1998, 'Cog, a Humanoid Robot, and the Question of the Image of God', *Zygon*, 33:1, pp. 91–111.

Fotopoulou, A. and K. O'Riordan, 2017, 'Training to Self-Care: Fitness Tracking, Biopedagogy and the Healthy Consumer', *Health Sociology Review*, 26:1, pp. 54–68.

Foucault, M., 1979, *Discipline and Punish: The Birth of the Prison*, London: Penguin.

_____, 1980, *Power/Knowledge: Selected Interviews and Other Writings 1972–1977*, New York: Harvester Wheatsheaf.

_____, 2000, 'The Ethics of the Concern for Self as a Practice of Freedom', in R. Rabinow (ed.), Michel Foucault, *Ethics: Subjectivity and Truth (The Essential Works of Foucault 1954–1984)*, volume 1, London: Penguin Books, pp. 281–301.

FRA, 2017, 'Surveillance by Intelligence Services: Fundamental Rights Safeguards and Remedies', Field Perspectives and Legal Update: FRA: European Union Agency for Fundamental Rights, available at https://op.europa.eu/en/publication-detail/-/publication/b7f98a74-afc2-11e7-837e-01aa75ed71a1/language-en, accessed 16.10.20.

Francis, 2013, *Evangelii gaudium*, available from www.vatican.va/content/francesco/en/apost_exhortations/documents/papa-francesco_esortazione-ap_20131124_evangelii-gaudium.html, accessed 17.06.20.

_____, 2014, 'Address of Pope Francis to Rectors and Students of the Pontifical Colleges and Residences of Rome – 12 May 2014', available at www.vatican.va/content/francesco/en/speeches/2014/may/documents/papa-francesco_20140512_pontifici-collegi-convitti.html, accessed 15.03.20.

_____, 2015, *Laudato si'*, available from www.vatican.va/content/francesco/en/encyclicals/documents/papa-francesco_20150524_enciclica-laudato-si.html, accessed 26.06.20.

_____, 2016, Message for the 50th World Communications Day, 2016 – 'Communication and Mercy: A Fruitful Encounter', available from www.vatican.va/content/francesco/en/messages/communications/documents/papa-francesco_20160124_messaggio-comunicazioni-sociali.html.

_____, 2018, Message for the 52nd World Communications Day, 2018 – '"The Truth Will Set You Free" (John 8:32), Fake News and Journalism for Peace', available from www.vatican.va/content/francesco/en/messages/communications/documents/papa-francesco_20180124_messaggio-comunicazioni-sociali.html.

_____, 2019, Message for the 53rd World Communications Day, 2019 – '"We Are Members One of Another" (Eph. 4.25). From Social Network Communities to the Human Community', available at http://w2.vatican.va/content/francesco/en/messages/communications/documents/papa-francesco_20190124_messaggio-comunicazioni-sociali.html.

Freire, P. and M. B. Ramos, 1972, *Pedagogy of the Oppressed*, London: Sheed & Ward.

Friesen, S. J., 2003, 'The Beast from the Land: Revelation 13:11–18 and Social Setting', in David L. Barr (ed.), *Reading the Book of Revelation: A Resource for Students*, Atlanta, GA: Society of Biblical Literature, pp. 49–64.

Fuchs, C., 2010, 'Labor in Informational Capitalism and on the Internet', *The Information Society*, 26:3, pp. 179–96.

_____, 2012, 'Critique of the Political Economy of Web 2.0 Surveillance', in Christian Fuchs et al. (eds), *Internet and Surveillance: The Challenges of Web 20 and Social Media*, Abingdon: Routledge, pp. 31–70.

_____, 2017, *Social Media: A Critical Introduction*, 2nd edn, London: Sage.

Fussey, P. and D. Murray, 2019, 'Independent Report on the London Metropolitan Police Service's Trial of Live Facial Recognition Technology', Colchester: Human Rights Centre, University of Essex.

Gailus, M., 2008, '"Hier werden täglich drei, vier Fälle einer nichtarischen Abstammung auggedeckt": Pfarrer Karl Themel und die Kirchenbuchstelle Alt-Berlin', in Manfred Gailus (ed.), *Kirchliche Amtshilfe: Die Kirche and die Judenverfolgung im 'Dritten Reich'*; Göttingen: Vandenhoeck & Ruprecht, pp. 82–100.

Gandy Jr, O. H., 2012, 'Statistical Surveillance: Remote Sensing in the Digital Age', in Kirstie Ball, Kevin D. Haggerty and David Lyon (eds), *Routledge Handbook of Surveillance Studies*, London and New York: Routledge, pp. 125–32.

Gangadharan, S. P., 2017, 'The Downside of Digital Inclusion: Expectations and Experiences of Privacy and Surveillance among Marginal Internet Users', *New Media and Society*, 19:4, pp. 597–615.

Gellman, B. and L. Poitras, 2013, 'U.S., British Intelligence Mining Data from Nine U.S. Internet Companies in Broad Secret Program', *The Washington Post*, 7 June, available at www.washingtonpost.com/investigations/us-intelligence-mining-data-from-nine-us-internet-companies-in-broad-secret-program/2013/06/06/3a0coda8-cebf-11e2-8845-d970ccb04497_story.html, accessed 2.12.19.

Gilens, M. and B. I. Page, 2014, 'Testing Theories of American Politics: Elites, Interest Groups, and Average Citizens', *Perspectives on Politics*, 12:3, pp. 564–81.

Good News Network, 2020, '9 Apps that Supercharge Your Spiritual Practical and Positive Thinking', *Good News Network*, available at www.goodnewsnetwork.org/9-apps-supercharge-spiritual-practice-positive-thinking/, accessed 20.04.20.

Gopal, P., 2004, 'Reading Subaltern History', in Neil Lazarus (ed.), *The Cambridge Companion to Postcolonial Literary Studies*, Cambridge: Cambridge University Press, pp. 139–61.

Goss, R., 1993, *Jesus Acted Up: A Gay and Lesbian Manifesto*, San Francisco, CA: HarperSanFrancisco.

Graham, E., 2013, *Between a Rock and a Hard Place: Public Theology in a Post-Secular Age*, London: SCM Press.

_____, 2017, 'Reflexivity and Rapprochement: Explorations of a "Postsecular" Public Theology', *International Journal of Public Theology*, 11:3, pp. 277–89.

Graham, S., 2010, 'Laboratories of War: Surveillance and US-Israeli Collaboration in War and Security', in Elia Zureik, David Lyon and Yasmeen Abu-Laban (eds), *Surveillance and Control in Israel/Palestine: Population, Territory, and Power*, London: Routledge, pp. 133–52.

Grassl, W., 2011, 'Hybrid Forms of Business: The Logic of Gift in the Commercial World', *Journal of Business Ethics*, 100, pp. 109–23.

Greenberg, I., 1977, 'Cloud of Smoke, Pillar of Fire: Judaism, Christianity, and Modernity after the Holocaust', in Eva Fleischner (ed.), *Auschwitz: Beginning of a New Era? Reflections on the Holocaust*, New York: Jewish Life Network.

Greenberg, M., 1997, 'Ezekiel 21–37', *The Anchor Bible*, New Haven, CT: Yale University Press.

Greenwald, G., 2014, *No Place to Hide: Edward Snowden, the NSA, and the U.S. Surveillance State*, New York: Picador.

Griffiths, B., 2015, 'Markets and the Common Good', in Nicholas Sagovsky and Peter McGrail (eds), *Together for the Common Good: Towards a National Conversation*, London: SCM Press, pp. 139–52.

Groome, T. H., 1991, *Sharing Faith: A Comprehensive Approach to Religious Education and Pastoral Ministry – the Way of Shared Praxis*, San Francisco, CA: HarperSanFrancisco.

Gutiérrez, G., 2001 [1974], *A Theology of Liberation*, London: SCM Press.

_____, 2005 [1984], *We Drink from our Own Wells*, London: SCM Press.

Gutzler, M. D., 2014, 'Big Data and the 21st Century Church', *Dialog*, 53:1, pp. 23–9.

Guzman, A. L. and S. C. Lewis., 2019, 'Artificial Intelligence and Communication: A Human – Machine Communication Research Agenda', *New Media & Society*, advance online, pp. 1–17.

Habermas, J., 1996, *Between Facts and Norms: Contributions to a Discourse Theory of Law and Democracy*, William Rehg (trans.), Cambridge: Polity Press.

Harari, Y. N., 2017, *Homo Deus: A Brief History of Tomorrow*, London: Vintage.

Hardt, M. and A. Negri, 2019, *Assembly*, New York: Oxford University Press.

Hauerwas, S., 1990, *Naming the Silences: God, Medicine, and the Problem of Suffering*, Edinburgh: T&T Clark.

Healey, K. and R. H. Woods Jr, 2017, 'Processing is not Judgment, Storage is not Memory: A Critique of Silicon Valley's Moral Catechism', *Journal of Media Ethics*, 32:1, pp. 2–15.

Hecht, I., 1985, *Invisible Walls and to Remember is to Heal*, Evanston, IL: Northwestern University Press.

Held, D., 1996, *Models of Democracy*, 2nd edn, Cambridge: Polity Press.

Hern, A., 2020, 'Facebook Moderators Join Criticism of Zuckerberg over Trump Stance', *The Guardian*, 8 June, available at www.theguardian.com/technology/2020/jun/08/facebook-moderators-criticism-mark-zuckerberg-donald-trump, accessed 16.06.20.

Heyen, N. B., 2016, 'Self-Tracking as Knowledge Production: Quantified Self between Prosumption and Citizen Science', in Stefan Selke (ed.), *Lifelogging: Digital Self-Tracking and Lifelogging – between Disruptive Technology and Cultural Transformation*, Wiesbaden: Springer Fachmedien Wiesbaden, pp. 283–301.

Hick, J., 1977, *Evil and the God of Love*, 2nd edn, London: Macmillan.

Hillygus, D. S. and T. G. Shields, 2008, *The Persuadable Voter: Wedge Issues in Presidential Campaigns*, Princeton, NJ: Princeton University Press.

Hintz, A., L. Dencik and K. Wahl-Jorgensen, 2019, *Digital Citizenship in a Datafied Society*, Cambridge: Polity Press.

Hobbes, T., 1968, *Leviathan*, C. B. Macpherson edn, Harmondsworth: Penguin.

Hoffmann, S., E. Taylor and S. Bradshaw, *The Market of Disinformation*, OXTEC: Oxford Technology & Elections Commission, available at https://oxtec.oii.ox.ac.uk/wp-content/uploads/sites/115/2019/10/OxTEC-The-Market-of-Disinformation pdf, accessed 28.10.19.

Hollenbach, D., 1996, 'Social Ethics under the Sign of the Cross', *The Annual of the Society of Christian Ethics*, pp. 1–18.

_____, 2002, *The Common Good and Christian Ethics*, Cambridge: Cambridge University Press.

hooks, b., 2015, *Black Looks: Race and Representation*, 2nd edn, New York: Routledge.

Howard-Brook, W. and A. Gwyther, 1999, *Unveiling Empire: Reading Revelation Then and Now*, Maryknoll, NY: Orbis Books.

Human Rights Council, 2019, 'Visit to the United Kingdom of Great Britain and Northern Ireland: Report of the Special Rapporteur on Extreme Poverty and Human Rights', *General Assembly of the United Nations*, Forty-first session, 24 June–12 July 2019, available from https://undocs.org/A/HRC/41/39/Add.1, accessed 14.09.20.

Human Rights Watch, 2018, 'China: Big Data Fuels Crackdown in Minority Region', 26 February, *Human Rights Watch*, available at www.hrw.org/news/2018/02/26/china-big-data-fuels-crackdown-minority-region, accessed 04.05.20.

Humphreys, L., 2018, *The Qualified Self: Social Media and the Accounting of Everyday Life*, Cambridge, MA: The MIT Press.

IBM, 2001, 'IBM Statement on Nazi-Era Book and Lawsuit', *IBM*, 14 February, available at www-03.ibm.com/press/us/en/pressrelease/1388.wss, accessed 01.05.20.

ICO, 2018a, 'Democracy Disrupted? Personal Information and Political Influence', Information Commissioner's Office, available from https://ico.org.uk/media/2259369/democracy-disrupted-110718.pdf, accessed 18.09.20.

_____, 2018b, 'ICO Issues Maximum £500,000 Fine to Facebook for Failing to Protect Users' Personal Information', Information Commissioner's Office, 25 October, available at https://ico.org.uk/facebook-fine-20181025, accessed 29.02.20.

_____, 2018c, 'Investigation into the Use of Data Analytics in Political Campaigns', Information Commissioner's Office, available at https://ico.org.uk/media/action-weve-taken/2260271/investigation-into-the-use-of-data-analytics-in-political-campaigns-final-20181105.pdf, accessed 05.11.19.

_____, Letter from Elizabeth Denham to Julian Knight MP, chair of Digital, Culture, Media and Sport Select Committee, 2 October 2020; reference ICO/O/ED/L/RTL/0181; available at https://ico.org.uk/media/action-weve-taken/2618383/20201002_ico-o-ed-l-rtl-0181_to-julian-knight-mp.pdf, accessed 16.10.20.

IDEA, 'Political Finance Database', *Institute for Democracy and Electoral Assistance*, available at www.idea.int/data-tools/data/political-finance-database, accessed 19.06.20.

iDisciple, 'Growth Plans', *iDisciple*, available at www.idisciple.org/growthplans, accessed 11.06.20.

International Conference of Information Commissioners, 2019, 'Johannesburg Conference Statement', *International Conference of Information Commissioners*, available at www.informationcommissioners.org/icic-2019, accessed 27.01.20.

Ipsos MORI, 2020, 'Public Attitudes Towards Online Targeting', Ipsos MORI for the Centre for Data Ethics and Innovation, and Sciencewise, https://assets. publishing.service.gov.uk/government/uploads/system/uploads/attachment_data/ file/863025/1901705901_Attitudes_to_Online_Targeting_Report_FINAL_PUB LIC_030220.pdf, accessed 17.09.20.

Isherwood, L., 2015, 'When the Flesh is Word, Debt Economy is not a Thing for Heaven', *Feminist Theology*, 23:3, pp. 284–91.

Jackelén, A., 2002, 'The Image of God as Techno Sapiens', *Zygon*, 37:2, pp. 289–302.

James, H., 2001, 'Corporate Guilt Exaggerated (Book Review)', *New Leader*, 84:2, pp. 23–4.

Jantzen, G. M., 1998, *Becoming Divine: Towards a Feminist Philosophy of Religion*, Manchester: Manchester University Press.

Jeffrey, G. R., 2000, *Surveillance Society: The Rise of Antichrist*, Toronto: Frontier Research Publications.

Jesuit Media Initiatives, 'About', Prayasyougo, available at https://pray-as-you-go. org/about/, accessed 11.06.20.

Jewish Virtual Library, 'The Nuremberg Laws: Background & Overview', Jewish Virtual Library, available at www.jewishvirtuallibrary.org/background-and-overview-of-the-nuremberg-laws, accessed 22.05.20.

John Paul II, 1981, *Laborem exercens*, available from www.vatican.va/content/ john-paul-ii/en/encyclicals/documents/hf_jp-ii_enc_14091981_laborem-exercens. html.

———, 1991, *Centesimus annus*, available at www.vatican.va/content/john-paul-ii/ en/encyclicals/documents/hf_jp-ii_enc_01051991_centesimus-annus.html.

John XXIII, 1963, *Pacem in terris*, available at www.vatican.va/content/john-xxiii/ en/encyclicals/documents/hf_j-xxiii_enc_11041963_pacem.html, accessed 23.02.20.

Jones, T., 1979, *Monty Python's Life of Brian*, Warner Bros. Pictures.

Jordan, T., 2015, *Information Politics: Liberation and Exploitation in the Digital Society*, London: Pluto Press.

Kahn, A. E., 1966, 'The Tyranny of Small Decisions: Market Failures, Imperfections, and the Limits of Economics', *Kyklos*, 19:1, pp. 23–47.

Kaiser, B., 2019, *Targeted*, London: HarperCollins.

Kaneda, T. and C. Haub, 2020, 'How many People have ever Lived on Earth?', *PRB*, 23 January, available at www.prb.org/howmanypeoplehaveeverlivedon earth/, accessed 15.05.20.

Kaplan, E. A., 1997, *Looking for the Other: Feminism, Film, and the Imperial Gaze*, New York and London: Routledge.

Kastenberg, J. E., 2007, 'Tactical Level PSYOP and MILDEC Information Operations: How to Smartly and Lawfully Prime the Battlefield', *The Army Lawyer*, 61, pp. 61–71.

Keys, M. M., 2006, *Aquinas, Aristotle, and the Promise of the Common Good*, Cambridge: Cambridge University Press.

Khan, S., 2018, 'Punjab Government's Safe Cities Project: Safer City or Over Policing', *Digital Rights Foundation*, available at https://drive.google.com/file/d/1ZqZ-b6dTcRo1znrylZVDGlqRShj5ktMd/view, accessed 25.01.20.

Kleinig, J., 2009, 'The Ethical Perils of Knowledge Acquisition', *Criminal Justice Ethics*, 28:2, pp. 201–22.

Kotsko, A., 2018, *Neoliberalism's Demons: On the Political Theology of Late Capital*, Stanford, CA: Stanford University Press.

Kraemer, F., K. van Overveld and M. Peterson, 2011, 'Is there an Ethics of Algorithms?', *Ethics and Information Technology*, 13:3, pp. 251–60.

Kraybill, J. N., 1996, 'Imperial Cult and Commerce in John's Apocalypse', *Journal for the Study of the New Testament Supplement*, Series 132, Sheffield: Sheffield Academic Press.

Kristensen, D. B. and C. Prigge, 2018, 'Human/Technology Associations in Self-Tracking Practices', in Btihaj Ajana (ed.), *Self-Tracking: Empirical and Philosophical Investigations*, Cham, Switzerland: Palgrave Macmillan, pp. 43–59.

Kymlicka, W., 1995, *Multicultural Citizenship: A Liberal Theory of Minority Rights*, Oxford: Clarendon Press.

Laczniak, G. R., 1998, 'Reflections on the 1997 Vatican Statements Regarding Ethics in Advertising', *Journal of Public Policy & Marketing*, 17:2, pp. 320–4.

Law Society, 2019, 'Algorithms in the Criminal Justice System', The Law Society of England and Wales, https://www.lawsociety.org.uk/topics/research/algorithm-use-in-the-criminal-justice-system-report, accessed 16.10.20.

Levi, P., 1993, 'People in a Landscape: Theokritos', in Peter Green (ed.), *Hellenistic History and Culture*, Berkeley, CA: University of California Press, pp. 111–26.

Levinas, E., 1969, *Totality and Infinity: An Essay on Exteriority*, Pittsburgh, PA: Duquesne University Press.

Levine, A.-J., 2014, *Short Stories by Jesus: The Enigmatic Parables of a Controversial Rabbi*, New York: HarperOne.

Lewis, B., 2018, 'Social Media, Peer Surveillance, Spiritual Formation, and Mission: Practising Christian Faith in a Surveilled Public Space', *Surveillance & Society*, 16:4, pp. 517–32.

Locke, J., 1988, *Two Treatises of Government*, 2nd edn, Cambridge: Cambridge University Press.

Lucas, L. and E. Feng, 2018, 'Inside China's Surveillance State', *Financial Times*, 20 July, available at www.ft.com/content/2182eebe-8a17-11e8-bf9e-8771d5404543, accessed 15.02.19.

Lupton, D., 2016, *The Quantified Self: A Sociology of Self-Tracking*, Cambridge: Polity Press.

Lyon, D., 1995, 'Whither Shall I Flee? Surveillance, Omniscience and Normativity in the Panopticon', *Christian Scholars Review*, 14:3, pp. 302–12.

_____, 2001, *Surveillance Society: Monitoring Everyday Life (Issues in Society)*, Buckingham: Open University Press.

_____, 2009, *Identifying Citizens: ID Cards as Surveillance*, Cambridge: Polity Press.

_____, 2014, 'Surveillance and the Eye of God', *Studies in Christian Ethics*, 27:1, pp. 21–32.

_____, 2018a, *The Culture of Surveillance*, Cambridge: Polity Press.

_____, 2018b, 'God's Eye: A Reason for Hope', *Surveillance & Society*, 16:4, pp. 546–53.

Machiavelli, N., 1989, *The Chief Works and Others*, 1, Durham, NC: Duke University Press.

Machlup, F., 1962, *The Production and Distribution of Knowledge in the United States*, Princeton, NJ: Princeton University Press.

Maltby, S. and H. Thornham, 2012, 'The Dis/Embodiment of Persuasive Military Discourse', *Journal of War & Culture Studies*, 5:1, pp. 33–46.

Marsilius of Padua, 2018, *The Defender of the Peace*, Cambridge: Cambridge University Press.

Matzner, T., 2018, 'Grasping the Ethics and Politics of Algorithms', in Ann Rudinow Sœtnan, Ingrid Schneider and Nicola Green (eds), *The Politics of Big Data: Big Data, Big Brother?*, London: Routledge, pp. 39–45.

Maybaum, I., 1965, *The Face of God after Auschwitz*, Amsterdam: Polak and Van Gennep.

McAdams, D. P., 1993, *The Stories We Live By: Personal Myths and the Making of the Self*, New York; London: The Guilford Press.

McClintock Fulkerson, M., 2012, 'Receiving from the Other: Theology and Grass-Roots Organizing', *International Journal of Public Theology*, 6:4, pp. 421–34.

McKane, W., 1986, *A Critical and Exegetical Commentary on Jeremiah*, vol. 1, Edinburgh: T&T Clark.

McLuhan, M., 2001 [1964], *Understanding Media*, London: Routledge.

Mein, A., 2001, *Ezekiel and the Ethics of Exile*, Oxford: Oxford University Press.

Merton, T., 1976, *The Power and Meaning of Love*, London: Sheldon Press.

_____, 1980, *Contemplation in a World of Action*, London: Unwin Paperbacks.

Metz, J.-B., 1984, 'Facing the Jews: Christian Theology after Auschwitz', in Elisabeth Schüssler Fiorenza (ed.), *The Holocaust as Interruption*, Edinburgh: T&T Clark, pp. 26–33.

Metzger, B. M., 1993, *Breaking the Code: Understanding the Book of Revelation*, Nashville, TN: Abingdon Press.

Míguez Bonino, J., 1977, 'Poverty as Curse, Blessing and Challenge', *Iliff Review*, 34:3, pp. 3–13.

Mill, J. S., 1989 [1859], *On Liberty*, Cambridge: Cambridge University Press.

Milton, S., 1997, 'Registering Civilians and Aliens in the Second World War', *Jewish History*, 11:2, pp. 79–87.

Miravelle, J.-M., 2017, 'Resisting the Less Important: Aquinas on Modesty', *Journal of Moral Theology*, 6:2, pp. 166–74.

Moltmann, J., 1974, *The Crucified God*, London: SCM Press.

_____, 1985, *God in Creation: An Ecological Doctrine of Creation*, London: SCM Press.

Mouffe, C., 1993, *The Return of the Political*, London and New York: Verso.

Murphy, P. E., 1998, 'Ethics in Advertising: Review, Analysis, and Suggestions', *Journal of Public Policy & Marketing*, 17:2, pp. 316–19.

Myers, C., 1988, *Binding the Strong Man: A Political Reading of Mark's Story of Jesus*, Maryknoll, NY: Orbis Books.

MyFitnessPal app, 'Fitness Starts with What You Eat', Under Armour, available at www.myfitnesspal.com/, accessed 19.03.20.

Nielsen Global Connect, 'Shaping a Smarter Market™', available at www.nielsen.com/us/en/solutions/nielsen-global-connect/, accessed 19.03.20.

Nielsen Global Media, 'Truth Is Our Only Agenda', available at www.nielsen.com/us/en/solutions/nielsen-global-media/, accessed 19.03.20.

Nissenbaum, H., 2010, *Privacy in Context: Technology, Policy, and the Integrity of Social Life*, Stanford, CA: Stanford Law Books.

Noble, S. U., 2018, *Algorithms of Oppression: How Search Engines Reinforce Racism*, New York: New York University Press.

Noddings, N., 1989, *Women and Evil*, Berkeley, CA: University of California Press.

Norris, P., 2001, *Digital Divide: Civic Engagement, Information Poverty, and the Internet Worldwide*, Cambridge: Cambridge University Press.

O'Neil, C., 2016, *Weapons of Math Destruction*, London: Allen Lane.

O'Donovan, O., 2017, 'The Common Good: Does It Represent a Political Programme by Oliver O'Donovan' (Video Recording), Centre for Theology and Public Issues, available at https://ctpi.div.ed.ac.uk/resources/common-good-represent-political-programme-oliver-odonovan/, accessed 24.02.20.

Papageorgiou, A. et al., 2018, 'Security and Privacy Analysis of Mobile Health Applications: The Alarming State of Practice', *IEEE Access*, 6, pp. 9390–403.

Pasquale, F., 2015, *The Black Box Society: The Secret Algorithms that Control Money and Information*, Cambridge, MA: Harvard University Press.

Pattison, S., 2007, *The Challenge of Practical Theology: Selected Essays*, London: Jessica Kingsley.

Paul VI, 1967, *Populorum progressio*, available at http://w2.vatican.va/content/paul-vi/en/encyclicals/documents/hf_p-vi_enc_26031967_populorum.html, accessed 31.12.15.

Phillips, D. Z., 2004, *The Problem of Evil and the Problem of God*, London: SCM Press.

Plantinga, A., 1973, 'The Free Will Defence', in W. L. Rowe and W. J. Wainwright (eds), *Philosophy of Religion: Selected Readings*, New York: Harcourt Brace Jovanovich, pp. 217–30.

Pontifical Council for Social Communications, 1997, 'Ethics in Advertising', 22 February, available at www.vatican.va/roman_curia/pontifical_councils/pccs/documents/rc_pc_pccs_doc_22021997_ethics-in-ad_en.html, accessed 1.11.19.

Pope, S. J., 1993, 'Proper and Improper Partiality and the Preferential Option for the Poor', *Theological Studies*, 54:2, pp. 242–71.

Porat, M. U., 1977, *The Information Economy: Definition and Measurement*, Office of Telecommunications Special Publications 77–12(1), US Department of Commerce/Office of Telecommunications, available from https://files.eric.ed.gov/fulltext/ED142205.pdf.

Pridmore, J. and Y. Wang, 2018, 'Prompting Spiritual Practices through Christian Faith Applications: Self-Paternalism and the Surveillance of the Soul', *Surveillance & Society*, 16:4, pp. 502–16.

Privacy Commissioner of Canada, 2019, 'Privacy Law Reform: A Pathway to Respecting Rights and Restoring Trust in Government and the Digital Economy – 2018–2019 Annual Report', Gatineau, Quebec: Office of the Privacy Commissioner of Canada.

PSA, 'Guide to PSA Readiness', Advancing Pretrial Policy and Research, available at www.psapretrial.org/implementation/guides/readiness/guide-to-psa-readiness, accessed 04.05.20.

Public Health Scotland, 'Measuring Function/Dependency: Older People in the Community – What is the Indicator of Relative Need (Iorn)', Public Health Scotland, available at www.isdscotland.org/Health-Topics/Health-and-Social-

Community-Care/Dependency-Relative-Needs/In-the-Community/, accessed 04. 05.20.

Pulitzer Prizes, The, 2019, 'Finalist in National Reporting: Staff of the New York Times, with Contributions from Carole Cadwalladr of the Guardian/the Observer of London', The Pulitzer Prizes, available at www.pulitzer.org/finalists/ staff-new-york-times-contributions-carole-cadwalladr-guardianthe-observer-london, accessed 15.01.20.

Punt, J., 2008, 'Intersections in Queer Theory and Postcolonial Theory, and Hermeneutical Spin-Offs', The Bible and Critical Theory, 4:2, pp. 24.1–16.

Raab, C. D., 2009, 'Identity: Difference and Categorization', in Ian Kerr, Valerie Steeves and Carole Lucock (eds), Lessons from the Identity Trail: Anonymity, Privacy and Identity in a Networked Society, Oxford: Oxford University Press, pp. 227–44.

Raphael, M., 2003, The Female Face of God in Auschwitz, London: Routledge.

Rawls, J., 1993, Political Liberalism, New York: Columbia University Press.

Reddie, A. G., 2012, Black Theology, London: SCM Press.

Reed, E. D., 2015, 'Wealth and Common Good', in Nicholas Sagovsky and Peter McGrail (eds), Together for the Common Good: Towards a National Conversation, London: SCM Press, pp. 49–64.

Reeves, J., 2016, 'Automatic for the People: The Automation of Communicative Labor', Communication and Critical/Cultural Studies, 13:2, pp. 150–65.

Reich, R. B., 2018, The Common Good, New York: Alfred A. Knopf.

Rettberg, J. W., 2018, 'Apps as Companions: How Quantified Self Apps Become Our Audience and Our Companions', in Btihaj Ajana (ed.), Self-Tracking: Empirical and Philosophical Investigations, Cham, Switzerland: Palgrave Macmillan, pp. 27–42.

Ringold, D. J., 1998, 'A Comment on the Pontifical Council for Social Communications Ethics in Advertising', Journal of Public Policy & Marketing, 17:2, pp. 332–5.

Riordan, P., 2008, A Grammar of the Common Good: Speaking of Globalization, London: Continuum.

_____, 2011, 'Human Happiness as a Common Good: Clarifying the Issues', in John R. Atherton, Elaine Graham and Ian Steedman (eds), The Practices of Happiness: Political Economy, Religion and Wellbeing, London: Routledge, pp. 207–15.

Ritzer, G. and N. Jurgenson, 2010, 'Production, Consumption, Prosumption: The Nature of Capitalism in the Age of the Digital "Prosumer"', Journal of Consumer Culture, 10:1, pp. 13–36.

Rivera, M., 2007, The Touch of Transcendence: A Postcolonial Theology of God, Louisville, KY: Westminster John Knox Press.

Roberts, S. R., 2018, 'The Biopolitics of China's "War on Terror" and the Exclusion of the Uyghurs', Critical Asian Studies, 50:2, pp. 232–58.

Rodrigues, C. A., 2019, '"Digital Gangsters": Are Facebook and Google a Challenge to Democracy?', Amsterdam Law Forum, 11:3, pp. 30–41.

Roman Catholic Church, 1999, Catechism of the Catholic Church, rev. edn, London: Burns & Oates.

Rosato, D., 2020, 'What Your Period Tracker App Knows about You', Consumer Reports, 28 January, available at www.consumerreports.org/health-privacy/ what-your-period-tracker-app-knows-about-you/, accessed 05.02.20.

Roth, J. K., 2004, 'Theistic Antitheodicy', *American Journal of Theology and Philosophy*, 25:3, pp. 276–93.

Rowland, C., 1993, *Revelation*, Epworth Commentaries, London: Epworth Press.

Rowlands, A., 2015, 'The Language of the Common Good', in Nicholas Sagovsky and Peter McGrail (eds), *Together for the Common Good: Towards a National Conversation*, London: SCM Press, pp. 3–15.

Russell, J. A., 2003, 'Core Affect and the Psychological Construction', *Psychological Review*, 110:1, pp. 145–72.

Ryan, D. E., 1996, *The Holocaust and the Jews of Marseille: The Enforcement of Anti-Semitic Policies in Vichy France*, Urbana, IL: University of Illinois Press.

Sacks, J., 1995, *Faith in the Future*, London: Darton, Longman & Todd.

Sagovsky, N. and P. McGrail, 2015, 'Introduction', in Nicholas Sagovsky and Peter McGrail (eds), *Together for the Common Good: Towards a National Conversation*, London: SCM Press, pp. xvii–xxx.

Sandel, M. J., 2009, *Justice: What's the Right Thing to Do?*, London: Allen Lane.

Sartre, J.-P., 1956, *Being and Nothingness: A Phenomenological Essay on Ontology*, Hazel E. Barnes (trans.), New York: Washington Square Press.

Scally, D., 2001, 'German Pastor sent Names of "Non-Aryan" Christians to Nazis', *Irish Times*, 26 October, available at www.irishtimes.com/news/german-pastor-sent-names-of-non-aryan-christians-to-nazis-1.334107, accessed 22.05.20.

Schleifer, R., 2014, 'Propaganda, Psyop, and Political Marketing: The Hamas Campaign as a Case in Point', *Journal of Political Marketing*, 13:1–2, pp. 152–73.

Schüssler Fiorenza, E., 1991, *Revelation: Vision of a Just World*, Edinburgh: T&T Clark.

Second Vatican Council, 1965, *Gaudium et spes*, available from www.vatican.va/archive/hist_councils/ii_vatican_council/documents/vat-ii_cons_19651207_gaudium-et-spes_en.html.

Seltzer, W., 1998, 'Population Statistics, the Holocaust, and the Nuremberg Trials', *Population and Development Review*, 24:3, pp. 511–52.

Settanni, M., D. Azucar and D. Marengo, 2018, 'Predicting Individual Characteristics from Digital Traces on Social Media: A Meta-Analysis', *Cyberpsychology, Behavior, and Social Networking*, 21:4, pp. 217–28.

She Reads Truth, 'Subscribe and Never Miss a Day in God's Word', available at https://subscription.shopshereadstruth.com/, accessed 20.04.20.

Sigurdson, O., 2016, *Heavenly Bodies: Incarnation, the Gaze, and Embodiment in Christian Theology*, Carl Olsen (trans.), Grand Rapids, MI: Eerdmans.

Simonite, T., 2019, 'The Best Algorithms Struggle to Recognize Black Faces Equally', *Wired*, 22 July, available at www.wired.com/story/best-algorithms-struggle-recognize-black-faces-equally/, accessed 04.05.20.

Smith, J. Z., 1987, *To Take Place: Toward Theory in Ritual*, Chicago, IL: University of Chicago Press.

Smyczek, P. J., 2005, 'Regulating the Battlefield of the Future: The Legal Limitations on the Conduct of Psychological Operations (PSYOP) under Public International Law', *Air Force Law Review*, 57, pp. 209–40.

Snodgrass, K., 2008, *Stories with Intent: A Comprehensive Guide to the Parables of Jesus*, Grand Rapids, MI: Eerdmans.

Snowden, E., 2019, *Permanent Record*, London: Macmillan.

Sorkin, A., 2019, 'An Open Letter to Mark Zuckerberg', *New York Times*, 31 October, available at www.nytimes.com/2019/10/31/opinion/aaron-sorkin-mark-zuckerberg-facebook.html, accessed 1.11.19.

Sperling, S., 2011, 'The Politics of Transparency and Surveillance in Post-Reunification Germany', *Surveillance & Society*, 8:4, pp. 396–412.

Stark, L. and K. Levy, 2018, 'The Surveillant Consumer', *Media, Culture & Society*, 40:8, pp. 1202–20.

Stewart, K., 2019, *The Power Worshippers: Inside the Dangerous Rise of Religious Nationalism*, New York: Bloomsbury.

Stoddart, E., 2011, *Theological Perspectives on a Surveillance Society: Watching and Being Watched*, Aldershot: Ashgate.

———, 2014a, '(In)visibility before Privacy: A Theological Ethics of Surveillance as Social Sorting', *Studies in Christian Ethics*, 27:1, pp. 33–49.

———, 2014b, *Advancing Practical Theology: Critical Discipleship for Disturbing Times*, London: SCM Press.

———, 2018, 'Wolves in the Airport: Jesus' Critique of Purity as a Challenge to 21st Century Surveillance', *Practical Theology*, 11:1, pp. 54–66.

Stone, K., 2005, *Practicing Safer Texts: Food, Sex and Bible in Queer Perspective*, London: T&T Clark.

Strava, 'Features', available at www.strava.com/features, accessed 14.03.20.

Strava Metro, 'Better Data, Better Cities', available at https://metro.strava.com/, accessed 14.03.20.

Sturken, M. and L. Cartwright, 2018, *Practices of Looking: An Introduction to Visual Culture*, 3rd edn, Oxford: Oxford University Press.

Sugirtharajah, R. S., 1998, 'Biblical Studies after the Empire: From a Colonial to a Postcolonial Mode of Interpretation', in R. S. Sugirtharajah (ed.), *The Post-Colonial Bible*, Sheffield: Sheffield Academic Press, pp. 12–22.

———, 1999, *Asian Biblical Hermeneutics and Postcolonialism*, The Biblical Seminar, Sheffield: Sheffield Academic Press.

Sung, J. M., 2007, *Desire, Market and Religion*, London: SCM Press.

Surveillance Camera Commissioner, 2019, 'Annual Report 2017/18', available at www.gov.uk/government/publications/surveillance-camera-commissioner-annual-report-2017-to-2018, accessed 27.01.20.

Swinburne, R., 1998, *Providence and the Problem of Evil*, Oxford: Clarendon Press.

Swinton, J., 2007, *Raging with Compassion: Pastoral Responses to the Problem of Evil*, Grand Rapids, MI: Eerdmans.

Swinton, J. and H. Mowat, 2006, *Practical Theology and Qualitative Research*, London: SCM Press.

Tajfel, H., 1981, *Human Groups and Social Categories: Studies in Social Psychology*, Cambridge: Cambridge University Press.

Tamez, E., 1982, *Bible of the Oppressed*, Maryknoll, NY: Orbis Books.

Tanner, K., 2005, *Economy of Grace*, Minneapolis, MN: Fortress Press.

Taylor, C., 1995, *Philosophical Arguments*, Cambridge, MA: Harvard University Press.

———, 2004, *Modern Social Imaginaries*, Durham, NC; London: Duke University Press.

Taylor, C. Z., 2002, 'Religious Addiction: Obsession with Spirituality', *Pastoral Psychology*, 50:4, pp. 291–315.

Thimmes, P., 2003, 'Women Reading Women in the Apocalypse: Reading Scenario 1, the Letter to Thyatira (Rev. 2.18–29)', *Currents in Biblical Research*, 2:1, pp. 128–44.

Thorson, E. et al., 2019, 'Exposure to Presidential Candidate Advertising on Television, Website, and Social Media during 23 Days of the 2016 Primary', *Journal of Current Issues & Research in Advertising*, 40:1, pp. 73–89.

Tilley, T. W., 2000, *The Evils of Theodicy*, Eugene, OR: Wipf & Stock.

Tilly, C., 1998, *Durable Inequality*, Berkeley, CA: University of California Press.

Tirole, J., 2017, *Economics for the Common Good*, Princeton, NJ: Princeton University Press.

Toffler, A., 1980, *The Third Wave*, London: Collins.

Toops, S., 2016, 'Spatial Results of the 2010 Census in Xinjiang', *Asia Dialogue: The Online Magazine of the University of Nottingham Asia Research Institute*, 7 March, available at http://theasiadialogue.com/2016/03/07/spatial-results-of-the-2010-census-in-xinjiang/, accessed 21.02.19.

Tracy, D., 1983, 'The Foundations of Practical Theology', in Don S. Browning (ed.), *Practical Theology: The Emerging Field in Theology, Church and World*, San Francisco, CA: Harper & Row.

Trible, P., 1984, *Texts of Terror: Literary-Feminist Readings of Biblical Narratives*, London: SCM Press.

Trozzo, E., 2019, *The Cyberdimension: A Political Theology of Cyberspace and Cybersecurity*, Eugene, OR: Cascade Books.

UCLA, 2019, 'UCLA Anderson School of Management Announces 2019 Gerald Loeb Award Winners', Cision PR Newswire, 28 June, available at www.prnewswire.com/news-releases/ucla-anderson-school-of-management-announces-2019-gerald-loeb-award-winners-300877656.html, accessed 15.01.20.

UNESCO, 2015, 'Rethinking Education: Towards a Global Common Good?', SDG 4 Education, available at www.sdg4education2030.org/rethinking-education-unesco-2015, accessed 13.06.20.

UNHCR, 'Stateless around the World', available at www.unhcr.org/statelessness-around-the-world.html, accessed 29.02.20.

United Healthcare, 'Get Rewarded Instantly!', available at https://broker.uhc.com/assets/UHCEW645218_RewardMe_Flyer%20FINAL.pdf, accessed 12.03.20 (flyer no longer available).

United Nations, 'Microplastics', UN Environment Programme, available at www.unenvironment.org/resources/report/microplastics, accessed 19.06.20.

Vallina-Rodriguez, N. and S. Sundarsan, 2017, '7 in 10 Smartphone Apps Share Your Data with Third-Party Services', *Scientific American*, 30 May, available at www.scientificamerican.com/article/7-in-10-smartphone-apps-share-your-data-with-third-party-services/, accessed 5.02.20.

van Dijk, J., 2013, 'Inequalities in the Network Society', in Kate Orton-Johnson and Nick Prior (eds), *Digital Sociology: Critical Perspectives*, Basingstoke: Palgrave Macmillan, pp. 105–24.

_____, 2014, 'Datafication, Dataism and Dataveillance: Big Data between Scientific Paradigm and Ideology', *Surveillance & Society*, 12:2, pp. 197–208.

Vanderheyden, P. A., 1999, 'Religious Addiction: The Subtle Destruction of the Soul', *Pastoral Psychology*, 47:4, pp. 293–302.

Vaughan, A., 2019, 'UK Launched Passport Photo Checker it Knew Would Fail with Dark Skin', *New Scientist*, 9 October, available at www.newscientist.com/

article/2219284-uk-launched-passport-photo-checker-it-knew-would-fail-with-dark-skin/, accessed 14.10.19.

Vedder, A. H., 1995, *The Values of Freedom*, Utrecht: Aurelio Domus Artium.

Walzer, M., 1990, 'Nation and Universe', in G. B. Peterson (ed.), *The Tanner Lectures on Human Values*, 11, Salt Lake City: University of Utah Press, pp. 509–56.

Watts, F. N., R. Nye and S. B. Savage, 2002, 'Unhealthy Religion', in *Psychology for Christian Ministry*, London: Routledge, pp. 59–76.

Welby, J., 2018, *Reimagining Britain: Foundations for Hope*, London: Bloomsbury.

WHO, 2015, 'Global Action Plan on Antimicrobial Resistance', World Health Organization, available at www.who.int/antimicrobial-resistance/publications/global-action-plan/en/, accessed 19.06.20.

Williams, R., 2005, '"Today is not an Occasion for us to focus on Fear" – Sermon in St Paul's Cathedral', *The Guardian*, 1 November, available at www.theguardian.com/uk/2005/nov/01/july7.politics, accessed 22.05.20.

_____, 2012, *Faith in the Public Square*, London: Bloomsbury.

Wimbush, V. L., 2000, 'Introduction: Reading Darkness, Reading Scriptures', in Vincent L. Wimbush (ed.), *African Americans and the Bible: Sacred Texts and Social Textures*, New York: Continuum, pp. 1–43.

Wojtyla, K., 1979, *The Acting Person*, A. Potocki (trans.), Dordrecht, Holland; Boston, MA: D. Reidel Publishing Company.

_____, 2008, *Person and Community: Selected Essays*, New York: Peter Lang.

Wright, N. T., 2012, 'Revelation and Christian Hope: Political Implications of the Revelation to John', in Richard B. Hays and Stefan Alkier (eds), *Revelation and the Politics of Apocalyptic Interpretation*, Waco, TX: Baylor University Press, pp. 105–24.

Wu, L., S. Zeng and Y. Wu, 2018, 'Affect Heuristic and Format Effect in Risk Perception', *Social Behavior and Personality*, 46:8, pp. 1331–44.

Wylie, C., 2019, *Mindf*ck: Inside Cambridge Analytica's Plot to Break the World*, London: Profile Books.

Yamamoto, M., S. Nah and S. Y. Bae, 2019, 'Social Media Prosumption and Online Political Participation: An Examination of Online Communication Processes', *New Media & Society*, 22:10, pp. 1885–902.

Young, L. C., 2017, 'Administration II – the Nazi Census and Making up People', in *List Cultures: Knowledge and Poetics from Mesopotamia to Buzzfeed*, Amsterdam: Amsterdam University Press, pp. 85–108.

YouVersion, 2018, 'Bible App', YouVersion, available at www.youversion.com/products/, accessed 23.03.18.

_____, 2019, '2019 Verse of the Year', YouVersion, available at www.youversion.com/share2019/, accessed 20.04.20.

Zamagni, S., 2012, 'Reciprocity and Fraternity', in Daniel K. Finn (ed.), *The Moral Dynamics of Economic Life: An Extension and Critique of Caritas in Veritate*, Oxford: Oxford University Press, pp. 73–6.

Zang, J. et al., 2015, 'Who Knows What About Me? A Survey of Behind the Scenes Personal Data Sharing to Third Parties by Mobile Apps', *Technology Science*, 30 October.

Zedner, L., 2006, 'Neither Safe nor Sound? The Perils and Possibilities of Risk', *Canadian Journal of Criminology and Criminal Justice*, 48:3, pp. 423–34.

Zuboff, S., 2019, *The Age of Surveillance Capitalism: The Fight for a Human Future at the New Frontier of Power*, London: Profile Books.

Zuckerberg, M., 2019, 'Standing for Voice and Free Expression: Transcript of Speech Given at Georgetown University 17 October 2019', *The Washington Post*, 17 October, available at www.washingtonpost.com/technology/2019/10/17/zuckerberg-standing-voice-free-expression/, accessed 1.11.19.

Zuiderveen Borgesius, F. J. et al., 2018, 'Online Political Microtargeting: Promises and Threats for Democracy', *Utrecht Law Review*, 14:1, pp. 82–96.

Index of Biblical References

10.29–33	105
10.33	13
11.17	114
11.45–46	176
15	15
15.4–6	15
15.1–7	14
15.8–9	13
15.4	208
15.29–30	14
16.19–23	12
22.47–48	162
23.18	69

John

7.12	69
7.31	69
7.45	69
7.43	69
10.12–13	14
10.11	15
18.39–40	69

Acts

1.26	71, 162
14.19	70
18.3	118
19	70, 117

1 Corinthians

6.9–11	118
6.16	118
6.19	118, 208

2 Corinthians

6.14–16a	118
6.16	118, 208

2 Peter

2.1	68

1 John

4.1	69

Revelation

2.18–29	69
2.20	69
3.1	137
3.17	137
13.16	116
14.9, 11	116
16.2	116
18.2–3, 9–11	114
18.7	114
18.11	114
18.17	114
20.4	116

Index of Names and Subjects